Alain Resnais: Interviews

Conversations with Filmmakers Series
Gerald Peary, General Editor

# ALAIN RESNAIS
INTERVIEWS

Edited by Lynn A. Higgins
with translations by T. Jefferson Kline

University Press of Mississippi / Jackson

The University Press of Mississippi is the scholarly publishing agency of
the Mississippi Institutions of Higher Learning: Alcorn State University,
Delta State University, Jackson State University, Mississippi State University,
Mississippi University for Women, Mississippi Valley State University,
University of Mississippi, and University of Southern Mississippi.

www.upress.state.ms.us

The University Press of Mississippi is a member
of the Association of University Presses.

Publication of this volume was made possible in part
by a generous donation from Dartmouth College.

Copyright © 2021 by University Press of Mississippi
All rights reserved

First printing 2021
∞

Library of Congress Control Number: 2021938282
Hardback ISBN 978-1-4968-3394-5
Trade paperback ISBN 978-1-4968-3393-8
Epub single ISBN 978-1-4968-3395-2
Epub institutional ISBN 978-1-4968-3396-9
PDF single ISBN 978-1-4968-3397-6
PDF institutional ISBN 978-1-4968-3398-3

British Library Cataloging-in-Publication Data available

Contents

Introduction   vii

Chronology   xxiii

Filmography   xxix

A Stoic Filmmaker: Interview with Alain Resnais   3
  Jean Michel Carta and Michel Mesnil / 1960

Trying to Understand My Own Film   13
  André Labarthe and Jacques Rivette / 1962

Interview with Alain Resnais: *The War Is Over*   20
  Robert Benayoun, Michel Ciment, and Jean-Louis Pays / 1966

Alain Resnais, Antidoctrinary   36
  O. Revault d'Allonnes / 1967

Interview with Alain Resnais   42
  Jacques Belmans / 1968

Memories of Resnais   47
  Richard Roud / 1969

Conversations with Resnais: There Isn't Enough Time   60
  James Monaco / 1975

Facts into Fiction: An Interview with Alain Resnais   68
  Richard Seaver / 1975

Interview with Alain Resnais: On *Mon Oncle d'Amérique*   77
  Robert Benayoun / 1980

Of Mice and Men: An Interview with Alain Resnais   82
   Tom Milne / 1980

Interview with Alain Resnais: on *L'Amour à mort*   87
   Alain Masson and François Thomas / 1984

Tracking Some Angles: A Talk with Alain Resnais   99
   Frederic Tuten / 1984

When the Cinema Emerged from Its Shell: An Interview with Alain Resnais   110
   Jean-Daniel Roob / 1986

Interview with Alain Resnais: On *Mélo*   127
   François Thomas / 1986

Interview with Alain Resnais   139
   Birgit Kämper and Thomas Tode / 1995

Alain Resnais: On *The Same Old Song*   148
   François Thomas / 1999

Alain Resnais's *Not on the Lips*   154
   Pascal Mérigeau / 2003

A Conversation with Alain Resnais: A Persistent Shadow   158
   François Thomas / 2006

An Auteur in Spite of Himself: An Interview with Alain Resnais   167
   Gary Crowdus and Richard Porton / 2010

A Conversation with Alain Resnais on *You Ain't Seen Nothin' Yet*   173
   François Thomas / 2012

A Conversation with Alain Resnais on *The Life of Riley*   176
   François Thomas / 2014

Additional Resources   185

Index   187

Introduction

Now considered one of the most innovative and influential filmmakers of the twentieth century, Alain Resnais (1922–2014) did not set out to become a director. In the interviews here, he more readily considers himself a "craftsman" than an "artist," citing the practical choices that shaped his career. (His early films were commissions, for example.) What can we make of a filmography that includes a pathbreaking short documentary about the Nazi extermination camps (*Nuit et brouillard / Night and Fog*, 1955) and a feature juxtaposing the German Occupation of France with the bombing of Hiroshima (*Hiroshima mon amour*, 1958) on the one hand, but also a short documentary advertising a plastics factory (*Le Chant du styrène*, 1958) and a formalist jewel (*L'Année dernière à Marienbad/Last Year at Marienbad*, 1960) that seems disconnected from any reality at all external to itself? And those are just the early years! Resnais went on to experiment with musical comedies, operettas, adaptations from theater and one from a novel, animation, and more. His range of genres should nevertheless not surprise us, given the far-flung passions that inspire his work, from Breton mythology to comic books and from Surrealism to neuroscience. Yet, viewed retrospectively, Resnais's corpus of work has remarkable continuity, and his career was foreshadowed as far back as his early childhood. Both the variety of his choices and the overall coherence of his artistic vision are readable in the interviews collected here.

Born in 1922, Resnais was the only child of a pharmacist in Vannes, a small city in Brittany full of medieval buildings, in a region known for its mysterious Stone Age formations and ancient Celtic legends. The provincial town was also stolidly bourgeois, and children were expected to conform to rigorous norms of behavior and belief. Raised as a strict Catholic, the young Resnais was allowed to visit only the parish movie house, not the secular one next door. His horizons further limited by asthma, he was home schooled as a child and inclined toward quiet entertainments, such as reading comic strips and adventure stories. And from the beginning, there were movies. At the age of eight, he invited friends to enjoy silent Laurel and Hardy comedies projected on a wall and accompanied by recorded music.[1] Anticipating his future vocation as a film editor, he cobbled together leftover snippets of advertising footage to illustrate stories of his own invention. For his thirteenth birthday, his parents gave him a Kodak 8mm camera, with which he filmed his friends starring in adventures drawn from popular novels about the fictional criminal Fantômas.

At fourteen, Resnais was sent to school in Paris. Finally, he could see whatever movies he liked, without parental or church supervision. Throughout his life, he retained vivid memories of films viewed during the 1930s and 1940s. He loved the Surrealist silent short *Un Chien Andalou* (1929), by Luis Buñuel and Salvador Dali. The 1933 American musical *42nd Street*, with its kaleidoscopic dance numbers choreographed by Busby Berkeley, stirred his ambition to make a musical. He was impressed by the social and psychological subtleties of Jean Renoir's *La Règle du jeu* (*The Rules of the Game*, 1939), and he appreciated the musicality and spare allegorical sensibility of Robert Bresson. He discovered Luchino Visconti, King Vidor, and Michael Curtiz, and of course, he loved the silent *Fantômas* adaptations by Louis Feuillade.

Shortly before the outbreak of the Second World War, Resnais headed south to prepare his baccalaureate exams. He never did complete his "*bac*," but in Nice, he became friends with Frédéric de Towarnicki, who would later be known as a journalist, translator, and author. Sharing a passion for comic strips, especially the fictional detective Harry Dickson (whose adventures Resnais had collected since childhood), the two youths focused their energies on adapting this "American Sherlock Holmes" to the screen. They would pursue this venture for more than two decades before abandoning it.[2] In the meantime, the project brought Resnais into contact with a network of interested supporters that included writer-musician Boris Vian, producers Pierre Braunberger and Anatole Dauman, and eventually the author of the Dickson stories, Jean Ray. Back in Paris during the German Occupation, the two young men remained friends, and when Towarnicki, a Polish Jew, was forced into hiding, Resnais crisscrossed Paris on a bicycle to take him meals.

Also during the Occupation, Resnais decided to study acting and enrolled in the Cours Simon, a Parisian school for the performing arts. He soon concluded he lacked the temperament to become an actor, however, and so in 1943, he applied and was accepted into the newly created national school for advanced study in cinematic arts (the IDHEC). What he chose to study was editing (*le montage*). Over the next few years, he would edit his own short films and others made by friends, including François Truffaut's first short film, *Une Visite*, and Agnès Varda's first feature, *La Pointe Courte* (both 1954). Originally a photographer in the theater, Varda gave the young Resnais a Leica camera, with which he shot studio portraits for actors. Later, he would publish a volume of photos with commentary by Spanish expatriate author and anti-Franco activist Jorge Semprun.[3] Resnais and Varda remained friends, and he would call on Semprun to collaborate on scripts for several of his own films.

Military service after the Liberation brought additional important encounters. Resnais's asthma precluded combat, but as part of the postwar occupation of Germany, he was conscripted into a cultural outreach service in the Rhine and Danube region, an assignment that introduced him to critic and future *Cahiers du cinéma* founder André Bazin, the world-famous mime Marcel Marceau, and essayist-critic-novelist-filmmaker Chris Marker. Marker, who had participated in the Resistance, brought his studies of philosophy and anthropology to the crafting of carefully researched documentaries that adopted a subjective, poetic, and sometimes polemical or militant point of view. In collaboration with Marker, Resnais would make short films, several of which were explicitly political and ran afoul of the censors, who were particularly vigilant during the French colonial wars in Indochina and Algeria of the 1950s and early 1960s. Marker and Resnais, along with Varda, were later grouped together and given the label "Left Bank" Filmmakers.

It was a good time to be making short films, thanks to the "Group of Thirty," a collective of film professionals organized to protect and promote the short film as a distinct art form and to monitor distribution and government funding for filmmakers.[4] After the Liberation, Resnais began to establish his reputation as a director of commissioned short-subject documentaries. The earliest ones were about art and artists, shot in black-and-white. In *Van Gogh* (1948), a dynamic camera zooms into the paintings to trace the brushstrokes that reveal the vision and feelings of a turbulent artist. The film triumphed at the Venice Biennale and won an Oscar. *Guernica* (1950) offers an analogous visual journey through Picasso's famous antiwar painting. In contrast to these two bold experiments, Resnais was disappointed with his *Gauguin* (1949), which he felt had failed to forge the sort of new forms of visual communication that would move him forward.

The interviews in this volume testify to Resnais's lifelong commitment to experimentation. Beginning with his earliest work, he sought to explore a broad range of genres, styles, visual techniques, and approaches to storytelling, constantly testing the boundaries of intelligibility. Yet the personality you will encounter here is relaxed and congenial, amusing and approachable, often professing unawareness of the taboos he has broken or the conventions he has shattered. He will not consent to pin down the meaning of his cryptic films—he leaves you the freedom to receive them as you will—but he nevertheless helps you appreciate how and why they are put together as they are.

Resnais and Marker's *Les Statues meurent aussi* (*Statues Also Die*, 1953), with voice-over narration written by Marker, was a commission from *Présence Africaine*, the flagship journal by African and Caribbean writers and visual artists of the Parisian *Négritude* movement. The film documents the uprooting of African pottery, masks, and other objects from their origins in ritual and community to be displayed in the alienating universe of European anthropological museums. Official government censors recognized the film for what it was: an anti-colonialist manifesto condemning cultural imperialism. Despite (or thanks to) the resulting controversy, the film won the Jean Vigo Prize in 1954.[5]

The debate around *Statues Also Die* was minor compared to the storm that erupted over Resnais's most enduring and disturbing short film. *Nuit et brouillard* (*Night and Fog*, 1956) was the first French movie to address the still-taboo history of the Nazi extermination camps. Commissioned for a museum on the Second World War, the film alternates black-and-white newsreel footage of the liberation of the camps by Allied troops with leisurely tracking shots, in the present and in color, through a postwar Auschwitz, its train tracks and barracks overgrown with grass, disconcertingly inoffensive in the sun. A voice-over composed and recited by poet, Resistance veteran, and concentration camp survivor Jean Cayrol calls upon our empathy and imagination to help us recognize this shameful history and prevent such genocidal barbarities from reoccurring. Warning that man's deadly inhumanity can reappear at any moment, the film's conclusion was a transparent allusion to the French atrocities of the ongoing Algerian war. Unsurprisingly, the film also encountered opposition from the censors.[6]

Meditative tracking shots, one of Resnais's formal signatures, reappear in *Toute La Mémoire du monde* (1956), a visit in black-and-white to the backstage machinery of the National Library. In *Le Chant du styrène* (1958), a commissioned advertisement for a plastic manufacturing company, the same technique, in garish color, follows the path of rubber and other raw materials as they flow through industrial tubes and gears to produce everyday household objects. With its playful cinematography by Sacha Vierny, its musical score by Georges Delerue, and its voice-over in classical Alexandrine verse composed by poet-novelist-playwright Raymond Queneau, a member of the experimental OuLiPo group,[7] the film's abstract forms portray the poetry of machinery in motion—there is only one brief glimpse of a human hand—in an effervescent paean to the activity of making things, whether plastic bowls or movies.

After 1958, Resnais would tackle only one further short subject, a 1992 documentary about George and Ira Gershwin, commissioned for television. As already noted, shorts were considered a distinct artistic "career track" at the time, and after a decade of ringing success with short documentaries, it did not go without saying that Resnais would move on to sign twenty fiction features over the next half century. Despite their origins as commissions, his early short films provided a laboratory in which he could refine his personal vision and hone the cinematic and narrative techniques necessary to realize it. Some of these—his use of tracking shots and his collaborations with writers—are obvious; others will come to prominence as we examine his films in a sequence of clusters.

On June 10, 1959, Resnais's first feature-length film, *Hiroshima mon amour* (1958), hit Parisian screens like a thunderclap. The project began as a commissioned documentary about the atomic bomb, but Resnais found himself morally and artistically reticent to carry out the assignment. He had read a recent novel, Marguerite Duras's *Moderato Cantabile* (Editions de Minuit, 1958), in which a woman ritually reenacts a traumatic scene she witnessed. Almost on a whim, the filmmaker contacted the novelist, who agreed to write a screenplay. Both the subject matter and the style of *Hiroshima mon amour* were shocking: a French actress's memories of her love affair with a German soldier during the German Occupation return with a vengeance during a trip to Hiroshima, where she discovers the tragic history of that city during a brief love affair with a Japanese architect. Just as there were personal and creative elements in Resnais's documentaries, his first feature film would thus incorporate a conspicuous documentary dimension. With *Hiroshima*, Resnais continues his search for forms that will express the shattered realities of a postwar world. Recounted in fragments as experienced subjectively by the nameless French woman, past and present (hi) stories blend together and overlap, are never explicit, never resolved. The camera tracks the woman as she wanders the city in a trance, while Delerue's discordant and hallucinatory musical score, nuanced black-and-white cinematography by Sacha Vierny, and editing by Henri Colpi (who had edited *Night and Fog*) combine to make the film into an enduring masterpiece and a milestone in world cinema history.

While *Hiroshima mon amour* has much in common with Resnais's previous documentary work, it also forms a kind of trilogy with his next two features, *L'Année dernière à Marienbad* (*Last Year at Marienbad*, 1960) and *Muriel ou le temps d'un retour* (*Muriel, or The Time of Return*, 1963). The impenetrable, gamelike structure of *Marienbad* involves three mysterious, nameless characters: a woman ("A," played by Delphine Seyrig) and two men, "X" and "M." Resnais described the film as "open to many myths," and indeed countless interpretations are possible. All that can be said is that X tries to persuade A that she promised to go away with him, while A resists his advances and his story. Resnais created the film in collaboration with Alain Robbe-Grillet, a leading figure of the contemporaneous "New Novel" movement. Artists who adopted "New" approaches to both cinema and prose fiction were suspicious of closed and conventional bourgeois forms of narrative and sought instead to liberate the imagination by opening up new options for fiction in their respective media.

Muriel (1963) touched on another taboo topic: the French colonial war that had culminated in Algerian independence the previous year. Here again, two interwoven stories are complicated by a layering of present and past: Bernard, a young man returned from military service in Algeria, lives with his aunt, Hélène

Aughain (Seyrig again), who receives an unexpected visit from her former lover, whom she has not seen since the outbreak of the Second World War. The blind spot at the heart of the narrative is the French military's use of torture in Algeria, a repressed knowledge that invades Bernard's behavior as well as the film's overall plot and structure. Once again, Resnais called on Resistance poet Jean Cayrol to write the screenplay.

All three films were received as explorations of memory, with critics placing the filmmaker in a twentieth-century narrative tradition that began with Proust. Resnais himself, however, found this analysis too narrow, asserting instead that what interested him were the workings of the mind more generally. In the wake of the Surrealists, Resnais experiments with representing how the objective world and our subjective responses flow together and become indistinguishable. Despite their differences, these three films have much in common: each seeks the precise cinematic techniques most suitable to convey the spirit and rhythms—the "voice"—of a woman's inner experience, from the lyrical black-and-white cinematography of *Hiroshima* and the crisper black-and-white geometry of *Marienbad*, to Hélène Aughain's blocked movements and static responses in *Muriel*, captured in muted browns by a stationary camera.

As a second cluster, we might juxtapose *La Guerre est finie* (*The War Is Over*, 1965) with *Stavisky . . .* (1973). Although separated by almost a decade, the two titles allow us to notice Resnais's approach to questions of identity, self-creation, and politics. In contrast to his three previous films, each of these showcases a male protagonist. *La Guerre est finie* takes place in the 1960s and focuses on Diégo (Yves Montand), a middle-aged professional organizer of anti-fascist resistance in Franco's Spain. Despite its precise historical setting, however, the film focuses on its character's mission and his self-doubts. As he shuttles back and forth across the Franco-Spanish border, we wonder how he will reconcile the disconnected facets of his life: his political commitments, the women he loves, his relation to an emerging new generation of revolutionaries with a different vision. What will the story of his life look like? Far from being an activist tract, the film offers a poignant portrait of a man who is aging, discouraged, and weary of the struggle.

Stavisky . . . was inspired by the historical figure of Serge Alexandre Stavisky (played by Jean-Paul Belmondo), a Jewish émigré, embezzler, and con man responsible for the 1934 financial scandal that triggered riots and almost brought down France's Socialist government. Stavisky's story is interwoven with the wheeling and dealing of several government ministers and with Leon Trotsky's visit to France. His most public face, however, is that of a theater owner and impresario, and Resnais explores theatricality and performance as his protagonist's preferred mode of being.[8] Like Diègo, Stavisky suggests he might tell (or invent) the story of his life. He fashions himself as Alexander the Great; he views his financial and political machinations through the filters of Sacha Guitry, Giraudoux, and Shakespeare. He is at once his own scriptwriter, director, costume designer, and editor, and he tries to control how and when his curtain will fall. In short, the film is a portrait of a public figure in a world where politics and spectacle have become indistinguishable. Resnais is primarily interested not in the facts of the case, however, but in the drama of an exemplary personality in specific historical circumstances.

In visual style, the two films differ greatly. Filmed in sober black-and-white, *La Guerre est finie* resembles documentary or *cinéma vérité*. *Stavisky...*, on the other hand, features lavish color, lush costumes, elaborate decors, and a musical score by Stephen Sondheim. A meticulous period piece, it belongs in the nostalgic *mode rétro* or heritage film trend that began in the early 1970s. Yet both films allow us to examine Resnais's politics. His work in documentary, and his readiness to take on controversial topics, have often raised the question of whether he is a political filmmaker, an *artiste engagé*. His willingness to take a militant stand outside his filmmaking (for example, by signing the 1960 *Manifeste des 121* in support of young men refusing to fight in France's war in Algeria) and his repeated tangles with government censorship suggest that his work conveys a strong ideological message. With Chris Marker, he would participate in overtly activist collective productions like *Loin du Vietnam* (1967) and *Ciné-Tracts* (1968). Yet Resnais's voice is quiet and self-effacing, never didactic or confrontational. His portraits are open-ended and his plots unresolved. He often expresses surprise when his work draws official attention. While his choices in public life are left-leaning, then, I would suggest that his overall filmmaking choices are less political than deeply ethical. For example, on several occasions he felt he lacked moral authority to take on a project, and his ethical scruples determine how he inflects his topics as well as his choices of scriptwriter, voice-over, and point of view. One could say that Resnais's manner of being *engagé* is to be found within his characters and *their* engagements with the world, where political perspectives are among the forces determining subjectivity and behavior. The political elements in his films are thus better seen as the side effects or consequences of storytelling, not its origin or purpose.

A third cluster of films—including *Je t'aime, je t'aime* (1967), *Providence* (1976), and *Mon Oncle d'Amérique* (1979)—explores what is perhaps Resnais's most persistent preoccupation: how to represent the workings of the human mind. Each can be understood as an investigation into the complex interweaving of subjective experience with objective conditions. The protagonist of *Je t'aime, je t'aime* (Claude Rich) volunteers to participate in a time-travel experiment during which he floats free from any clearly delineated past, present, or future. He dives repeatedly into water and then re-emerges, living a single moment of his life over and over, in a subjective representation of guilt and obsession. As in *Marienbad*, this film fits together more like a mosaic than a narrative. In *Providence*—Resnais's first English-language film—a dying novelist (John Gielgud) spends a night of drunken delirium reviewing the events of his life. His ruminations are punctuated by vivid responses to his pain, memories of dinners, quarrels with his son (Dirk Bogarde), and feverish imaginings. *Mon Oncle d'Amérique* weaves the life stories and inner thoughts of three fictional characters together with scientific theories as explained by real-life experimental neuroscientist Henri Laborit, in order to probe an important question: to what extent is our behavior determined by biology?

Resnais's project in these films calls to mind nineteenth-century writer Emile Zola, who, inspired by the development of scientific methods of investigation in medicine, composed a cycle of twenty "experimental" novels in order to trace interactions of heredity and environment within an extended family. Not unlike Zola, Resnais puts his characters under a microscope seeking to understand and represent the web of reflexes, perceptions, thoughts, memories, and emotions that make up human consciousness. But while Zola left the frame of external events and objective reality more or less in place, Resnais looks out from inside the minds of his characters. (Remember that the filmmaker was already erasing boundaries between mind and matter in *Van Gogh*, where he literally discards the frame and plunges through his paintings into the mindset of the artist.) While Resnais frequently calls himself an "anti-illusionist," he does not reject realism per se, but instead strives to portray a different reality, that of subjective experience. Yes, the fictional biographies sometimes illustrate Laborit's neurobiological research, but what is even more striking is the way human behavior escapes categorization and scientific theorizing. Imagination (or creativity, or free will, or even the soul) transcends biology, making humans unpredictable and unique, eluding scientific understanding.

Resnais once referred to *Providence* as "a documentary about the imagination,"[9] a remark that describes all three films, which take on the challenge of representing human consciousness without reference to the temporal or spatial signposts of traditional narrative. Instead, seeking to give the films the architecture of the mind itself, he reveals his affinities with one of the most fundamental influences on his worldview: even as a child, Resnais was drawn to Surrealism, and especially to the poet André Breton. (The filmmaker recounts that he once crossed paths with Breton, but he was too awed to approach the man known as the "pope" of Surrealism, and whom Resnais describes as his "idol.") Reflecting on his enduring fascination with the fictional criminal Fantômas, Resnais identifies Surrealist elements in stories that were dreamlike and fantastical, neither linear nor chronological. Following Freud, the Surrealist painters and poets thought of dreams as the "royal way" to the unconscious, and their poetry and parlor games (such as "automatic writing," which Resnais mentions repeatedly here and sometimes practices as he plans his films) were designed to unveil the mysterious forces and dreamlike thought processes at play in everyday life. Such too is Resnais's project. In *Providence*, a shadowy band of primitive and seemingly prehistoric barbarians pops up periodically from a rocky landscape, intrusive visual remnants, perhaps, of an ancient Breton mythology, that embody the old man's atavistic fears and yearnings. Twenty years later, in *On Connaît la chanson* (*Same Old Song*, 1997), the unconscious bubbles up periodically in the form of animated jellyfish that float transparently above the characters' heads to convey their thoughts and feelings. Images such as these are both experimental and playful, and with the Surrealists, Resnais does not think of them as "non-realistic." Rather, he proposes them as a different dimension of realism, representing the reality of the mind. His affinity with Surrealism also suggests a subliminal recognition that, just as the Surrealists of the 1920s were responding to the recent trauma of the "Great War," Resnais began his career in the wake of the unthinkable catastrophes of the Second World War.

The critic who has best understood Resnais's experiments with mental realism is the philosopher Gilles Deleuze. Deleuze believes Resnais exemplifies a new method of representing time in something he calls the modern "time image." Contrasted with the action or "movement image" of classical cinema, the "time image" breaks with conventional narrative and instead represents the subjective experience of time's passing. Life is not a chronological succession of past, present, and future, like beads on a string. Deleuze observes that in Resnais's films, there is no fixed center (or string) to which characters can confidently refer. Instead, perceptions of the present are colored by traumas and nostalgia subsisting from the past along with anxious or curious anticipations of the future. In other words, Resnais's films accurately represent our experience of past, present, and future as "three implicated presents."[10] Some of the films that seem illegible become more understandable in this light. It is helpful to think of them as deliberately dissolving conventional "coherence" in favor of characters and stories that contradict and repeat themselves, as if ruminating.

During the first half of his career, Resnais sought out an expansive galaxy of the era's stars, engaging them for two films at most: Delphine Seyrig, Yves Montand, Jean-Paul Belmondo, Claude Rich, John Gielgud, Dirk Bogarde, Gérard Depardieu . . . Beginning in 1982, however, there is a striking evolution in his approach to casting: Resnais began to work intensively with a core troupe of three actors. Pierre Arditi, who had appeared in *Mon Oncle d'Amérique*, would star in eight of Resnais's eleven remaining features. André Dussollier would appear in seven of them, and Sabine Azéma would star in all but one. Resnais and Azéma married in 1998. The trio's ensemble work sparkles with uncommon synergy and would garner many awards and much critical acclaim.

This new concept of casting is part of a broader strategy of collective creation. Resnais always preferred to work in close harmony with carefully chosen collaborators. Reluctant to call himself an auteur, he sooner sees himself as the leader of a theatrical or musical ensemble. Notable among his long-term collaborators was his first wife, Florence Malraux, who served as his assistant director from *Marienbad* in 1960 through *Mélo* in 1986. Albert Jurgenson edited nine Resnais films between 1968 and 1993, and Sacha Vierny was director of photography for seven feature-length films over a period of more than twenty-five years, beginning with *Night and Fog*. Jacques Saulnier created production designs for an impressive record of eighteen Resnais films beginning with *Marienbad* and ending with the director's last film in 2013. Then there are the literary writers whom he has brought into his fold: Queneau, Cayrol, Semprun, Duras, Robbe-Grillet, and English playwright and director Alan Ayckbourn, just to name the most prominent. His collaboration with Henri Laborit for *Mon Oncle d'Amérique* is a unique experiment in collaboration between an artist and a scientist blending documentary and fiction. Resnais is a team builder for many reasons, including ethical ones—his reluctance to speak for victims and his desire to bring in experts—and simply for the pleasure of creating in partnership with others.

Working with his chosen "family" of actors, three of Resnais's titles of the decade might be seen as a trilogy. In *La Vie est un roman* (*Life Is a Bed of Roses*, 1983), a motley assembly of characters (played by Azéma, Arditi, Dussollier, with Fanny Ardant and others) attempts to reinvent life in the aftermath of the first World War. Blending fairy-tale magic, science-fiction speculation, and operatic style, the characters engage in games and experiments, hoping to find a reliable route out of horror toward renewed happiness. *L'Amour à mort* (*Love unto Death*, 1984) visualizes the subjective experience of the death of a loved one. Simon (Arditi) falls ill and dies and then comes back to life. Elisabeth (Azéma), who loves him passionately, is eager to begin life anew with him. When Simon dies again for good, Elisabeth vows to follow him, so that they can be resuscitated together. Dialogue is almost unnecessary to convey the emotional force of Elisabeth's refusal to accept Simon's death. The scenes are punctuated by slow fades with a sprinkling of stars or snow against black background. *Mélo* (1986), adapted from a play by Henri Bernstein, gives us three musicians entangled in a love triangle (Azéma, Arditi, and Dussollier again), in a story involving jealousy, suicide, and dramatic declamation, with a score by Bach and Brahms. A red velvet curtain and changes of set divide the movie into scenes, mimicking a theatrical production. Here, theater furnishes not only a source text, but also a cinematic conceit and a formal challenge.

The first of these titles—*Mélo*—suggests we might consider the three films under an additional rubric: melodrama. In fact, many defining features of the melodramatic mode are present in abundance throughout Resnais's career. The 1980s trilogy stretches depiction of extreme emotion almost to the breaking point, with themes of love and death presented with hyperbolic excess, stylized and overdramatized affect, and extravagant use of color for symbolic purposes. Resnais adopts these melodramatic conventions to experiment with new ways of engaging the spectator on an emotional level. And, of course, as literally "musical drama," the genre seeks to elicit emotion directly through music. The three protagonists of *Mélo* are professional musicians, *Life Is a Bed of Roses* explicitly declares that music is the main source of hope in the quest to forge new "harmonies" in a post-traumatic world, and in In *L'Amour à mort*, Resnais uses musical rhythms to define his characters and to structure the film's overall composition. Close attention to the musicality of voices, dialogues, and the rhythms of the scenes seeks to bypass cognitive coherence and aim directly for feeling.

Melodrama originated on the stage, so it should not surprise us that Resnais would continue to concentrate his efforts on discovering what theater has to offer the cinema. Of his eight remaining features after *Mélo*, five are adaptations from theatrical texts and two more are heavily indebted to stage performance. This orientation evokes his early ambition to become an actor, to be sure, but more important, as he declares repeatedly in the interviews here, it highlights an approach to filmmaking that incorporates his understanding of dramatic texts (unlike novels, for example) as works in progress, not fully realized until their incarnation on the stage or screen. Décors, costumes, colors, sound, and especially actors are essential contributors to such a process.

Resnais affords his characters an open-ended freedom similar to the flexibility he builds into his plots: like Stavisky, they are all performers of their own lives, and he shows them in all their foolishness, fragility, and pathos, but he also treats them with playful affection. In these ways, Resnais's untiring research into cinematic form embraces the full implications of the term "play." He is aware that, like scientific research, aesthetic advances depend on multiple sources and demand some wiggle room be left for chance, for the "play" of competing forces, for asking the question "What if . . . ?" (These are key tenets of Surrealism as well.) Also part of the game is a calculated intermingling of genres: comedy and tragedy, comic strip, musical review, vaudeville, variety singing, animation, and special effects all make an appearance. And while his topics may sometimes be grim, we should never underestimate his capacity for playfulness. Harry Dickson and Fantômas are never far from mind.

Both *Smoking/No Smoking* (1993) and *Coeurs* (*Private Fears in Public Places*, 2006) were adapted from works by British playwright Alan Ayckbourn. The first of these—two full-length features best understood as a single film in two panels—stars only Azéma and Arditi playing four or five roles each. The characters include a rural schoolmaster, his wife, a gardener, neighbors, townspeople, and a maid. Humor lies in the ordinary but slightly off-kilter situations and in the sheer ingenuity of staging (and the suspense of watching) interactions in which various characters played by a single actor very nearly appear on-screen at the same time. The plot advances through a series of scenarios articulated by the proposition "Ou bien . . ." ("Or else . . ."): at any moment, things could turn out differently. Narrative, like life, defies linearity; the deck can always be reshuffled to start another round.

Resnais appreciated Ayckbourn for writing plays not necessarily intended to be staged—in fact, some never were—and he recognized their potential for cinematic adaptation. *Coeurs* (*Private Fears in Public Places*, 2006) takes place in Paris and stars Resnais's favorite trio plus a few others. This time, the heterogeneous collection of characters includes a crotchety old man (voice only), a real estate agent, an unemployed drunk, a sympathetic bartender, and a bored young woman who videotapes herself in a striptease. Like *Smoking/No Smoking*, this film offers another set of mix-and-match quests for love that eventually (almost) intersect.

Still drawing on the conventions of theater, two further experiments incorporate forms of popular culture: comic strips and operetta. *I Want to Go Home* (1988), scripted by cartoonist Jules Feiffer and starring Adolph Green and Gérard Depardieu, incorporates stylized singing numbers and animated comic strip characters such as Popeye and Tarzan. The film was intriguing and fun, but neither a box-office nor a critical success. *Pas sur la bouche* (*Not on the lips*, 2003) was adapted from a 1925 operetta and stars, once again, Azéma and Arditi, this time alongside Lambert Wilson and Audrey Tautou (of *Amélie* fame). The dialogue is almost entirely sung, while couples form and reconfigure in dizzy sequence, until a set of ingeniously choreographed coincidences brings them all together in the same place. Frivolous and playful, the film mocks bourgeois codes of behavior and indulges in nostalgia for earlier (if not more innocent) forms of popular entertainment. Opulent sets and beautiful costumes, masterful directing, acting, and singing, and its sheer over-the-top silliness captured the hearts of audiences almost in spite of themselves.

Also immersed in the world of theater, *Vous n'avez encore rien vu* (*You Ain't Seen Nothin' Yet*, 2011) establishes an entirely different mood. Adapted from two plays by Jean Anouilh, there are no traces of popular culture here. Resnais instead challenged himself to film a potentially infinite regress of temporal layers and plays-within-plays. A dead man leaves a message convoking his actor friends to his house to view a filmed rehearsal of a play in which all the friends had once played roles. A figure appears who might be Satan or God or Fate, and at least one character dies twice, while past and present, filmed and recited versions of the play echo and impinge upon each other in counterpoint. The fact that the play in question is *Eurydice* echoes Resnais's other "Orphic" films, including *Amour à mort*, *Je t'aime, je t'aime*, and even *Hiroshima mon amour*, where a character undertakes a literal or metaphorical "voyage" to the underworld to rejoin a dead companion. Although there is little singing, *Vous n'avez encore rien vu* is a choral movie for many voices.

Resnais's final film, *Aimer, boire et chanter* (*The Life of Riley*, 2013) begins with a couple in their garden rehearsing their lines for a play. Other couples appear, and as in the Ayckbourn-inspired movies, these individuals have had other, secret relationships with each other in the past or will in the near future. The film is not drawn from an existing play, but instead mimics one. Very much in the mood and style of Ayckbourn, the script was written by three writers among whom is one Alex Réval, a pen name Resnais had already adopted on previous occasions. In all his theatrically inspired work, Resnais pushes beyond theatrical representation by experimenting with techniques only available in cinema, such as split screen and close-ups.

Resnais's most beloved film, *On Connaît la chanson* (*Same Old Song*, 1997), is neither theatrical in itself nor adapted from a play, but it is heavily indebted to the stage nonetheless. The screenplay was written by playwright-actor couple Agnès Jaoui and Jean-Pierre Bacri, who had previously adapted *Smoking/No Smoking*. Like *Pas sur la bouche*, *On connaît la chanson* is a kind of musical or operetta, but with a twist: this time, at moments of intense emotion, our favorite actors—Azéma, Arditi, Dussollier, and Wilson, along with Jaoui and Bacri, in leading roles—open their mouths and (surprise!) lip-sync familiar numbers sung by well-loved singers such as Charles Aznavour, Josephine Baker, Maurice Chevalier, Eddy Mitchell, and Edith Piaf, all to delightful comic and melodramatic effect. The film won numerous prizes, among them eight César Awards for best directing, acting, writing, editing, and sound.

In this final, large cluster of films that closes Resnais's filmography, one outlier confirms the rules while shedding light on the entirety of the director's career. With *Les Herbes Folles* (*Wild Grass*, 2008), the director undertook what he always vowed he would never do: adapt a novel. Like the film, the novel in question— Christian Gailly's *L'Incident* (1996)—relates an unlikely series of "incidents" that bring a man (Dussollier) together with a woman (Azéma) whose stolen wallet he finds on the street. Asked in interviews why he broke his vow to stay away from novels, Resnais answers in terms reminiscent of his theatrical ventures: he was drawn to the "voice" of the novel's narrator, appreciated the open-ended plot that left ample room for chance, and was inspired by the mixture of comic and tragic elements. Writing as Alex Réval (and at the age of eighty-six!), Resnais wrote the screenplay himself. Despite its novelistic origins, the film succeeds in maintaining the primacy of emotion over narration and of character over plot, while taking advantage of an unpredictable sequence—reminiscent of André Breton's Surrealist novel, *Nadja* (1928)—of chance encounters and coincidences. The film's title is meant to evoke weeds that sprout up unexpectedly, as in the cracks between paving stones.

It is difficult if not impossible to summarize the career of an artist like Alain Resnais. I have presented his films in "clusters" as a descriptive convenience that aims to frame the interviews below, as they chart a career characterized by both immense variety and remarkable coherence. This apparent paradox perhaps derives from Resnais's deep familiarity with all aspects of his craft. During the sixty-eight years of his working life, he delved into virtually every corner of filmmaking: he worked as director of short subjects and of feature films, of course, but in addition, at one time or another, as screenwriter (uncredited or as Alex Réval), assistant director, actor, camera operator, cinematographer, editor, special effects coordinator, technical consultant, and even author of source material. There was almost no aspect of filmmaking he did not practice himself.

Resnais's oeuvre is not reducible to his plots, nor can it be identified by specific themes or even narrative techniques. What you will discover here instead are the constellations of themes and the marvelously complex intersections of plot incidents with inventive combinations of techniques that convey unconventional points of view. I would propose that the unity of his work can be most easily understood as a function of his original choice of what he calls his "vocation": *le montage*.

Montage is not quite the same thing as "editing." With the exception of the early one-minute, single-shot movies of the Lumière brothers—and possibly a few longer experiments since—all films are cut and assembled in order to join one shot to another. Resnais's conception of *montage* is not that of Hollywood continuity editing, however, nor did he adopt André Bazin's recommendations for creating an illusion of visual and emotional reality. His approach is different, too, from Eisenstein's dialectical montage, where meaning—often political meaning—arises between shots from their juxtaposition. Resnais does not make a movie and then edit it. His vision for the editing is present from the beginning. Nothing much happens in his films; the editing *is* the story. It is the way the shots are assembled that produces each film's musical rhythms and harmonies, its contrapuntal layering of past and present moments, its emotional complexities, in an echo chamber of competing perceptions or alternative worlds. Even death is reversible! Resnais's *montage* does more than bring together bits of film into a whole: it's more akin to lace, where meaning is created not by the threads alone, but by their elegant interactions with empty spaces. This is what Resnais means by "anti-illusionism"; it's more like a dream (hence the Surrealist connection, one last time) or tapping into the unconscious. And it's closer to what Deleuze called the "time image," where movies can represent the workings of thought. This conception of *montage*—this conception of cinema itself—is a worldview, an ethic, and an aesthetic rolled into one. Resnais's films—whether they're about the Occupation and the atomic bomb or a bourgeois couple at home, a plastics factory or a passionate love affair, whether they take place in an otherworldly manor inhabited by characters named only "X," "A," and "M" or in the bowels of the national library—all manage somehow to reveal what you will encounter again and again in these interviews: a creator who is at once an intellectual, a philosopher, an entertainer, a craftsman, and an artist.

LAH

Notes

1. For additional biographical details, see Robert Benayoun, *Alain Resnais: Arpenteur de l'imaginaire* (Stock, 1980); Suzanne Liandrat-Guigues and Jean-Louis Leutrat, *Alain Resnais: Liaisons secrètes, accords vagabonds* (Cahiers du cinéma, 2006); and Jean-Luc Douin, *Alain Resnais* (La Martinière, 2013).
2. Tawarnicki would eventually publish their script as *Les Aventures de Harry Dickson, scénario pour un film (non-réalisé)* par Alain Resnais et Frédéric Towarnicki (Capricci, 2007).
3. *Repérages: photographies d'Alain Resnais, texte de Jorge Semprun* (Chêne, 1974).
4. For more about the Group of Thirty, see Steven Ungar, "Quality Wars: The Groupe des Trente and the Renewal of the Short Subject in France, 1953–1963," *South Central Review* 33, no. 2 (summer 2016): 30–43.
5. For further discussion, see Sam Di Iorio, "The Fragile Present: *Statues Also Die* with *Night and Fog*," *South Central Review* 33, no. 2 (summer 2016): 15–29.
6. See Sylvie Lindeperg *Nuit et brouillard: Un Film dans l'histoire* (Jacob, 2007).
7. The Ouvroir de Littérature Potentiel or OuLiPo continues today as a workshop on writing following more or less Surrealist principles.
8. See Dudley Andrew and Steven Ungar, *Popular Front Paris and the Poetics of Culture* (Harvard University Press, 2005), 16–51.
9. DVD bonus interview with Resnais accompanying *Providence* (Jupiter Films).
10. Gilles Deleuze, *Cinema 2: The Time Image*, trans. Hugh Tomlinson and Robert Galeta (University of Minnesota Press, 1989), 101.

Chronology

1922   Alain Resnais born in Vannes, Brittany, on June 3, 1922, the only son of Pierre Resnais, a pharmacist, and Jeanne Gachet, who lived in la rue Mené. His parents wanted him to take up pharmacology, but he didn't feel the courage to prepare such a heavy degree.

1929   Resnais turns seven the year the talkies are introduced. He attended Catholic school at Saint-François Xavier until age fourteen.

1935   Receives 8mm movie camera from his father for his thirteenth birthday. Alain built a little movie theater to show films. Alain makes *L'aventure de Guy*, his first feature film. He also did an early film project on *Brave New World* that has disappeared. Shoots a version of *Fantômas* with his friends. His memorable early moviegoing experiences included a documentary on the growth of a bean, a Harold Lloyd silent comedy called *Haunted Spooks* (1920), and *The Awakening of Professor Mecanicas*, a science-fiction cartoon by R. Lortac.

              He also gradually built up a collection of comic books that was to become one of the finest collections in all of France. He would later report that it was from reading comics that he learned how to shoot and edit a film.

1939   Resnais heads to Paris to study at the Collège Frédéric-Leplay and spends Thursday and Sunday afternoons at the movies. Lives on the rue de Courcelles, where Proust had lived. Enrolled in the acting school René Simon for two years, where he meets Danielle Delorme and shows movies such as *Metropolis* to her and other friends. Resnais did not become an actor, but became a a great fan of actors.

1940   The war forces him to head south to Nice, thinking to reach Algeria, but he ends up back in Paris. During the 1940s, he took thousands of still photographs with his Leica. Later they were published as *Repérages* (1974) with an introduction by Jorge Semprun, who wrote that "their beauty comes from an explosive mixture of everyday platitudes and furtive interrogation that bring them their depth."

1942   Becomes assistant to Georges Pitoëff at the Mathurins Theater, and works in a bookstore.

1943   Enters IDHEC with an interest in editing, but quits after a year and a half, finding the courses too theoretical.

1945   Leaves Paris to do military service and spends nineteen months in Germany. There Resnais meets André Voisin. The two form a theater troupe called *Les Arlequins* and collaborate on theatrical shows.

1946   Resnais returns to Paris where (thanks to his parents) he takes up residence at 70 rue des Plantes near the Gare Montparnasse. There he convinces his downstairs neighbor, Gérard Philippe, to act in a Surrealist short entitled, *Ouvert pour Inventaire*, also starring Danièle Delorme. The film has disappeared.

1947   Resnais makes a short film, *Visites*, with Max Ernst and also works as editor for Nicole Vedrès's *Paris 1900*.

1948   Resnais makes a film, *Les Chateaux de la Loire*, as he rides his bike through the Loire Valley with his camera on his back. Makes *Van Gogh*, a short film, commissioned by Pierre Braunberger, to coincide with a show of the artist's work that had just opened in Paris. The film wins a prize that year at the Venice biennale, and an Oscar in 1950. Later that year he meets François Truffaut and serves as editor on Truffaut's first film, a silent 16mm short entitled *Une Visite* (now lost).

1950   Resnais makes two short films, *Gauguin*, and *Guernica*, the latter on Picasso's 1937 antiwar painting with a text by Paul Eluard and read by Maria Casarès.

         Jean-Luc Godard praises Resnais's short films as having "reinvented the cinema." With Chris Marker, Resnais also makes *Les Statues meurent aussi* (*Statues Also Die*), a political film on the destructive effect of French colonialism on African art.

1954–55   Resnais signs on as editor of Agnès Varda's *La pointe courte*. Varda recalls, "At that time the only film of Alain's I knew was *Guernica*. That was enough for me to dare ask him to edit *La Pointe courte*, which I had just shot instinctively, intuitively, as a revolt, an isolated act. I sent him the script. He replied immediately in a very long and attentive letter. He explained that it was just not possible for him: this cinema corresponded too closely to what he dreamed of doing himself. All the same, he accepted a little later. The editing was very slow, six months, here in this very room at rue Daguerre where we had installed a hired viewing machine. [. . .] For me it was a time of reflection. Like an apprenticeship in the kind of cinema I had to continue, in which Alain was able to give me confidence. When he could have arranged things, made them follow his own inclination, he did nothing of the sort. He wanted above all to leave me responsible for my errors and also for a certain personal accent. This is his integrity. Thanks to him, I understood my own work. By scrupulously editing my film he allowed me to clarify my own thoughts. And he sent me to the cinema—I hardly ever went at that time—made me really love it. Yes, that was a vital encounter for me and if he did not have any direct influence on my first film, it is to him that I owe becoming what I now am" (Agnès Varda, "Dans une chambre haute," in Bounoure).

1955 Resnais makes *Nuit et brouillard* (*Night and Fog*), with Jean Cayrol, about the Nazi concentration camps. Considered too political, the film is withdrawn from the Cannes Film Festival.

1956 Resnais makes *Toute la mémoire du monde*, a short film about the French National Library.

1958 Resnais shoots *Le Chant du Styrène*, made for the Pechiney company to celebrate their product. The text, by Raymond Queneau, is written in classical Alexandrine verse. It traces the production of polystyrene backwards from production towards the raw material, towards abstract matter.

Late in the year, Resnais is approached to do a documentary on the atomic bomb. He refuses, but tells the producer that he might reconsider if someone like novelist Marguérite Duras were involved. The result is *Hiroshima mon amour*, with a screenplay by Duras. Resnais calls the film a "false documentary."

1959 Resnais meets Jean-Raymond Kremer, the Belgian author, to discuss making a film of *Les Aventures de Harry Dickson*. By 1960, Resnais has a completed script of the film, but it's far too long and takes seven years to whip into shape. It remains on his wish list for the rest of his life.

Resnais meets (and will later marry) Florence Malraux, daughter of the author of *Man's Fate*.

1960 Resnais signs the *Manifesto of the 121*, a protest against French military policy in Algeria.

1961 *L'Année dernière à Marienbad* (*Last Year at Marienbad*), made in collaboration with the French New Novelist, Alain Robbe-Grillet, premieres at the Venice Film Festival, winning the Golden Lion.

1962 Resnais begins shooting *Muriel* in November.

1964 Resnais approaches Jorge Semprun with a proposal to do a film together.

1966 *La Guerre est finie* (*The War Is Over*), their collaboration, is shown at Cannes, but, after an objection by the Spanish government, it is shown "out of competition."

1967–68 *Je t'aime, je t'aime* is shot in the autumn and premieres in Paris in April, 1968 during "the events" of May. The film was to be lost in the chaos of *les événements*. English-speaking audiences would not see the film until four years later. Resnais also participates with Chris Marker and Jean-Luc Godard in a collective film about the war in Vietnam, *Loin du Vietnam* (*Far from Vietnam*).

1969 Resnais marries Florence Malraux, who had been his assistant on every film since *Marienbad*.

1970 Resnais gets a commitment from Dirk Bogarde to play the Marquis de Sade, but the film never materializes.

1972 Resnais visits New York City and spends time at MOMA with Penelope Mortimer, hoping to produce a screenplay and then a film of *The Home*, but it remains only a wishful discussion. He later meets with Jorge Semprun to discuss *Stavisky* . . . .

1973 Resnais contributes an episode of *L'An '01* a collective film organized by Jacques Doillon.

1974 *Stavisky* . . . opens in May.

1977 Resnais collaborates with David Mercer on *Providence*, starring John Gielgud and Dirk Bogarde, about a novelist struggling with conflicting versions of his past as he lies dying.

1980 After having studied the work of neurobiologist Henri Laborit, Resnais shoots *Mon oncle d'Amérique* (*My American Uncle*), interweaving three fictional stories intended to illustrate Laborit's theories. The film wins the Grand Prix at Cannes.

1983 With a group that will become his "team" for the rest of his career, Resnais works with Sabine Azéma, Pierre Arditi, and André Dussollier to make *La vie est un roman* (*Life Is a Bed of Roses*), a comic fantasy that tends toward the operatic.

1984 With the same group of actors, Resnais shoots *L'Amour à mort* (*Love Unto Death*), a film that imagines the return to life of a man who cannot die without his wife.

1986 In *Mélo*, Resnais adapts playwright Henri Bernstein's work to the screen. Resnais and Florence Malraux are divorced.

1989 In *I Want to Go Home*, with a screenplay by Jules Feiffer, Resnais delves into the world of comic books and cartoons.

1992 Resnais explores the life and work of the American composer in *Gershwin*, a TV documentary.

1993 Now fascinated by Alan Ayckbourn's writing for the theater, Resnais adapts the British playwright's *Smoking/No Smoking* for the screen.

1997	*On Connaît la chanson* (*Same Old Song*) brings a series of popular songs to a dramatic plot.
1998	Resnais marries his longtime leading lady, Sabine Azéma.
2003	Resnais makes *Pas Sur La Bouche* (*Not on the Lips*), based on an operetta from the 1920s and experiments with having actors, rather than dubbed singers, sing the songs.
2006	Resnais returns to his fascination with Alan Ayckbourn's work in *Coeurs* (*Private Fears in Public Places*).
2009	At age eighty-seven and nowhere near depletion, Resnais films *Les Herbes Folles* (*Wild Grass*), based on a novel by Christian Gailly.
2012	*Vous n'avez encore rien vu* (*You Ain't Seen Nothin' Yet*) proves that Resnais has not tired of his long career. The film is based on two plays by Jean Anouilh.
2014	Resnais shoots his last film, *Aimer, boire et chanter* (*Life of Riley*), inspired by the work of Alan Ayckbourn. Three weeks before his death, Resnais learns the film has won a prize at the Sixty-fourth Berlin International Film Festival. Resnais dies on March 1 in Paris at the age of ninety-one. He is buried in the Cimetière Montparnasse.

Filmography

As Actor, Assistant Director, or Technical Assistant (Selected)

1942   LES VISITEURS DU SOIR (dir. Marcel Carné), actor
1947   PARIS 1900 (dir. Nicole Vedrès), assistant director
          JEAN EFFEL (dir. Sylvain Dhomme), director of photography
          MALFRAY (dir. Robert Hessens), assistant director
          HAUSSMANN ET LA TRANSFORMATION DE PARIS (dir. Pierre Mignot and Jean Leduc), special effects
1953   AUX FRONTIERES DE L'HOMME (dir. Nicole Védrès), editor
1955   LA POINTE COURTE (dir. Agnès Varda), editor
1957   L'OEIL DU MAITRE (dir. Jacques Doniol-Valcroze), editor
1958   NOVEMBRE A PARIS (dir. François Reichenbach), editor

Short Films

VAN GOGH (1948)
Director: **Alain Resnais**
Concept: Robert Hessens, Gaston Diehl
Music: Jacques Besse
Editing: **Alain Resnais**
Cinematography: Henri Ferrand
Pantheon Production
B&W, 20 minutes
Award: Academy Award for Best Short Subject, 1950

PAUL GAUGUIN (1950)
Director: **Alain Resnais**
Concept: Gaston Diehl
Cinematography: Henry Ferrand
Music: Darius Milhaud
Editing: **Alain Resnais**

Pantheon Production
B&W, 12 minutes

GUERNICA (1950)
Director: **Alain Resnais**, Robert Hessens
Text: Paul Eluard
Cinematography: André Dumaître
Music: Guy Bernard
Editing: **Alain Resnais**
Pantheon Production.
B&W, 12 minutes
Awards: Punta del Este, Prize for Best Film on Art, 1952

LES STATUES MEURENT AUSSI (STATUES ALSO DIE) (1950–53)
Director: **Alain Resnais**
Text: Chris Marker, read by Jean Negroni
Cinematography: Ghislain Coquet
Music: Guy Bernard
Sound: Henri Colpi
Editing: **Alain Resnais**
Production: Tadié Cinéma, Présence Africaine
B&W, 29 minutes

NUIT ET BROUILLARD (NIGHT AND FOG) (1956)
Director: **Alain Resnais**
Text: Jean Cayrol, read by Michel Bouquet
Cinematography: Ghislain Cloquet
Music: Hanns Eisler
Sound: Henri Colpi
Editing: **Alain Resnais,** Henri Colpy, and others
Argos Films, Como Films
B&W and color, 32 minutes
Award: Prix Jean Vigo

TOUTE LA MEMOIRE DU MONDE (1956)
Director: **Alain Resnais**
Text: Rémo Forlani
Cinematography: Ghislain Cloquet
Music: Maurice Jarre, directed by Georges Delerue

Sound: Studios Magnan
Editing: **Alain Resnais** and others
Films de la Pléiade (Pierre Braunberger)
Cast: François-Régis Bastide, Monique Le Porrier, Joseph Rovan, Agnés Varda
B&W, 22 minutes
Awards: Prix de la C.S.T., 1957; Cannes Film Festival, Best Photography, 1957; Gold Medal in Mannheim, 1958

LE MYSTERE DE L'ATELIER QUINZE (1957)
Director: **Alain Resnais,** André Heinrich.
Text: Chris Marker
Cinematography: Ghislain Cloquet
Music: Pierre Barbaud
Sound: Studios Marignan
Editing: Anne Sarraute
Producer: Jacqueline Jacoupy
18 minutes

LE CHANT DU STYRENE (1958)
Director: **Alain Resnais**
Text: Raymond Queneau
Cinematography: Sacha Vierny
Music: Pierre Barbaud, directed by Georges Delerue
Sound: Studios Marignan
Editing: **Alain Resnais**, Claudine Merlin
Films de la Pléiade (Pierre Braunberger)
Color, 14 minutes
Awards: Venice Film Festival, Mercure d'or, 1958

CONTRE L'OUBLI (1991)
Contribution called "Pour Esteban Gonzalez (Cuba)," 1991

GERSHWIN (TV documentary) (1992)
Text: Edward Jablinski, read by Pierre Arditi, Sabine Azéma, Lambert Wilson
A2, Telemax, CNC, Ministry of Culture and Communication, Conseil de l'Europe, Sofica Cofimage 3, RAI 2, Channel 4
Cinematography: Ned Burgess
Editing: Albert Jurgenson
Color, 52 minutes
Feature Films

HIROSHIMA MON AMOUR (1958)
Director: **Alain Resnais**
Screenplay: Marguérite Duras
Cinematography: Takahashi Michio (Japan); Sacha Vierny (France)
Music: Giovanni Fusco and Georges Delerue
Sound: Yamamoto, Pierre Calvet
Editing: Henri Colpi, Jasmine Chasney, Anne Sarraute
Argos Films, Como Films, Daïeï, Pathé Overseas
Cast: Emmanuelle Riva, Eiji Okada, Bernard Fresson, Stella Dassas, Pierrre Barbaud
B&W, 91 minutes
Awards: Presented "out of competition," Cannes Film Festival, 1959; Cannes Film Festival, prize from the FIPRESCI and the Société des écrivains de cinéma, 1959; Critics' and Distributors' Prize, New York, 1960

L'ANNEE DERNIERE A MARIENBAD (LAST YEAR AT MARIENBAD) (1961)
Director: **Alain Resnais**
Screenplay: Alain Robbe-Grillet
Cinematography: Sacha Vierny
Music: Francis Seyrig
Sound: Guy Villette
Sets: Jacques Saulnier
Editing: Henri Colpi, Jasmine Chasney
Terra Film, Société nouvelle des films Cormoran, Argos Films, Tamara, Cinetel, Como Films
Cast: Delphine Seyrig, Giorgio Albertazzi, Sacha Pitoëff
B&W, 93 minutes
Awards: Venice Film Festival, Golden Lion, 1961; Prix Méliès

MURIEL OU LE TEMPS D'UN RETOUR (MURIEL, OR THE TIME OF RETURN) (1963)
Director: **Alain Resnais**
Screenplay: Jean Cayrol
Cinematography: Sacha Vierny
Music: Hans Warner Henze, Georges Delerue
Sound: Antoine Bonfanti
Editing: Kenout Peltier
Argos Films, Alpha Productions Éclair, Films de la Pléiade, Dear Films
Color, 116 minutes

Cast: Delphine Seyrig (Hélène), Jean-Pierre Kérien (Alphonse), Nita Klein (Françoise), Jean-Baptiste Thierrée (Bernard), Claude Sainval (Roland de Smoke), Laurence Badie (Claudie), Jean Champion (Ernest Choisy), Jean Dasté (goatherd)

LA GUERRE EST FINIE (THE WAR IS OVER) (1966)
Director: **Alain Resnais**
Screenplay: Jorge Semprun
Cinematography: Sacha Vierny
Music: Giovanni Fusco
Sound: Antoine Bonfanti
Sets: Jacques Saulnier
Editing: Eric Pluet
Socfracima, Europa Film
Cast: Yves Montand (Diègo Mora), Ingrid Thulin (Marianne), Geneviève Bujold (Nadine Sallanches), Jean Dasté (network leader), Paul Crauchet (Roberto), Dominique Rozan (Jude), Gérard Lartigau (chief of revolutionary action group), Laurence Badie (Bernadette Pluvier), Michel Piccoli (an inspector), Jorge Semprun (narrator)
B&W, 121 minutes

LOIN DU VIETNAM (FAR FROM VIETNAM), sequence "Claude Ridder" (1967)
Director: **Alain Resnais**
Screenplay: Jacques Sternberg
Cinematography: Denys Clerval
Sound: Antoine Bonfanti
Editing: Colette Leloup
Cast: Bernard Fresson (Claude Ridder), Karen Banguernon (young woman)
Production: S.L.O.N. (Chris Marker)
15 color, 15 minutes

JE T'AIME, JE T'AIME (1968)
Director: **Alain Resnais**
Screenplay: Jacques Sternberg
Cinematography: Jean Boffety
Music: Krzysztof Penderecki
Sound: Antoine Bonfanti
Editing: Colette Leloup, Albert Jurgenson
Parc Film, Fox Europa

Cast: Claude Rich (Claude Ridder), Olga Georges-Picot (Catrine), Anouck Ferjac (Wiana), Georges Jamin (the surgeon), Van Doude (head of the clinic), Dominique Rozan (the doctor), Alain Robbe-Grillet (Press attaché), Catherine Robbe-Grillet (secretary)
Color, 91 minutes

L'AN 01, sequence "New York" (1972)
Director: **Alain Resnais**
Screenplay: Gébé
Editing: Noëlle Boisson
U.Z. Productions (Anne-Marie Prieur)
Cast: Lee Falk (the banker), David Pascal (newspaper salesman), Frederic Tuten (speaker)
4 minutes

STAVISKY . . . (1974)
Director: **Alain Resnais**
Screenplay: Jorge Semprun
Cinematography: Sacha Vierny
Music: Stephen Sondheim
Sound: Jean-Pierre Ruh, Bernard Bats
Editing: Albert Jurgenson
Cérito Films, Ariane Films, Euro International
Cast: Jean-Paul Belmondo (Stavisky), François Perier (Albert Borelli), Anny Duperet (Arlette), Michael Lonsdale (Dr. Mézy), Roberto Bisacco (Juan Montalvo), Claude Rich (Inspector Bonny), Charles Boyer (Baron Raoul), Pierre Vernier (Maitre Grammont), Marcel Cuvelier (Inspector Boussaud), Gérard Départdieu (Inventor of the Matriscope), Yves Peneau (Leon Trotsky), Catherine Sellers (Natalya Trotsky), Niels Arestrup (Trotsky's secretary), François Leterrier (André Malraux)
Color, 115 minutes

PROVIDENCE (1976)
Director: **Alain Resnais**
Screenplay: David Mercer
Cinematography: Ricardo Aronovitch
Music: Miklós Rósza
Sound: René Magnol
Sets: Jacques Saulnier
Editing: Albert Jurgenson

Action Film, S.F.P., F.R.3, Citel Film
Cast: Dirk Bogarde (Claude Langham), Ellen Burstyn (Sonia Langham), Sir John Gielgud (Clive Langham), David Warner (Kevin Woodford), Denis Lawson (Dave Woodford), Elaine Stritch (Molly Langham), Tanya Lopert (Miss Lister), Anna Wang (Karen), Cyril Luckham (Mark Edington)
Color, 110 minutes
Awards: César Awards for Best Film and Best Director

MON ONCLE D'AMERIQUE (MY AMERICAN UNCLE) (1980)
Director: **Alain Resnais**
Screenplay: Jean Gruault, based on the work of Henri Laborit
Cinematography: Sacha Vierny
Music: Arié Dzierlatka
Sound: Jean-Pierre Ruh
Sets: Jacques Saulnier
Editing: Albert Jurgenson
Producers: Phillippe Dussart, Andrea Films, T.F. 1
Cast: Guillaume Boisseau, Damien Boisseau, Jean-Philippe Puymartin, Roger Pierre (Jean Le Gall), Ina Bédard, Stéphanie Lousteau, Nicole Garcia (Janine Garnier), Ludovic Salis, François Calvez, Gérard Depardieu (René Ragueneau), Professor Henri Laborit (himself), Catherine Frot, Nelly Borgeaud (Arlette Le Gall), Valérie Dréville, Marie Dubois (Thérèse Raguenaud), Pierre Arditi (Zambeau), Catherine Serre (his secretary), Gérard Darrieux, Laurence Badie (Léon Veestrate and his wife), Jean Dasté (Monsieur Louis)
Color, 125 minutes
Awards: Cannes Film Festival, Special Jury Prize, 1980; Grand Prix du Cinéma Français, 1980

LA VIE EST UN ROMAN (LIFE IS A BED OF ROSES) (1983)
Director: **Alain Resnais**
Screenplay: Jean Gruault
Cinematography: Bruno Nuytten
Music: M. Philippe-Gérard
Sound: Pierre Lenoir
Sets: Jacques Saulnier, Enki Bilal
Editing: Albert Jurgenson
Produced by Philippe Dussart, Soprofilms, Films A.2, Fideline Films, Films Ariane, Filmedis
Cast: Vittorio Gassman (Walter Guarini), Ruggero Raimondi (Count Forbek), Geraldine Chaplin (Nora Winkle), Fanny Ardant (Livia), Pierre Arditi (Robert

Dufresne), Sabine Azéma (Elizabeth Rousseau), Robert Manuel (Georges Leroux), Martine Kelly (Claudine Obertin), André Dussollier (Raoul)
Color, 111 minutes

L'AMOUR A MORT (LOVE UNTO DEATH) (1984)
Director: **Alain Resnais**
Screenplay: Jean Gruault
Cinematography: Sacha Vierny
Music: Hans Werner Henze
Sound: Pierre Gamet
Sets: Jacques Saulnier
Editing: Albert Jurgenson
Produced by Philippe Dussart, Films Ariane, Films A2
Cast: Sabine Azéma (Elisabeth Sutter), Pierre Arditi (Simon), Fanny Ardant (Judith), André Dussollier (Jérôme), Jean Dasté (Dr. Rozier), Geneviève Mnich (André Jourdet's widow), Jean-Claude Weibel (the specialist), Louis Castel (friend of the Jourdets), Françoise Morhange (Madame Vigne)
Color, 112 minutes

MÉLO (1986)
Director: **Alain Resnais**
Screenplay: from the play by Henri Bernstein
Cinematography: Charles Van Damme
Editing: Albert Jurgenson
Music: M. Philippe-Gérard
Sound: Henri Morelle
Producers: Marin Karmitz, M.K.2 and Films A.2.
Cast: Sabine Azéma (Romaine), Fanny Ardant (Christiane), Pierre Arditi (Pierre), André Dussollier (Marcel) Jacques Dacqmine (the doctor), Hubert Gignoux (the priest).
Color, 112 minutes
Awards: Césars for Best Actress (Azéma), Best Actor (Dussollier), Best Supporting Actor (Arditi)

I WANT TO GO HOME (1989)
Director: **Alain Resnais**
Screenplay: Jules Feiffer
Cinematography: Charles Van Damme
Music: John Kander
Editing: Albert Jurgenson

Producer: Marin Karmitz, MK2
Cast: Adolphe Green (Joey Wellman), Laura Benson (Elsie Wellman), Linda Lavin (Lena Apthrop), Gérard Depardieu (Christian Gauthier), Micheline Presle (Isabelle Gauthier), John Ashton (Harry Dempsey), Geraldine Chaplin (Terry Armstrong)
Color, 105 minutes

SMOKING and NO SMOKING (1993)
Director: **Alain Resnais**
Screenplay: Agnès Jaoui and Jean-Pierre Bacri, from Alan Ayckbourn's play, *Intimate Exchanges*
Cinematography: Renato Berta
Sound: Bernard Bats and Gérard Lamps
Music: John Pattison
Sets: Jacques Saulnier
Editing: Albert Jurgenson
Producer: Bruno Pésery, Michel Seydoux, Pyramide Distribution,
Cast: Sabine Azéma (Celia Teasdale, Rowena Coombes, Sylvie Bell, Irene Pridworthy, Josephine Hamilton), Pierre Arditi (Toby Teasdale, Miles Coombes, Lionel Hepplewick, Joe Hepplewick)
298 minutes (146 minutes and 147 minutes)
Awards: Silver Bear, Berlin Festival; Louis Delluc Prize; Césars for Best Film, Best Director (**Alain Resnais**), Best Actor (Pierre Arditi), Best Actress (Sabine Azéma), Best Cinematography (Renato Berta), Best Editing (Albert Jurgenson), and Best Sound (Bernard Bats and Gérard Lamps)

ON CONNAIT LA CHANSON (SAME OLD SONG) (1997)
Director: **Alain Resnais**
Screenplay: Agnès Jaoui, Jean-Pierre Bacri
Cinematography: Renato Berta
Music: Henri Christiné, Bruno Fontaine
Sound: Pierre Lenoir, Jean-Pierre Laforce, Michel Klochendler
Sets: Jacques Saulnier
Editing: Hervé de Luze
Producer: Bruno Pésery, AMLF, Arena Films, Caméra One, Vega Films
Color, 120 minutes
Cast: Pierre Arditi (Claude Lalande), Sabine Azéma (Odile Lalande), Jean-Pierre Bacri (Nicolas), André Dussollier (Simon), Agnès Jaoui (Camille), Lambert Wilson (Marc Duveyrier), Jane Birkin (Jane), Jean-Paul Roussillon (Odile's father), Claire Nadeau (the guest)

Awards: Louis Delluc Prize, 1997; César Awards for Best Film, Best Actor, Best Supporting Actor, Best Supporting Actress, Best Writing, Best editing, Best Sound, 1998; Berlin Festival Silver Bear (Resnais for outstanding artistic contribution), 1998

PAS SUR LA BOUCHE (NOT ON THE LIPS) (2003)
Director: **Alain Resnais**
Screenplay: Alain Resnais From the operetta by André Barde and Maurice Yvain
Cinematography: Renato Berto
Music: Maurice Yvain, Bruno Fontaine
Sound: Jean-Marie Blondel, Gérard Hardy, Gérard Lamps
Sets: Jacques Saulnier
Editing: Hervé de Luze
Producer: Bruno Pésery, Pathé
Cast: Sabine Azéma (Gilberte Valandray), Pierre Arditi (Georges Valandray), Isabelle Nanty (Arlette), Daniel Prévost (Faradel), Jalil Lespert (Charley), Audrey Tautou (Huguette), Lambert Wilson (Eric Thomson), Darry Cowl (Madame Foin)
Color, 115 minutes
Awards: César Awards for Best Sound, Best Costumes, and Best Supporting Actor (Darry Cowl); Etoile d'or for Best Film from Academy of French film journalists, 2004; Prix Lumière for best director awarded by International Press in Paris, 2004.

COEURS (PRIVATE FEARS IN PUBLIC PLACES) (2006)
Director: **Alain Resnais**
Screenplay: Jean-Michel Ribes, adapted from play by Alan Ayckbourn
Cinematography: Eric Gautier
Music: Mark Snow
Sound: Jean-Marie Blondel
Sets: Jacques Saulnier
Editing: Hervé de Luze
Producer: Bruno Pésery
Cast: Sabine Azéma (Charlotte), Lambert Wilson (Dan), Pierre Arditi (Lionel), Laura Morante (Nicole), Isabelle Carré (Gaëlle), André Dussollier (Thierry)
Color, 120 minutes
Awards: Venice Film Festival, Silver Lion for Best Director (**Alain Resnais**) and Best Actress (Laura Morante), 2007; European Film Awards, Etoile d'Or for Best Director; FIPRESCI Prize, 2007

LES HERBES FOLLES (WILD GRASS) (2009)
Director: **Alain Resnais**

Screenplay: Alain Resnais (as Alex Réval), Laurent Herbiet, from novel by Christian Gailly
Cinematography: Eric Gautier
Music: Mark Snow
Sound: Jean-Marie Blondel
Sets: Jacques Saulnier
Editing: Hervé de Luze
Producers: Jean-Louis Livi, Julie Salvador; Studio Canal
Cast: Sabine Azéma (Marguerite Muir), André Dussollier (Georges Paalet), Anne Consigny (Suzanne), Emmanuelle Devos (Josépha), Mathieu Amalric (Bernard de Bordeaux), Michel Vuillermoz (Lucien d'Orange), Sara Forestier (Elodie), Vladimir Consigny (Marcelin), Edouard Baer (narrator)
Color, 104 minutes
Award: Cannes Film Festival, Special Jury Prize at Cannes Festival for Resnais "as a lifetime achievement award for his work and exceptional contribution to the history of cinema," 2009

VOUS N'AVEZ ENCORE RIEN VU (YOU AIN'T SEEN NOTHIN' YET) (2012)
Director: **Alain Resnais**
Screenplay: Laurent Herbiet, **Alain Resnais** (as Alex Réval), from two plays by Jean Anouilh
Cinematography: Eric Gautier
Music: Mark Snow
Sound: Jean-Pierre Duret, Gérard Hardy, Gérard Lamps
Sets: Jacques Saulnier
Editing: Hervé de Luze
Producers: Jean-Louis Livi, Julie Salvador, Studio Canal Alamode Film
Cast: Mathieu Amalric (Monsieur Henri), Sabine Azéma (Eurydice 1), Anne Consigny (Eurydice 2), Pierre Arditi (Orphée 1) Lambert Wilson (Orphée 2), Michel Piccoli (Orphée's father), Anny Duperey (Eurydice's mother), Denis Podalydès (Antoine), Michel Vuillermoz (Vincent)
Color, 115 minutes

AIMER, BOIRE ET CHANTER (LIFE OF RILEY) (2014)
Director: **Alain Resnais**
Screenplay: Laurent Herbiet, Alain Resnais (as Alex Réval)
Cinematography: Dominique Bouilleret
Music: Mark Snow
Sound: Jean-Pierre Duret
Sets: Jacques Saulnier

Editing: Hervé de Luze
Cast: Sabine Azéma (Kathryn), André Dussollier (Simeon), Sandrine Kiberlain (Monica), Michel Vuillermoz (Jack), Caroline Sihol (Tamara), Alba Gaïa Kraghede Bellugi (Tilly).
Color, 108 minutes
Award: Berlin Film Festival, Prix Alfred Bauer, 2014

Alain Resnais: Interviews

A Stoic Filmmaker: Interview with Alain Resnais

Jean Michel Carta and Michel Mesnil / 1960

From *Esprit* 28, no. 6 (June 1960). Reprinted by permission. Translated by T. Jefferson Kline.

Jean Michel Carta and Michel Mesnil: Do you have the feeling of belonging to a group or school of film directors?

Alain Resnais: Neither I, nor any of the young directors I know, has this feeling. That said, there are some commonalities among us; for example, we often love the same films, and we frequent Langlois's Cinémathèque.

J-MC and MM: But you have special affinities with such directors as Agnès Varda and Chris Marker.

AR: Of course, personal affinities with them, but since we don't talk much about what we're working on, I don't see how we could influence each other. It's shared tastes that unite us rather than influences we might have on each other's work.

J-MC and MM: Like everyone else, you deny that there's any homogeneity among the "New Wave" directors, and yet you don't have the feeling that you're working in the tradition of your predecessors like, for example, Autant-Lara.

AR: So maybe it's a question of an opposition between what one might call "a theatrical" vs "a novelistic" cinema. We dream of having a cinema that's much freer and more constantly improvised in each sequence. So it's in the dramatic construction of our work rather than a style of acting that there's a difference. The traditional recipes for filmic construction (everything coming together in the last third of the film) are just one of the possible ways to make films.

J-MC and MM: In this same issue, Marie-Claire Wuilleumier tries to characterize the modern cinema by grouping you with Antonioni, Varda, Rouch . . . and notes that, among those shared characteristics are the use of moments where nothing is happening.

AR: That's true, but we're certainly not alone in this. It's what gives Becker's *Grisbi* its unexpected quality. It's not at all in the tradition of Henry Bernstein, where the explosion between the couple is accompanied by frantic cries. But, you know, I don't think I operate according to any one system. For *Hiroshima*, the film just happened that way; the style of the film simply imposed itself on Marguerite Duras and me. We ended up dropping certain scenes that were more anecdotal and that we had planned on adding to the film to enrich the Nevers story simply because that would have given the impression that the girl was reflecting on her situation before talking.

J-MC and MM: The construction of *Hiroshima* seems to break away from anything we've seen in traditional film: introduction, crisis, resolution. On the contrary, your film is the story of a crisis and a separation that begins with the first images of the film only to be consummated at the film's end in total anguish—it's a decrescendo.

Indeed, it's customary to place at the beginning of the last third of the film the reemergence of the elements that are necessary to lead to the work's resolution.

AR: Marguerite Duras and I were well aware that in abandoning this rule and replacing it with a musical structure, we risked boring our audience, and, sure enough, a number of the viewers found the film soporific. Still, we preferred taking this risk.

At the recommendation of the distributors and taking account of the many sensible criticisms that I'd heard from colleagues, I took pains to shorten the final version that was intended for the neighborhood and provincial movie houses. Well, the result was catastrophic. The film seemed even longer than before, nearly incomprehensible, bizarre, fortuitous, and, in any case, no less boring.

J-MC and MM: You mentioned the musical structure of your film just now. Is music very important to you?

AR: It's of capital importance: often when doing the storyboard, I start with an image from which all the other images in the film flow and are arranged like notes in a musical composition. Even *Toute la mémoire du monde* was inspired by a few measures of Kurt Weil's operetta *Lady in the Dark*. That provided a series of long tracking shots, separated by very short breaks, that I would liken to the great movements of a baroque composition, wholly appropriate to the baroque construction of the National Library. I was also very influenced by Stravinsky, including his recent works. For me, his Apollo is a major work.

J-MC and MM: You've also said that what you were aiming for was a kind of comic-opera, that you were trying to transcend the realism of the photographic image.

AR: What I wanted was to achieve the equivalent of reading, to allow the film's viewers as much freedom of imagination as they would have reading a novel. That around the image, behind the image, and even within the image, they could allow their imagination to run wild, while still under the spell of the images on the screen.

J-MC and MM: Doesn't this relationship to your viewers connect you to certain tendencies of the French "New Novel"?

AR: I worked with Jean Cayrol on *Night and Fog*, and while working on *Hiroshima*, I often thought about the conversations we'd had. Three months ago, I discovered Robbe-Grillet's work. We worked together on a scenario and we got along very well.

J-MC and MM: It's obvious, indeed, that Robbe-Grillet's objective and minute descriptions of things might be the equivalent of the apparently neutral images in your films (and here I'm thinking of the tracking shots in *Hiroshima* that move at a constant speed—and of the tracking shots in Nevers). So your editing might be the equivalent of the construction of a novel.

AR: We are so conscious of these similarities (and Robbe-Grillet's novels give the impression of being ready in advance for a film shoot with all the cinematic notations already in place) that in a way they're somewhat limiting. We are aware that in the remarkable resemblances between the two arts there are traps that have to be avoided in assuming that they are equivalent. It's precisely when the novel seems the most "cinematic" that we have to get away from literary descriptions.

J-MC and MM: So you have the impression that we're approaching a cinema that is attempting to distance the viewer from the spectacle?

AR: Well, that's what I'd like: to have the viewers identify not so much with the hero, but rather, at times, with the feelings of the hero. There should be moments of identification but also moments of distance. That they should be drawn into the emotion that they share with the hero but that they retain their judgment. In Godard's *Breathless*, what I love is the exchange of feelings between Jean Seberg and Belmondo, but I also like it that I have permission to find them antipathetic. Some people feel that this film is immoral because of its fascistic glorification of the gangster but others identify with the film's hero. This kind of freedom has long been recognized in the theater and the novel. Of course, you can also fall into a sort of complacency of the voyeur, the kind of feelings you have when you witness an accident.

Vis-à-vis the heroine of *Hiroshima*, I also think that you should feel a combination of sympathy for her, mingled with some reserve, some annoyance . . . but isn't this what happens constantly in friendship and in love? During the shooting we exchanged all kinds of stories about her, for example, that she's a mythomaniac and that the story she tells to her Japanese friend never happened, or else that she's not really in Hiroshima but in an asylum and she's inventing the whole story. You can see to what degree this character might escape us and escape the spectator. It's also in order to give the viewers their freedom that we didn't suggest that the German soldier was anti-Nazi, which was, in our minds, implicit, but we refused to say it in order not to clear the heroine of any wrongdoing, to avoid making her too easily sympathetic, of not favoring the viewers' desired identification with her.

J-MC and MM: Speaking of "distanciation" we thought that Queneau's commentary in *Le Chant du Styrène* was intended to be parodic, a way of distancing himself from the "subject" of the film.

AR: I don't think that was understood; I was thinking of Boileau's didactic poetry and of Malherbe, and it seemed to me that a text in verse would be more effective, pedagogically, and then I felt that there was some connection between the *alexandrine* verse form and CinemaScope; but I have a certain taste for the mixture of salt and sugar, for unusual associations. It may seem paradoxical, but Péchiney initially didn't want to use Queneau's commentary and had had a more classical, sober commentary written but after trying it we realized vaguely that there was something important in the Queneau text whereas the classical commentary was less perceptible. Now Péchiney has circulated the Queneau version. I wasn't asked, by the way, to explain the fabrication of styrene, but simply to show that it was a noble substance and that its fabrication was very complex, and required a very advanced knowledge of chemistry.

J-MC and MM: Aren't you afraid that this "literary cinema" isn't going to lead to a break with the larger public?

AR: Well, for the moment, anyway, the public seems to accept this cinema quite easily. Of course, there's a very sure way of judging this: the attitude of the producers who are supporting the young cinema.

J-MC and MM: Do you think that the cinema is essentially realistic?

AR: It's not so evident; there have always been two tendencies: the realistic one and the imaginary one. From the very beginning of cinema there was the Méliès school and the Lumière school and those two tendencies have continued ever since.

In *Hiroshima*, the opening scene is not the representation of the couple, it's a poetic image. And the ashes on the bodies do not refer to any specific anecdotal reality, it's just a thought. As for the commentary, it's sort of like what you might say when you're half-asleep in the morning, or what you might blurt out at an exultant moment in the street.

In the same way, the use of color might be done in a realistic way or the opposite. A priori it seems to me that a film is always a sound film and shot in color. From there, you can begin to experiment: to make it a silent film and in black-and-white, for example. In *Night and Fog*, I just tried to make the color realistic, to achieve the most faithful reproduction possible of the place. In *Le Chant du*

Stryène, on the other hand, there are transpositions, there are dominants that are used quite consciously.

J-MC and MM: Would you ever be able to make fantasy films?

AR: Certainly. Why couldn't we make the cinematic equivalent of *Alice in Wonderland*? Personally, I don't think I have the requisite imaginative qualities for such a project; it's very difficult to sustain something like that for an hour and a half. But that's no reason not to make the attempt to master it.

J-MC and MM: Well, aside from Cocteau's *Orpheus*, the French fantastic genre is pretty bad.

AR: The comic is just as bad. But I absolutely refuse to define any art by its past.

J-MC and MM: Nevertheless, if you show somebody walking upside down, the audience isn't going to accept it.

AR: If a director manages to make us believe in such a world, then he's won.

J-MC and MM: Do you believe in the virtue of techniques like automatic writing?

AR: For me, they're indispensable; you can't work without them. But it's really a question of the way you use such material. I think that once automatic writing has offered up its maximum potential, then you can work the results into your film. You get to choose from among the treasures that you've fished out of those waters. The first idea comes from a purely automatic process, but then if I can justify it rationally I'll use it, but, on the other hand if it doesn't seem to add anything I discard it. But still, if it keeps coming back obsessively to mind, then I'll use it, precisely because I *can't* justify it rationally! What I love in certain painters like Max Ernst, for example, is this kind of freedom, this oneiric quality of the mise en scène.

J-MC and MM: Does chance often play a role in your films?

AR: Yes, just as it does in all films, the moment you focus the camera on something: when, for example, you're about to shoot a scene, you set up the camera and look into the viewfinder and you see the counter-shot of what you were going to film, and this immediately gives you an idea of what you have to do. Chance has selected this image from among the 2000 possibilities that were open to you the minute you lifted the camera to put it in place. You have to be constantly open to such possibilities.

J-MC and MM: Doesn't the acting also introduce an element of chance into your work?

AR: Of course. You ask your actor for such and such a gesture and he'll do something unexpected that immediately strikes you as just right; obviously you jump on what he's just created.

J-MC and MM: Was it a great change to move from filming things to filming actors?

AR: It was a huge relief . . . If you only knew how tired you can get of framing an ashtray or lighting it a little more from the right or a little more from the left. It's very oppressive and tiring.

J-MC and MM: Legend has it that you began making films when you were very young.

AR: At thirteen. Unfortunately, I started with some very bad assumptions. I wanted to make a movie of *Fantômas*, and I thought that since the actors were kids, all I had to do to make them look like adults was to move the camera closer to them. But when I projected the film it didn't work like that at all. I was extremely disappointed and the actors quickly became discouraged. There was nothing unusual about shooting with an 8mm camera. The originality was to try to film with characters.

I don't seem to be able to think of film as a career; in the beginning it felt like the pharmacist feels when he locks up his shop and takes a pleasant stroll home. Still today, I feel as if its just tinkering. In order for a film to interest me, it has to have some experimental aspect, and that's what was missing in *Gauguin* and is the reason it's a bad film.

It's certain that I've never in my life been able to see cinema as my first priority. You see how many films I've made, and it's no accident. I don't like giving up my evenings to work. That strikes me as abnormal.

J-MC and MM: Marguerite Duras, however, said that you were inhabited by the cinema.

AR: Yes, when I'm shooting—just like everyone else—it's absolutely impossible to emerge from it. But when it's done, I don't try to rush to do another film, like some people do who have an urgent message to communicate. For each film I've done, it was material constraints that obliged me to accept each proposal. I've always done work on command and I've always wanted not to do the film that was proposed. I prefer editing films to directing them; it's less absorbing from every point of view. And then there's the difficulty of choosing. At the moment, I have three concrete proposals. Cayrol, Anne-Marie de Vilaine, and Robbe-Grillet are working for me (it's a little bit out of superstition, but I am tempted to tell a story that people don't know), but my dream would be that the three films be shot at the same time. I find it very disagreeable to have to make one and then wait a month before beginning the next one. I think I'd be more inspired if I were working on three films at once. It's too bad!

J-MC and MM: Was it lack of proposals that prevented you from making feature-length films earlier than you did?

AR: For a long time, people thought that a director of short subjects could never make feature-length films. It's true that someone proposed that I direct *La tête contre les murs*, but after *Night and Fog* and *Toute la mémoire du monde*,

I was afraid of locking myself up in an insane asylum, in another concentration camp; it was becoming an obsession, everywhere there were walls and prisons.

J-MC and MM: The success of *Hiroshima* was much greater than anyone expected.

AR: Yes, in almost every country except Japan. Its success was particularly marked in Italy, in South America, in Belgium, and in England . . .

J-MC and MM: How do you deal with success? Can you be a successful director and still manage to step out of the limelight to think about making other films?

AR: It's difficult. Success brings with it lots of obligations. For the first five or six months, I spent my time meeting with people in cafés, and I began a bit naïvely to attempt to answer all the letters I received and to read and criticize all the scenarios I received from would-be authors. Now I'm trying to be a brute, which is pretty painful. Perhaps I'll get back to shooting, but I began by being completely overwhelmed.

The other danger would, of course, be to become a sort of statue, to imagine that you've become the author that other people believe you to be and to attempt to provide them the merchandise they're expecting from you. I refused some pretty interesting projects in which there were lots of references to memory, forgetting, war, and death. I wanted to create the impression for myself that I wasn't going to do the same thing twice in a row. I've been conditioned, however, since I refuse to see certain resemblances.

J-MC and MM: Do you feel the same defiance vis-à-vis the influences others might exert on you?

AR: Yes. For example, right now I'm looking for an actress, but I turned down one who would have worked very well, but with whom it would have looked as if I was copying Hitchcock.

J-MC and MM: What are the films and/or directors that have most influenced you?

AR: Certainly, some of Buñuel's films, Cocteau's *Orpheus*, Antonioni, and then Welles and of course Eisenstein, Visconti. To say that my films are in any way equal to theirs is a bit ridiculous . . . and, ultimately, we don't really always know. Very recently, when I was watching Hitchcock's *Suspicion* (which I liked better this time than in 1944), I had the impression of seeing a shot that I'd unconsciously literally copied in *Hiroshima*. If there are influences, they are simultaneously very precise and subterranean. How to know?

J-MC and MM: Do you see a lot of films?

AR: Fewer than some others do, but I see about eighty to a hundred films a year.

J-MC and MM: How do you feel about having your own work distributed?

AR: As though one of my gestures has been propagated on a planetary scale. It's both a bit comical and a little immodest as well. The capacity for distribution of films is crazy. As for me, I find writing a book much more difficult and the effects are much slower. That doesn't seem fair to me.

J-MC and MM: And yet a lot of writers have admired *Hiroshima*.

AR: Yes, but Duras, wrote the book—or at least the quantity and quality of her work is the equivalent of what it takes to write a book—though she did complete the work in two and a half months.

J-MC and MM: She's so modest.

AR: Maybe she's neurotic, or else it's her way of maintaining her freedom.

J-MC and MM: In your films you seem preoccupied with the loss of substance following on forgetfulness. But the ultimate forgetfulness, i.e., death, doesn't seem to strike you. You seem more sensitive to the scandals of life rather than to the absolute scandal of death.

AR: That's true, and it's because death is, for the moment, beyond our reach, whereas we are fully responsible for life.

J-MC and MM: Your cinema is resolutely agnostic.

AR: That's right. I don't refuse the possibility of an afterlife, I just believe that it's beyond our comprehension or reach, and I prefer to take on what I can change. It isn't that mystical problems are old hat; they're just not part of my universe. Bergman, for example, whom I admire greatly, has founded his work on a certain number of metaphysical themes which are appropriate for him and which I respect. What I regret, on the other hand, is that he has adopted vis-à-vis the evolution of the world a position of resignation that leads him to affirm, for example, that to harp on the world's contradictions only risks alienating people further and, in the long run, it's better to just let things sort themselves out, or deteriorate, by themselves. As a director, my most cherished desire is, on the contrary, to provoke in my viewers some change, no matter how minute, or distant. My goal will have been attained if, for example, two weeks after seeing one of my films, one of my viewers experiences a sudden epiphany in the face of some event apparently unrelated to the subject of my film.

J-MC and MM: The flood of memories experienced by the heroine in *Hiroshima* seems to be set off by the sight of the Japanese man's hand on the bed that recalls the hand of her German lover. Is this a mechanism that is related to Proust's notion of involuntary memory?

AR: Indeed! I believe that at certain moments when we feel ourselves on a deeper level of existence, we can also recapture a past buried beneath our daily routines.

J-MC and MM: One of the possible objections to your film concerns its pessimism: the necessity of forgetting in order to go on living and the consciousness of the tragic betrayal constituted by forgetting, which together create a contradiction that could end up making life impossible. Your characters would thus be prisoners of their past, like those of Faulkner, according to Sartre.

AR: Well, that's certainly a plausible objection. And yet, *Hiroshima* doesn't end up affirming the impossibility of living. The two main characters meet, experience something together and then go off, each one having to face his/her separate responsibilities. The fact that it shows people who are suffering does not make *Hiroshima* a pessimistic film. Life isn't always amusing, but at least my characters have experienced these forty-eight hours; maybe they're as—or more—valuable than ten years of apparent but lethargic happiness. Real suffering comes from an empty rather than a painful life. Real suffering can be witnessed in the characters in, for example, Kurosawa's *Ikiru (To Live)*. In Antonioni's *Il Grido (The Cry)*, where the main character ends up committing suicide, the intensity of his suffering is a witness to man's grandeur.

J-MC and MM: In *Hiroshima*, it appears that there's an adversarial or antagonistic relationship between the individual and the social that are often presented as antagonists, not only in the case of war, but even in day-to-day existence. Is it symbolic that the French woman and the Japanese man are jostled by the antinuclear demonstration?

AR: I don't really like the word "symbolic." That just happened during the shooting. You could assign it that meaning, but I didn't stage it on purpose and would have found such an intention too obvious. Let's say that there isn't any necessary antagonism between individuals and happiness, but evidently there are always difficulties, if only in the way time is allotted and spent.

J-MC and MM: Why don't you make films about problems that are perceived as more urgent, as, for example, the Algerian war?

AR: I'd like to, but I haven't yet found the author who'd provide a text that would correspond to what I can do. I almost did one: Daniel Anselm's *La Permission (The Leave)*. We almost did it, but I realized I'd have a great deal of trouble finding the right tone for a subject as sociologically realistic as his text. I prefer to create a lyrical transposition than to do a documentary. However, one of the projects I'm working on with Anne-Marie Vilaine includes the reactions of several characters who've been marked by the Algerian war.

J-MC and MM: There's a campaign going on right now for a reinforcement of censorship that invokes moral arguments.

AR: Indeed, we are threatened with a veritable "Spanish-type" censorship, since, according to a recent decree, all screenplays must be approved by a commission. They're claiming it's for reasons of morality, but I don't really believe this.

J-MC and MM: Edgar Morin has pointed out that, even if they eliminated all forms of film censorship, it wouldn't lead to an increase in pornographic films.

Most obviously because a majority of people would refuse to see them as a matter of principle, but also because, even if they wanted to, the moral structures of our current society would forbid them from going. And, indeed, it's hard to imagine that in a small provincial town where everyone knows each other, respectable citizens would line up to go see such filth. After all, the "Midi-Minuit" in Paris, that specializes in international spicy films, has no competitors.

AR: I completely agree with this view. Moreover, thus far, the censors have always been pretty indulgent when it comes to questions of morality. The powers of the current commission have been quite adequate to rein in such unacceptable tendencies among French filmmakers. And if there was any impetus to change the rules, it would doubtless be to institute political intolerance. The maneuver they've thought of is to claim that there's an increase in smut in order to reinforce censorship in general. What threatens us is "general morality" in all its forms. It would be simple to find a solution: outside of forbidding minors from seeing certain films, it would be enough to list (as they do for the press) what kinds of ideas or attitudes (e.g., racism, certain violent positions) are unlawful to propagate. But what they really want to establish is the reign of the arbitrary.

Trying to Understand My Own Film

André Labarthe and Jacques Rivette / 1962

From *Films and Filming* VIII, no. 5 (February 1962). Reprinted by permission.

The Venice 1961 Golden Lion picture, Alain Resnais's *L'Année dernière a Marienbad*, is a "sealed" work of art. Some of its mysteries are unsealed by the director himself. Two young French writers—Andre Labarthe and Jacques Rivette—have been analyzing the film with Resnais. And Resnais, in turn, has been discussing its implications with its author, novelist Alain Robbe-Grillet. The debate started with a detail that may prove for many the big issue of *Marienbad* . . . a game played throughout by the two men, while the woman waits. What is the mystery of the game?

Alain Resnais: The game is the only point about which I am unable to tell you anything. I have never played it. Apparently it is very ancient; the Chinese played it three thousand years before Jesus Christ. It was the game of Nim, of which Robbe-Grillet has invented a variation without even knowing it existed.

André Labarthe and Jacques Rivette: But it functions less as a game than as a trap?

AR: Quite. My personal impression is that when Albertazzi loses, it is consciously and deliberately. Perhaps through a lack of concern. In any case, "X" has a very complex character: he has periods of violent willfulness and obstinacy, which abruptly give way to discouragement.

AL and JR: What is the hidden relationship between the game and the film?

AR: It is, I believe, the necessity of making a decision. Of course, the characters, while playing, may be allowing themselves a few moments' reflection while arriving at their decisions. In any case, the whole thing is possibly a part of the woman's stream of consciousness, as, on the point of deciding what to do, she recalls the various factors in a few seconds. I don't think there are any other meanings, except possibly that there may be a cyclic recurrence of one's problems. This would correspond to the element of musical form and to the obsessive qualities of dreams. But, so far as I'm concerned, *Marienbad* contains no symbols or allegories.

AL and JR: But there *are* things that one may take as symbols.

AR: Yes, of course, one may be reminded of the Grail, or anything else. But the film is open to any such myth. If you look for parallels to ten current themes, whether mythological or realistic, you will arrive at a correct interpretation of 60 to 80 percent of the film. But your interpretations will never hold good for the film as a whole. One of the themes which interests me in the film is that of a parallel universe. It is quite possible that all the characters are speaking the truth. We didn't deliberately premise the film around this possibility, but there is a certain connection with "automatic writing." The possibility of "automatism" can't be dismissed simply on the grounds that Robbe-Grillet's style is extremely precise and his vision very clear-cut. His way of working often reminds me of Le Douanier Rousseau, who used to start his canvas in the left-hand corner, filling in the smallest details, and then work across to finish in the right-hand corner. This is what was so fascinating about the film; we were forced to begin orientating it, I won't say without knowing how it would end, but, all the same, the last pages of the script had hardly been typed when we began shooting. The important thing was a constant fidelity to our intuition. It's the sort of film of which one says, "Once it's shot, there will be twenty-five ways of editing it." But, on the contrary, we always fell back on our original ideas. This is why Robbe-Grillet and I feel so *excluded* from the film, we look on it as something apart from ourselves. We wanted the film to work quite differently from a conventional entertainment; by a sort of contemplation, or meditation, a series of advances and retreats from the subject. We wanted to feel ourselves in the presence of a sculpture which one studies first from one angle, then from another, from near or farther away.

AL and JR: But there is still a resistance by the cinematic material, which has to be overcome.

AR: Yes. Personally, I see the film as an exploration of various themes, an attempt to discover which are the blind alleys and which are the real avenues of approach. Both are present in the film. For the time being, I'm too close to the film to see it clearly. Every morning I read what has been written about it, and I notice that some critics speak of a work that is as cold as the poems of Mallarmé, while others call it tender and passionate. Which doesn't enlighten me very much. Possibly both reactions are justified, the film may act as something like a mirror for every spectator.

AL and JR: Without setting out to make an exegesis of the film, isn't there a snag in the idea of leading the spectator towards the past or the future? Seeing it again, we have the impression that the film is not concerned with time so much as with the relationship of the real and the imaginary.

AR: The film is about *degrees* of reality. There are moments where it is altogether invented, or interior, as at the moments where the picture corresponds to the dialogue. The interior monologue is never in the soundtrack; it is almost always in the visuals, which, even when they show events in the past, correspond to the *present* thoughts in the mind of the character. So what is presented as the present or the past is simply a reality that exists while the character is speaking. The other day, I was talking to a girl who had just returned from India, and suddenly I visualized her wearing a blue dress and standing in front of the temple of Angkor. Yet she had never been to Angkor and the blue dress was the one she was wearing now.

AL and JR: There are a great many interpretations. When Robbe-Grillet summarizes the film, he describes it from the point of view of the man who suggests a past to the woman.

AR: That's right. If one accepts Truffaut's dictum, "Every film should be summarized in one word," then one can say, *L'Année dernière à Marienbad* or *Persuasion*. That's a solution but there are others.

AL and JR: One can also take the film as if the past was real, that the woman repudiates it, and that the man plays a role analogous to that of a psychoanalyst, forcing her to accept events which she has deliberately repressed.

AR: It's from this angle that I directed the film. Some psychoanalytic themes were introduced quite consciously, for example, the ostentatiously large rooms, indicating a tendency towards narcissism. At one point, Albertazzi hears shots and I finally cut them out during the editing, because they didn't conform to my idea of his character. Or perhaps because I was too aware of their psychological significance?

AL and JR: The moments of tension between Albertazzi and the girl correspond to those beween analyst and patient?

AR: I don't know if you remember that scene towards the end, where the man has his hand against the door, just after the hypothetical sequence of death, where she imagines that if she left with him, she would be killed and so on. When she says, as if in despair, "But I have never stayed so long anywhere," I get the impression, particularly from her intonation, of an acquiescence, which is total: so that the scene is real. It is so tempting to conceive of her as an invalid. First of all, that hotel has a special air. And I have always been intrigued by Sacha Pitoeff's words to the woman as she lies on the bed: "You must rest, remember that is why we came here." This always reminds me of *Caligari*, where the Doctor says, at the end, "Yes, he will be calmed, I shall cure him." There does seem to be a certain similarity. Perhaps the hotel is really a clinic.

AL and JR: There is another interpretation that you sensed: that Albertazzi is dead.

AR: Robbe-Grillet finally hit on the phrase "granite flagstone," and he realized that the description of the garden would fit a cemetery. On pursuing this line of thought, he realized that the film had affinities with the old Breton legends—the story of Death coming to fetch his victim and allowing him a year's respite. But we never attempted to make the film conform to any precise meaning; we always allowed a certain ambiguity.

Stray from Reality

AR: In the first quarter of the film, things seem to have a fairly high degree of reality; we stray further and further from it as the film proceeds; it is quite conceivable that at the end, suddenly, everything converges, that the conclusion of the film is the most real part of all.

AL and JR: And there'd be a big climax halfway through when she recognizes the statue.

AR: Yes, when she discovers the garden and realizes that the garden is, after all, only the place where they happen to be. This poses all the problems of the film's chronology.

AL and JR: There is a moment when she realizes that she is trapped. Is that when she laces her shoe?

AR: Exactly. From that moment, we can take it that she has *remembered*. If, perhaps, she is sincere at the beginning, if her refusal is not sheer coquetry or fear, then, from that moment she remembers. But, of course, we never really know if the scenes are occurring in the man's mind or the woman's. There is a perpetual oscillation between the two. You could even maintain that everything is told from her viewpoint. Several spectators have told me that the woman does exist, that she died long before, that everything is happening between two ghosts. But one only thinks of these possibilities after the film has been completed—not while shooting or even editing.

AL and JR: What was your guiding principle in organizing this material, which you were deliberately keeping vague; was it a feeling of affinity between theme and image, internal rhyming?

AR: Interestingly enough, I was not the only one to be guided as I was. During the whole shooting there was no disagreement, whether among the actors or among the technicians. Now and again, we discussed various possibilities. We talked about the shots beforehand, we said, "This is in the tone of the film, isn't it?" But such discussions never lasted more than a few moments. We were all compelled to follow the one path, from which we were not allowed to stray. It almost became teamwork of a sort; we were prisoners, not of a logical argument, but of a para-logic, which kept us in constant agreement from Philippe Brun to Sacha Vierny or Albertazzi. It would be most interesting to draw up a diary of "correspondences" in the selection of locations and actors. There was any number of bizarre coincidences, phenomena which would have delighted André Breton or Jean Cocteau. I have the impression that the form must have preexisted, I don't know how or where, and that somehow as one writes, the story automatically takes the mold.

Every time I make a film, I discover that one can't allocate gestures or words to the characters just as one pleases. There was a moment, during the preparation of *Marienbad*, where I arrived with my little black notebook and suggested to Robbe-Grillet that we should introduce the real world under the guise of conversations concerning a political problem, which would be insoluble, at least for those who were interested in it. But we realized that the real world would be introduced by the spectators themselves, as they watched the film, and that it was impossible to include them in it.

Not Free

AR: At one point, I also wanted the woman to be pregnant; I mentioned it to Robbe-Grillet, but it turned out to be hardly feasible. We were not free. I am convinced that we don't make these films as we choose.

For me, the film represents an attempt still crude and primitive, to approach the complexity of thought and of its mechanisms. But I must stress that it is only a small step forward compared to what we should achieve eventually. I have found that in each descent into the unconscious, an emotion is born.

I remember how I felt while watching *Le Jour se lève*, with its sudden moments of ambiguity, as when the image of the wardrobe begins to fade out, and another scene gradually materializes. In reality, we don't think chronologically; our decisions never conform to an ordered logic. We all have *clouds*, factors that determine our being, but are not successions of logical acts following a perfect sequence. I am interested in exploring that universe from the point of view of reality, if not actually of morality.

AL and JR: There is the danger of falling into a trap, rather like that which Paulhan mentioned in connection with language; what one thinks of as the height of liberty is likely to be for someone else totally arbitrary.

AR: The difficulty is inherent in all communication, whether between two people or ten million. One has to know how much of one's subjective reality one can share with others (for we have sight, hair, thought, and so on). One arrives naturally at the idea of a "global unconscious." I am attracted by the idea of applying disciplines rather different from those of the most contemporary films. It arouses my curiosity. In the cinema, I am drawn to the idea of popularization. A book or a painting first makes contact with a thousand people, while a film reaches millions straight away.

From this angle, it is interesting to recall the experiences of a writer in 1880 or a painter to only a few connoisseurs. I dislike sectarianism; and any attempt to demolish the walls of the *clique* delights me for its own sake. In any case, even if one wanted to repeat exactly what others have already done, the chemical composition of the cinema is very different. When Van Gogh amuses himself by copying Delacroix, or Picasso Velazquez, the result is a completely new painting. Of course, the cinema is rather clumsy with its concrete images. Its style is rather pachydermous. We are still afflicted by the old dichotomy between the realism of Lumière and the fantasy of Melies. We wobble between these two alternatives and often fall between two stools. *Lola*, for example: is it Lumière or Melies?

Form Important

AR: When I see a film, I am less interested in the characters than in the play of feelings. I think we could arrive at a cinema without psychologically defined characters, where the pattern of feelings exists freely, just as, in modern painting, the play of forms is more important than the "story."

AL and JR: What alarms us is the position René Clair pushes to its logical absurdity when he says, "Shooting is just a chore."

AR: For me, shooting is elucidation. I do make small sketches beforehand, but for the sake of peace.

AL and JR: While shooting, what attitude do you adopt toward your sketches?

AR: I still study them. It helps in my relationships with the actors and the cameramen. They save the actor from getting panicky eight or ten days before we shoot. If he has read the shooting script and has a clear idea of it, and then, while shooting, I place him in a position or a composition that hasn't been foreseen, he is apt to worry. And, as I like everyone to be as relaxed as possible on the set, I prefer arguments to be over before shooting. I'm all in favor of rehearsing the entire film before shooting begins.

For *Marienbad*, we drew up a complete chronology on squared paper. And before beginning any scene with the actors, we said: "In the editing, this scene follows such and such a scene, but in actual chronology it follows another scene, which will appear much later in the film." I frequently recorded a fragment of the preceding scene, so as to work from the continuity rather than from the cue. This chronological chart was drawn up after the scenario was finished. Obviously, all the changes of costume correspond to different "layers" of time.

Dilation of Time

AR: That isn't the key to the film, assuming there is one. But one could edit the film so as to restore the chronological order of the scenes. One might see the film as extended over a week, or with all that is shown in the present tense as taking place from Sunday to Sunday inclusive. This doesn't stop Robbe-Grillet from saying, "Maybe it all happens in five minutes." This is consistent with the dilation of time in dreams, at least as far as we understand the mechanism of dreams.

AL and JR: Your montage is, in a sense, the modern version of the "montage of attraction." For Pudovkin, the shots were the words of a sentence, whereas for Eisenstein each shot was in itself a living element.

AR: Eisenstein has more in common with the encounter between "an umbrella and a sewing machine on a dissecting table" [Breton's famous definition of beauty]. And insofar as I remain very aware of the Surrealist discipline, I feel much nearer Eisenstein's conceptions. Each shot retains its life.

AL and JR: There is an attitude of great humility before each of the elements, whether in reality or in creative work, which must preserve its organic life and at the same time be part of an organic whole.

AR: I would be reluctant to transform a setting, even in small details, to suit the camera. It is up to the camera to present the décor in the right way; it's not for the setting to conform to the camera. The same holds good for the actor. I have an immense respect for an actor's work. How rarely we alter the shooting to suit an actor's feelings, whereas we are constantly changing it on account of the weather!

Interview with Alain Resnais: *The War Is Over*

Robert Benayoun, Michel Ciment, and Jean-Louis Pays / 1966

From *Positif*, no. 79 (October 1966). Reprinted by permission. Translated by T. Jefferson Kline.

Robert Benayoun: You've been reproached for not making political films practically up until *Muriel* and certainly when you made *Marienbad*. Some accused you of hiding in the shadows while very serious things were happening. And yet you had projects that you weren't able to realize. *Muriel* was fairly political, but with *La Guerre est finie* (*The War Is Over*), you have tackled a political subject head on. Is this a kind of catharsis, an old idea that's finally come to the surface, or did things just evolve in this way?

Alain Resnais: Clearly in cinema, people have the impression that films are made without any clear reason, but a film director is a living being, and is sensitive to bunches of things that come and go and that are happening around him. It's very hard to define exactly what leads one to make a particular film. But it's definitely not the case that one wakes up one morning and says, "Now I'm going to make a film about dreams or about politics." I remember that the character of Okada in *Hiroshima* corresponded to an idea of this kind: he was an architect who was very political. One wonders whether he wasn't a kind of Japanese Diégo. You know, there are huge rocks that come from the moon, frozen meteorites. There's an extraordinary one in New York that's enormous, and you have the impression that one could film this meteorite in a long shot, or with surface lighting only, which would show another view of it, or you could enter each of its cavities, but ultimately, it's all part of one exploration. In each of my films, there's a point that's emphasized more than others. For example, I feel that Diégo, and Alphonse in *Muriel*, have many traits in common. Everything must in some way depend on their notion of the imaginary. I've always protested against the word "memory" but not against the word "imaginary" or against the word "consciousness." The imaginary plays a considerable role in our lives. It seems to me, in any case, an ideal subject for cinema. If cinema is not specifically a way of juggling time, it's nevertheless the best possible means of playing with this concept. Is all of this related or is it the same thing? As I was saying to Jean-Louis Pays the other day, how can we explain *Dickson* except by saying that Diégo may be reading *Dickson* every night?

RB: He's reading *Peanuts*.

AR: And curiously that wasn't my idea. I would have preferred not to have *Peanuts* involved at all, since that would mean I was projecting my own personal tastes on the hero. You sense right away that Diégo isn't the least bit interested in film—or in music, I think: those are his tastes, so *Peanuts* might have seemed strange, but, given the fairly sophisticated (in the good sense) side of Marianne, it was normal for the kid to be reading *Peanuts* and not *Mickey Mouse*. I think his mother would have given him *Spirou*, *Peanuts*, and things like that. So it's natural that, at that moment, Diégo would take that book and fall asleep over it. It would have felt completely false if he'd taken *Peanuts* into Marianne's room, given the other books there, it's entirely connected to the kid.

Jean-Louis Pays: I think there's been a political side to all of your films ever since your early short subjects, no?

AR: Not in *Le Chant du Styrène*. People tend to assign choices to us that seem evident to them, but they don't really correspond to real life. Of course, there are always choices to make, but it seems to me that you're not forced to dedicate your entire life to a single idea.

Michel Ciment: *Muriel* is the first of your films in which, as in *La Guerre est finie*, society is painted with a larger brush than in *Hiroshima*, in the sense that they could be considered a kind of panoramic whereas *Hiroshima* would be pure depth of field.

AR: When I hear you ask this kind of question, I'm really wary of answering, "Yes, I make political films!" just to make you happy! (The three interviewers protest.)

RB: You're saying we've exaggerated this theme of memory in your work . . .

AR: All I'm saying is that for neither Duras nor myself did this derive from a deliberate decision. I think the theme of memory is present every time you write a play or paint a picture, since writing and painting respond to a desire to stop time and struggle against death. As for me, I prefer the words "consciousness" and " the imaginary" to the word "memory," though consciousness is certainly a form of memory.

RB: Aren't all of the characters in your feature films people who are uprooted who perpetually arrive too late to their rendezvous, and who end up leading parallel lives?

AR: Yes, they're adrift, dissatisfied, and marginalized.

RB: And they prefer these situations. You sense this in the case of Diégo; he could have made himself useful and in a much more stable way, perhaps, but he just enjoys coming and going and never remaining in one place.

AR: This is certainly true as well. What I see as the connection between Alphonse and Diégo is that neither one can tolerate life as it is. So Alphonse invents a new life, almost by chance, and Diégo, for his part, wants to transform life itself. But it's this dissatisfaction with life that makes Alphonse such a likeable character.

J-LP: Diégo is a revolutionary, whereas Alphonse withdraws into a purely imaginary space, like opium. He destroys himself, whereas Diégo wants to achieve something.

AR: True enough. A Greek journalist asked me if Diégo didn't have a pathological side to him that I didn't want to show. But I find that, quite to the contrary, he's very balanced. Does he suffer the anguish of a forty-year-old man? Yes, I can sense that.

J-LP: I think that Diégo suffers from a kind of double anguish, that of the militant who's tired of having seen Spain live under fascism for thirty years. But there's also the wear and tear that accumulates on a man of his age, and he's physically worn out from the life he lives.

AR: And who feels that there don't seem to be any solutions to these problems. Especially since the story lasts only three days.

J-PL: But his anguish comes from his revolt and his desire to create something positive, and therefore it's not the same as trying to escape from reality. In fact, anguish is a perfectly appropriate response to his reality! There's no escaping it, whereas Alphonse is in perpetual flight.

AR: Yes, it's somewhat like some of Pirandello's characters who invent their lives, but if they do so it's because their lives are so unsatisfactory, and that's what moves us.

RB: I don't know whether this comes from Semprun or from you, but I was immensely pleased with Diégo's tirade when he angrily attacks Lorca.

AR: The first time I met with Semprun, I told him that in no case would we make a film about Spain. And he answered, "Definitely not!" In any case, I would not be capable of such a film since I have to admit that I don't understand Lorca and have had it up to here with him! Every time I open the newspaper, I see something about Lorca's politics and it annoys the hell out of me! And I'll add, it's not true! But what I like about Diégo's tirade is that its emotive value is much greater than its political value. At that moment, Diégo—who's completely exhausted by his all-night drive, and is frustrated to have missed Juan and to have gotten mixed up in this adventure—is very aware that he's not in a very good position morally. Of course, having slept with Nadine delighted him, but even so, if he'd known Marianne was there . . . so he feels both happy and unhappy.

When he gets to Marianne's place there are visitors there . . . and so he feels really stupid. After that, he's bawled out by Bill and especially by Agnes. He tells them he's already had supper but he's really hungry, then he drinks a whiskey to regain his composure and ends up half-drunk, and suddenly he launches into this tirade that he regrets and which makes the whole thing pretty incoherent. Generally incoherence in films belongs to the domain of feelings, whereas in this case there are elements of reality that enter into his incoherence. I understand that this scene is shocking, and you could see a political statement in it. But there isn't one. Where the documentary aspect of this comes in is the fact that this corresponds to a tendency of many Spanish intellectuals: in Goytisolo's articles, for example, he says, "Enough with this myth of Spain!" And, indeed, what characterizes Spain's situation is that almost the entire world, even if it's only a matter of sentiment, is anti-Franco. But this grand-scale opposition doesn't translate into any actions by other governments. But Spain is much more than Lorca or Dali, et cetera. If we'd wanted to make a film about Spain (and it seems to me that first we should make a film about France, since criticizing Spain seems to me to be a cop-out), it would have been better to make a documentary or start a press campaign. What I mean is, if the real goal were political, then hiding behind a fiction would be an act of cowardice. Which doesn't mean that fiction films don't have a role to play. When you see how furiously the interior minister of Spain reacted to this film, I confess I'm surprised. It would have been smarter to just let it pass without comment.

RB: That certainly would have been more diplomatic.

J-LP: Yes, as soon as they discovered from the Office of Cinema that the film was being made, they began to object.

AR: We had warnings. The Spanish embassy sent us a letter requesting information before they even knew what we were doing. The Spanish government worries most of all about anything that will draw attention to their country, any discussion, anything that feels like criticism. The question is, does one have the right to use real events in a fiction film. I understand all too well why people would contest this right. But, personally, I think it's simpler just to call a spade a spade. Moreover, we could have simply called the film "Garabain" and never pronounced the word Spain: it wouldn't have dramatically changed anything. But I have the impression that when the film was released and was then withdrawn from competition at Cannes, that its political nature was emphasized and gave it a certain celebrity that it wouldn't have had otherwise. It happens that the main character is a professional revolutionary, which seems to enrich the dramatic conflict of the work. So he's the focus of the work. But the difficulty of such an approach is to try to portray him without having him say things that are intended to be politically right-minded.

J-LP: You've been criticized for giving Diégo a privileged status vis-à-vis his comrades in the movement.

AR: Well, naturally. But doing so would have made an entirely different film. What's more, I find it interesting to imagine a film about the other members of his group. We were very conscious when we were shooting the film of all of its faults, and we knew that we'd be criticized for this and that the film would be badly received in some quarters, but we simply told ourselves that another film could be made that portrayed the progress of the movement and that had a wider view of events. But if you don't act, you're just marching in place. If you don't try to do *something*, you'll never amount to anything. I'm really afraid of these films that we dream up of an evening after dinner among friends. "Oh, if only we could do a film on . . . but the censors would never . . ." Of course, but we have to practice a politics of the possible, so we make the films that we can. If we always tried to make the ideal film we'd end up at ninety without having made anything. As for me, I know that in 1948–49, I gave up on some films and said to myself: no, I think so-and-so would be more worthy than I of treating this subject, and in fact he said he was going to shoot it. So I stayed in the background, as it were, and the film never got made.

J-LP: Was that the film on abortion?

AR: No, I never found a scenario that would have worked for that subject, and yet I really would have liked to do one. I would have focused more on birth control and the various procedures for preventing pregnancy. I began thinking about it in 1950, but sadly, nothing I looked at or tried, whether essays or scenarios, ever seemed to work out. It was a very difficult subject, perhaps too difficult.

RB: To come back to *La Guerre est finie*, the scene of the meeting seems very autobiographical on Semprun's part.

AR: Yes, but the film director should never try to expose certain secrets, but instead try to preserve the privacy of the person he's working with. Otherwise he's confronted with not daring to make certain things. I know that, at times, when I was feeling awkward, I tried erecting a wall in order to shoot without scruples, simply checking that everything worked and was done well.

RB: You know that at Cannes, the "unofficial" film showings got more attention than the official ones, despite many beautiful entries, and that everyone went to see *La Guerre est finie*. The day before, they'd shown Bresson's *Au Hasard Balthazar* and a lot of people were saying (you know who, of course), "After such a brilliant use of nonprofessional actors, how can one go back to using actors as well known as Yves Montand?"

AR: That whole discussion was skewed in a very artificial way, because Bresson was provoked into sounding disloyal to his friends by asking him questions about his work that forced him to take what sounded like inflexible positions that he ordinarily wouldn't adopt in less contentious circumstances.

RB: But he's had this theory about actors for a long time!

AR: Certainly! But you feel that through a series of leading questions one ends up sounding much more cutting than one feels. In any case those are questions that I constantly ask myself, but to which haven't yet found answers. You can see, and Renoir has already said this, that we're heading towards a cinema that's becoming radically different from what we've been used to. Why shouldn't cinema experience the same evolution that we've seen in music since the Middle Ages? A composer who is in his twenties today finds himself faced with three very different kinds of expression because today you can explore the *tonal* system, the *serial* system, or, let's say, the *concrete or electronic* system. They're three very different paths and it seems strange to have the choice of three such different languages. In the sixteenth or nineteenth centuries, a painter didn't ask himself what language to use in his painting. There have always been the academic vs. the non-academic, but ultimately there was a single tendency. But when the "Fauves" began exhibiting their work, everyone wanted to be a "Fauve" and then when the Cubists started, everyone wanted to be a Cubist, and yet one could feel a period of hesitation between such radically different possibilities. So why couldn't there be the same hesitation, the same possibility of radically different kinds of films today?

RB: In this use of nonprofessionals there's the direction that Bresson took, of course, but there's also the one Forman took which leads to a very deep sense of realism and not of abstraction.

AR: Bresson feels things in that way, and he's at ease with this approach despite the fantastical amount of work that his methods require. He might be compared to Meyerhold's conception of things, since his mises en scène had a very precise plastic idea that he wanted to achieve with his actors: he wanted to make them almost interchangeable in his mise en scène. It's a bit the same with Bresson. The "musical tonality" that he wants to achieve, he's afraid that the actors won't be able to give him what he's looking for. Indeed, it's not evident that a director as brilliant as Bresson might not need actors who are hypersensitive, incredibly flexible from whom he could obtain certain notes . . .

RB: Whereas you need professional actors.

AR: I derive enormous pleasure, personally, as a spectator, from the notion of an ensemble. I love going to Bergman's films, virtually any of them, just for that. Because I really like rediscovering the ensemble and seeing that the actor playing the garage mechanic had played the knight in the previous film. I'm fascinated by watching Jouvet in his different roles because of the variety of ways he has of creating a character. When I see an actor like Laurence Olivier, I'm much happier than if it were an unknown. Watching the various styles of actors totally fascinates me.

RB: To the point of giving Spanish roles to French actors.

AR: Well, that was tricky. But I had the impression that if I'd stuck a Spanish actor in the midst of all these French guys it would feel hypocritical.

RB: Well, it's true that when you see a film with Hardy Krüger un-dubbed with his beautiful accent and other foreigners dubbed, who are speaking without an accent, the film falls on its face.

AR: We always work within conventions. You either submit to the conventions or you use them; you either take advantage of them or you resist them. Chris Marker's formula, "Actors are like a postage stamps; they can only be used once," is funny but it doesn't work for me.

MC: Bresson thinks that the avenue he has opened up is the direction cinema ought to go. It's normal that he believes that in order to create. The problem is that the critics are saying, "You can't look at films any more now that you've seen Bresson's."

AR: Well, it's difficult, isn't it, because certain critics accept American actors simply because there's a certain exotic quality at work there, but that doesn't work for French actors because they know the actor and recognize his voice—and that's true for me as well. It's not a question of quality. It's just easier for us to imagine Cary Grant in a variety of different roles than Jean Gabin, for example. Must we struggle against this tendency? Because I too was inclined to say: "For Diégo we'll need an unknown—a new face." But maybe it's interesting when we're dealing with fiction film not to imitate documentary but present the thing for what it is, a fiction. That's why, certainly, there's an aspect of the film that didn't quite work: the problem of the narrator. But if I insisted on having this narrator in the film it was because it was also a way of saying: "We're at the movies. We'll present you realistic elements, of course, but we won't try to make you believe that this is anything but a movie." It's a kind of honesty and I don't believe this decreases one's emotion; quite the contrary, it enhances it when it works.

MC: Were you thinking about Butor's novel *La Modification*?

AR: Well, when the narrator uses the familiar "tu" form, yes, I wondered whether Butor hadn't done the same thing in his novel. But I didn't end up feeling there was really any connection between the two. Semprun and I both felt the commentator should always be using the future, but we couldn't make it work.

RB: As for Montand, wasn't it his physical presence that was the deciding factor in using him? I find he's reached exactly that age where his face has taken on a universal quality.

AR: We were looking at five different possibilities for the role, and I had a lot of trouble making up my mind. We were all pretty undecided, so what we did was to take the shot breakdown and go through it page by page imagining each of the five possibilities in each scene and Montand came out on top by a significant margin.

MC: The only other I can imagine in the role would be Serge Reggiani.

AR: We considered him as well. I think Reggiani is a very great talent.

RB: Montand has taken on one of those faces chiseled in marble and full of crevasses that certain great American actors have.

MC: Maybe it was the challenge you faced taking someone like Yves Montand and within ten minutes making everyone believe he was a revolutionary!

AR: We didn't choose him because of the challenge he posed. I had the impression that in Montand, there was the possibility that at some deeper level, certain equivalents in his own life might enable him to lend a lot of emotion to the role. It's also true that it's very interesting to displace someone from his normal life into something completely different. In his movie career, Jouvet always played the role of a cop, and it's really too bad. It would have been terrific to have him play some of the great leading roles. When Pagnol first used Fernandel in a dramatic role, everyone was wild about it.

RB: Or when the crooner Dick Powell became a private eye in *Murder My Sweet*.

AR: Yes, we got to see how well those brutal roles fit him!

MC: To come back to the discussion of the imaginary . . . in each of your films, there's a voice with a foreign accent . . . the Japanese in *Hiroshima*, Albertazzi in *Marienbad*, and the way you use Delphine Seyrig in *Muriel*, that gives her a different kind of elocution. Was this the reason you went for a co-production for *La Guerre est finie*?

AR: No, not at all; I had to impose Okada, at least his voice. The same for Thulin. It was a matter of co-production that had me choose Ingrid Thulin. It was after she accepted to play the role that Sweden offered to co-produce the film.

RB: I remember your saying, a propos of *Marienbad*, that to achieve that incantatory tone, you needed a foreign voice.

AR: Robbe-Grillet and I were entirely in agreement on that. And I wanted Albertazzi because I wanted a new face, which clearly contradicts what I've just said about actors. Delphine Seyrig and Emmanuelle Riva were also new faces. When I made *Hiroshima*, I had to choose between taking an excellent actress who was already well known and which would have presented three possibilities of co-production with the Japanese and would have added 20 million to our budget. But despite these advantages, I insisted on Riva. The foreign accents are pure chance and not a matter of taste, it just happens that way. In *Muriel*, there are no foreign accents.

MC: No but you make Delphine Seyrig use an unusual speaking style.

AR: True, but in that case I can explain why: the woman I was thinking of whom I'd known when I was a kid in Vannes, had a very particular way of speaking, and I'm very sensitive to people who have an unusual tone or a particular musicality in their voice, and there are lots of actors who have a special way of speaking. Playing "false" or playing "true" doesn't interest me at all. That's why I always want to have texts that are somewhat musical. People said both of *Hiroshima* and of *Marienbad*, that they had qualities in common with music or opera.

RB: In *La Guerre est finie*, there's this very beautiful phrase: "Death has brought sunlight into your life," that is linked to the sight of a cemetery for these young people.

AR: I'm not interested in creating literature like that of the theater or the novel, but I feel like there's a place for another kind of literature in a movie theater.

RB: At Cannes, certain critics reproached you for having made fun of these young people. But I think, on the contrary, that there's a kind of complicity between Diégo and them.

AR: Especially with Miguel. We tried to establish a sense of collusion between the two of them. Indeed, Miguel remains very attentive during their discussion.

RB: Don't you think this reproach surfaces because of generational differences?

AV: It's well known that in matters of this kind, everyone has his own fantasies and his own obsessions. Certain people said that these young people were the only sympathetic characters in the film. So that worked in both directions. But ultimately, these kids are a kind of superimposition of the Spanish Civil War on the War in Algeria. We could have done more with this subject, but it would have added an hour to the film.

RB: And aren't they simply upset with the idea that the police followed them even though they hadn't done anything?

J-LP: Well, there *was* the suitcase with the explosives.

AR: In my opinion, the criticism that one could make of the film, given that it is precisely situated in time (the action takes place between the 14th and 16th of April 1966, I think, and this is an important date in relation to the action of the entire film), and it's possible that these kids are really kids from 1964. So there's a disjuncture here and this scene should have been done differently. Semprun would be the best one to decide this matter and not me. We're aware, however, that Diégo arrived a year later, but in any case these are not young people of 1966.

J-LP: In any case these criticisms were addressed primarily to Semprun.

AR: Well, when I made *Hiroshima*, people said to me, "What a beautiful film! If only it didn't include Marguerite Duras's dialogues!" And my answer is, "You can blame me for everything and everyone involved in the film, because if these dialogues are bad, then all I had to do was not record them, given that I have carte blanche and complete freedom to make the film as I please!"

J-LP: It's been said as well that the order for a general strike was made up.

AR: Yes, I read that people reproached us for having twisted events in order to prove a thesis and claimed that we'd been forced to make up the bit about a general strike. However, the journal that called for a general strike is authentic, and that's what I filmed and it's an exact translation of that call for a strike that is read in the film. On the other hand, I remember perfectly that while we were writing the screenplay, I bought some newspapers and listened to the radio from May 1st on, to find out what was happening and what the situation was going to be in Spain, since that could entirely change the film. If the general strike had taken place, it would have been amazing, since it wouldn't have undone the film, but there would have been other repercussions. What would Marianne and Diégo have done? We would have written it exactly according to what was happening and it would have been an extraordinary event. I'd already experienced this sort of suspense when filming *Hiroshima*, though at a lesser level. We had no money, and we needed to organize a great demonstration for peace, but would anyone have come? The Japanese were pretty tired of peace demonstrations. So it was terrible. I was afraid of having this really pitiful parade, but then I reassured myself: in the end, what was the situation? We show a small production in which a young woman plays a role in a film that appears to be about peace. They're shooting this film and invite the population to join in, so ultimately we're doing the same thing; so if tomorrow morning half the population of Hiroshima shows up, that'll be great! We'd take home an amazing document showing a huge crowd. If only three people show up, well then, I'll show three people. It ended up being something in between: there were a few students, not too many, so it was a little parade. So people then criticized me for ridiculing Hiroshima, for showing a pathetic parade, et cetera. But that's the way it was. It seems that for some people there are simply things you can't talk about, that you have to hide, but I don't believe that there are truths that must be whispered simply because people don't want to hear them.

J-LP: So in the end the general strike never took place?

AR: No, there was a small demonstration at Bilbao that had no repercussions. But I must emphasize that in 1966 there was no call for a general strike.

J-LP: I was very surprised that people disputed your version of these events since, during the week the film was released, you had already discussed these events that you'd followed on the radio.

AR: Indeed, and I didn't think that anyone would criticize the film from that perspective. The tract was also authentic. Moreover it's unthinkable to imagine that we would have entirely made up such a story. But that's where everything gets contradictory. On the one hand, I used French actors, but even if I'd chosen Spanish actors it would have been impossible to hire real Spanish resistance fighters! Having them play themselves would obviously have compromised them! On the other hand, the scene of the political meeting is in some respects incomplete. We couldn't summarize eight hours of debate into seven minutes of celluloid, unless we transposed it, which does mean we falsified it.

J-PL: The voice-over commentary in the scene of the meeting gives the impression of having been added to break the charm that Diégo was enjoying, by providing a little distance on the event, so that he doesn't appear to be in a privileged position vis à vis his comrades.

AR: I wanted to break through that sort of sentimentalism, and I didn't want to present an unhappy hero. And I think I managed to give the impression that he's able to express his point of view and, even though the representative is a bit crusty, he listens carefully to what the guy has to say.

RB: You don't think he listens in a condescending way?

AR: Maybe a bit, but he's a veteran of the Spanish Civil War, he really lived through it, and so that comes into play. Diégo is a bit young. So the representative doesn't dismiss him. And we made many concessions. At first their language was a little overdosed with Marxist political phraseology, and we had to cut some of it to make it comprehensible.

J-LP: Well, you know that ever since Waldeck Rochet has appeared on the scene, people know how the communists express things.

AR: Sure, and when I saw Waldeck Rochet, I was very surprised because I'd never seen him physically, so I didn't have a very clear picture of him, but when I saw him I found that Jean Dasté bore a surprising resemblance to him!

J-LP: Three days after seeing your film, I saw Dasté in Gatti's *L'Homme Seul* at the theater in Saint-Etienne, where he was playing the role of a communist militant.

AR: That must have been very interesting. I'd love to see that play. What you'd need would be lots of money to spend five months a year traveling around France seeing plays in different cities.

J-LP: To film them?

AR: Filming them would cost half a million apiece. But I was on the verge of doing it. It's very rare that a company would be able to invest a half-million francs to record a play. And then you end up getting really exhausted, since it's extra work you have to add on to what you're already doing. It's very hard to get this kind of project going. What's more, it wouldn't have much commercial exposure. I'm often tempted to try it. It would be very difficult, but it should be done. We should realize too that there's another way of going about this. There's the new Kodachrome ultra-rapid film that would allow us to work more easily. But that would also mean an extra day of work for the actors.

RB: Jonas and Adolfas Mekas did *The Brig* in two nights clandestinely, under "wraps," and it was real cinema.

AR: I saw Brecht-Gorki's *The Mother* filmed in the same way and it was terrific. I'd seen the play in at the Berliner, and it was thrilling to see this film that had been shot ten years earlier, and to see what had changed.

J-PL: Don't you think Jean Bouise [who plays Ramon in *La Guerre est finie*] is the epitome of the anti-Bressonian actor?

AR: Well, I'm not so sure . . . perhaps if one were to introduce Bouise to Bresson, without mentioning that he's an actor, they would hit it off pretty well!

RB: There was a public reaction, picked up by some critics, saying that your film was less difficult than some of the others and that everyone could go and see it and understand it. But. in fact, in this film there is some use of advanced research on what we might call "blinkety blank" that shows things that happen in the blink of an eye, and that few people end up remembering having seen.

AR: Well, I'm not very well placed to judge this, but there's certainly something contradictory here. But after all, this isn' tragic; it's simply funny that I should be reproached with hermeticism one year and with the opposite the next season. The idea that my film is directed to too large an audience!

It seems to me that the role of the imaginary in daily life, the banal side of the imagination has never really been presented. Because dreams . . . we all love dreams, but because maybe there were effects to be gleaned from the fact that imagination often subtends reality. In any case, I limited myself to bringing in the imaginary in moments when the character is stuck and can't move. Evidently that was limiting, since why couldn't one do the whole film on the level of the imaginary. So I decided to bring in the imaginary without thinking too much about it. I think it roughly corresponds to moments when Diégo wants to do something he's forbidden to do at that precise moment. So these were the only imaginary bits that remained in the film.

MC: Was this all decided during the editing?

AR: No, almost all in the shot breakdown. Then I looked for the side of the imaginary that was outside of time. I don't think the film's viewers perceived it, and yet they could feel a sort of malaise due to the fact that these images are set in the future: it's true that in our imagination, we don't think chronologically. If I think, I'm going to see so-and-so in an hour, I don't watch myself leave the house, get in a taxi, arrive, climb the staircase, and ring the doorbell. No. I'm simply going to find myself in his apartment and then try to imagine how I got there. I think there are some very rich things to discover and that are hinted at in the film.

I'm interested, when we encounter scenes that correspond to a feeling of "déjà-vu," that they are, in some sense, "announced," and so I think that every character in the film is presented once in the imagination before being there in reality. It seemed to me that one could derive from such motifs that every cognition is a re-cognition. An English critic devoted four lines to the film: "*La Guerre est finie* was made in order to prove that if you're a Spanish revolutionary, you make love much more lyrically than other people . . ." et cetera. I laughed at this at the time, but in a way it's true that if you're in constant danger, and feel apprehensive about getting arrested and thrown in prison at any moment, there can be something exalting in the sudden difficulties of love . . .

RB: That's what Bataille said: it's what's forbidden that stimulates love. And while we're talking about the love scenes, which are very beautiful, doesn't one of them correspond to pure, fresh sensuality in a relaxed moment, whereas the other is a scene of passion?

AR: Passion and daily life. That also interests me, and I wanted (I'm not sure if this happens or not) to show that when a couple lives together for a very long time, there is a ritual side that doesn't prevent very deep emotions, but includes gestures that are a bit silly, but which are the gestures that are usually not shown in the cinema, where we always see people meeting, moments of physical revelation, the first night together. But here we have people who have been together a long time, so I tried to show how they acted when they were coming back together—habitual and old gestures.

RB: There's something I didn't understand. What was the meaning of the photos of arrows that he discovers in his wife's room and looks at a long time.

AR: There was no special meaning. When Diègo arrives, Marianne and her friends are looking for photos that they'd mislaid and that are part of an album on the city. Now arrows are very important in cities. They indicate directions and indeed, we're surrounded by arrows in 1966, so they arrive there, at the moment when he's in between, and rewriting his note starting from scratch, which annoys him. These are all opportunities to think about something else. And it happens that there are some photos of Marianne, and of course he thinks about the other world where Marianne is living, and which isn't his world, and he also looks at the images of the city. But there's no particular meaning other than that. I always try, when there's a set direction to a film, to say the opposite, which undoes the whole construction of the film, through a detail, or a zest of the irrational. This is a little superstitious, I think. In the sense that there's a constant direction to this film that completely loses its focus and doesn't lead anywhere.

J-LP: Do you think that the end of the film constitutes Marianne's "sudden realization" about Diégo's cause?

RB: She says several times in the film that she would like to go to Spain, to be with him.

AR: I've been reproached for not having given Marianne a political consciousness about Spain, but that would have been an oversimplified, idealized picture of her, because if she loves Diégo and what he's doing, what he represents, and if, doubtless, she leaves her husband for him, it's because he represents an entirely different universe than the one she aspires to. Marianne would also have loved, in a certain way, to have been totally involved, but she's Swedish and lives in France: it would feel completely artificial if her connection to the Spanish people were other than a sentimental one. I don't think you can suddenly decide to fight for ten years like that for a country you don't belong to. Ultimately, obviously, certain circumstances obtain that cause some people to make decisions that are entirely based on conviction. So what happened? Diégo's crisis is that he's going to remain in Paris. There's a moment when, in his mind, Diégo imagines his little drama: "Evidently it's sad I'm staying, but on the other hand, I'll be able to read, to see Marianne, see Nadine again, and I'll be able to write, so perhaps there are advantages to this situation." In a sense, that should represent Marianne's dream: finally, Diégo is going to stay. Obviously, she wants him to stay, especially after their life and those long years of separation . . . And then she realizes that it would be worse; from the moment that what you dreamed of seems attainable, but you haven't completely thought about the consequences, suddenly you realize that it's going to produce another kind of catastrophe. So for her, it's true, there's a certain kind of "realization": Diégo will never be anything else than a committed revolutionary.

J-LP: She doesn't end up blaming the Party, which she could have held responsible for the danger that Diégo is risking. It's quite the opposite: she behaves out of solidarity with his position.

RB: For Marianne, those are Diégo's friends.

AR: It's when they're faced with difficult decisions that people show their true colors. If good will is not always obvious in this film, the end, at least as I imagine it, is that she arrives in Barcelona, is reunited with Diégo and Juan, and says to them: 'Watch out. You've been spotted. They're going to arrest you when you try to return." So they'll take different routes to return. Or, maybe she and Diégo will remain in Spain.

MC: Did you have the feeling while you were making it, that this was the most direct of your films?

AR: You can't have feelings like that.

J-LP: There are definitely scenarios that require completely different approaches, for example *Marienbad*.

AR: That was the wonderful surprise about *Marienbad*. For the first two weeks, we were all sort of terrified, we really had the impression that we were involved in something we didn't understand at all, something scary and that we were forced to obey. With *Marienbad* we never had the impression of making a gratuitous or simply "decorative" film. Ultimately, we all felt caught up in it. It's strange, because if it had just been me, or a single actor or a single actress, one might have argued that it was because we liked Robbe-Grillet, that we were sensitive to this type of sound or literature; but it was the entire team, it was true of people who'd never read a single line of Robbe-Grillet, who found themselves completely absorbed by that atmosphere.

RB: When you shoot your films, your writers never visit the set?

AR: That's the way it happened with Marguérite Duras: she couldn't fly, and couldn't stay so long in Japan. Afterwards, I showed her the rushes and was able to discuss the work during the editing of the film. So, a whole section of the text was rewritten. It's interesting to me that the scriptwriters, from the moment that we begin to shoot, have no idea of what we're doing, with the inevitable result that, when I show them the film for the first time at such an advanced stage, there are things they will see with fresh eyes, which wouldn't be the case if they'd seen each of the rushes as they were shot. And since there are always things to rework, that's a way of getting completely involved—otherwise it would end up being a bit ordinary.

RB: Do you think that it's this way of working in stages that made Semprun and everyone who worked with you want to make films?

AR: I always like reversing propositions like that, so I'd answer: no, if I chose them, it was because I felt they were already leaning toward the theatrical arts, so the fact that they ended up wanting to make films proved it. I didn't choose them for their literary qualities, but for their dramatic bent. You might argue that I bully my collaborators by asking them not to come to the shoots, but it's often they who choose not to. Ultimately, it's very difficult if you know what you want to do, to have two people on the set. It's not a question of discussion, but of having a tendency to want to "please" and end up losing your way. I also think you ought to be able to make "mistakes" in two or three shots and end up feeling that an "error" that was made in a sequence can end up being justified by the last shot of that sequence and be something good. Whereas if you try to correct every shot, you could end up with something dreadful.

J-LP: Have you worked with all your scriptwriters the way you did with Semprun, by writing together?

AR: For the most part, yes. But it may turn out that with one, we'll work every day together whereas with another, it could be once a week. It varies a lot.

MC: What directives did you give Fusco for the music?

AR: It was he who proposed the choirs and I agreed immediately. What was interesting was to link, thanks to Fusco, love scenes and political scenes (by using the same musical theme) and thereby accentuate the mixing and interaction of these feelings. The Spanish theme—or rather the revolutionary theme—is a kind of steady *obbligato* that seeps into the more sentimental scenes, such as the funeral, to link them together. It's very tonal, very traditional music, but that's always a problem for film music. What's complicated in contemporary music is that its development is *horizontal*, which is to say that it develops through additions, through accretions, so that at the end of a movement, if you have a good ear and a good musical memory, you can "hear" the superposition of chords, in what ends up feeling to me like a horizontal progression. It seems to me, on the other hand, that dramatic music should, on the contrary, have a *vertical* development to better follow the development of the action. So it's very difficult to adopt a contemporary language for a story that, doubtless, obeys more ancient laws, provisionally.

Alain Resnais, Antidoctrinary

O. Revault d'Allonnes / 1967

From *La Revue d'Esthétique*, nos. 2–3 (1967). Reprinted by permission. Translated by T. Jefferson Kline.

O. Revault d'Allonnes: Your work represents a certain well-defined tendency in the current cinema that is said to be determined by the importance of the storyline—of what happens in your films. At least that's what's said about your cinema. Do you accept this definition? And if not, in what way does it distort your intentions?

Alain Resnais: All fiction films, or in any case 99 percent of them, tell a story. I don't know if the films I've directed could be singled out in this respect. My goal, in any case, is not to tell stories, but to create emotions. That's what counts the most for me. So maybe the difference between me and the other film directors you're thinking of is a difference in age. I'm ten years older than they are.

What I'm trying to create, to organize, is a kind of theater, which is to say, something that is universally necessary to mankind. Everywhere you go, you will find that people organize theatrical performances. This is mysterious and moving, this need: even under the bombs during the Korean War, even in Moscow in 1917, people who were dying of hunger went to the theater. If it were just a matter of the storyline in films or in plays, if the story were really the essential part of these shows, it would be enough just to write it and print it. Of course, in any film there's a story, but what really matters is that this story furnishes the occasion for, and the means of, a theatrical representation. If the story is important (and everything is important) it certainly isn't the most important thing in a film.

ORA: Have you ever felt the need to write, or do you think only about creating films?

AR: I regret that I don't know how to write; I'm not at all a writer. I don't feel the necessary nostalgia, and I even have the impression that I'd lose my freedom in writing. Some time ago, I tried to make a short film on grammar, but unfortunately it didn't work out. It's too bad: I might have learned how to manipulate language and use words and writing.

ORA: So, you might also be interested in working in theater?

AR: Technically, I'm not sure, but in terms of emotions, I think it would be easy for me. Leaving aside questions of stagecraft, of course. You know, I'm not really an *author* of films so much as a director: it's the theatricality of the art that is, if I might say, my domain. Even if I provide a theme, a sketch, or a line of dialogue, I have to have someone to write the screenplay to be happy.

Obviously, you could wonder whether the story doesn't end up, thanks to the author's work, being the primordial element in the films I collaborate on. And yet I don't believe that my films are "literary." The authors of most of my films are not just *writers*, they're also theater people. A film can be as important as a book for a writer, but you can't film a book. A book is a finished work, complete, unlike a screenplay. For example, it would never occur to me to make a film of a published novel, which is sufficient unto itself.

It's not just by chance that almost all of the authors with whom I've worked became film directors: Marguerite Duras, Robbe-Grillet, Cayrol, Jorge Semprun. I can't imagine the same thing happening with, for example, Faulkner! All I had to do was reveal, in bringing their work to the screen, the virtual theatricality of these authors.

ORA: But isn't it precisely your influence that drew these authors toward this theatricality?

AR: I don't think so. It simply proves that there are writers for films, if I may put it this way, and writers for books. It's true in the other arts, by the way. There is theatrical music—for example, Stravinsky's music—and I'm not just thinking about his ballets. There are also theatrical painters: Uccello is a theatrical painter par excellence! There is in those art forms something that may be called the aesthetic perception that one has in the theater.

ORA: What role do objects play in your films? Do you sometimes feel a kind of fascination for objects, as one might infer from *Marienbad* or *Muriel*?

AR: It's not the object in itself: the object is situated and treated in a realistic manner, and I show it just because it's there. But it's always seen from the perspective of a character. In *Muriel*, it's a bit a "fly's-eye view" of things. Spontaneously, I imagine a fly looking at one thing after another without settling on anything. I felt that the editing of this film had to be very dry.

ORA: Then why so many shots—all static ones—with a single long tracking shot at the end?

AR: The static shots accentuate the ruptures. In fact, there are seven hundred shots in two hours; that's a lot, although people have done more. It's not a great technical feat. Ultimately, camera movement follows the movements and the gaze of the character. I felt all that in a musical way. Of course, *Muriel* gains meaning in comparison with *Marienbad*, which was more or less the opposite: very fluid editing, with objects and sets gouverned by the characters' obsessions.

ORA: In a given shot or sequence, what is the element that first strikes you: the image, the word, the movement, or something else?

AR: It's different every time. Sometimes it's the voice, at others the image, an object or its rhythm. The main thing is to provoke an emotion. The technical side of the question never comes first: technical details are just a means to an end. In this sense, technical problems are agonizing, since it's a question, first and foremost, of inspiration. We don't know beforehand how we're going to do something, or even if a solution will come. It's not the technique that inspires the idea. Otherwise all you'd have to do would be to set about things and you'd be sure to reach your goal.

As for voices, yes, maybe a voice can produce an idea of an image. At other times it might be an object: everything depends on the situation in which the character finds himself. You begin with one element and then discover others from the emotion of the scene. If I film from a certain angle, edit in a certain way, and with a certain music, it's to produce as much pleasure as possible—or fear. I am always focused on the effect I want to produce. Everything must combine to move the spectators . . . so that they'll feel some emotion (so they'll want to talk about the film when they leave the theater).

ORA: Do you consider yourself a "politically engaged" artist, who has something to say to his audience?

AR: I don't think so. If people find me "politically engaged" so much the better, but I absolutely don't want to be trapped in the dilemma "message—no message." The filmmaker who decided a priori to make a film solely to say this or that, that this is good and that is bad, and derived his entire film from the mission he'd set for himself, would end up being dishonest to himself and to his audience.

What I'm looking for are characters who behave freely, whether they choose what they do or react to the concrete situation they find themselves in. At the beginning of a film, the character may seem like a symbol, and the viewer may expect that he'll do certain things or avoid certain things as a consequence. But if so, he'd remain only a sketch of a character with a very basic psychology. An interesting scenario is one in which the character *escapes* from all control and from all of our expectations, when he exists *independently*. Sometimes, directors try to graft a certain message onto this living, free character. They might, for example, try to add a sentence that will provide a moral lesson, or whatever. But in 95 percent of such cases, the sentence dies during the shooting and the graft simply doesn't take. It not that the actor doesn't know how to say the line: good actors will always manage to do what they need to do. But for the film overall, it just won't work. You simply can't tack something onto a character from the outside. So, for example, I completely approve of Godard's decision, in *Vivre sa vie*, when he has us listen to a long speech about prostitution pronounced off-screen. If he'd tried to put this speech in the mouth of one of his characters, it wouldn't have worked.

A truly "engaged" filmmaker would end up making all his films from the same political position. I'm too much prey to the spirit of contradiction. I refuse to appear politically engaged to "look good."

ORA: You were speaking of the audience. Is it your ongoing intent to reach a large audience?

AR: Like everyone else, I'm looking to appeal to the largest possible audience. I don't search for my audience in any systematic way, but I only feel I've succeeded if I reach them. My job is to tell my story in the best possible way.

ORA: And what about your connections to the world of cinema? For example, your relations with your producer, your actors, and all your collaborators?

AR: I feel that I have excellent relations with my collaborators. I feel very well integrated into this milieu. For me the most important relationships are with the author on the one hand and the actors on the other. After all, the film director is really a sort of coordinator. The creative work of the actor is just as important as that of the authors of the film, exactly in the perspective I was just describing in which the character begins to live his own life. It's at that point that you can see whether things are going to work or not, what's missing and what's overdone. The actor is a work of art in motion. He's the one who has to come up with the solutions.

ORA: What about your relations with the critics?

AR: After all, a critic is nothing more than a privileged member of the audience: unlike the other viewers, he gets to express himself in the press. I know my films won't please everyone. Obviously, if a critic runs me down, it bothers me, if he praises me, I'm happy, but it's the same for every viewer in the theater, the vast majority of whom don't get to express themselves publicly. That's just part of the rules of the game. I don't have the right to complain about the severity of the critics.

ORA: Do you have any sense of what direction your work will take in the future, at least in its main direction?

AR: None whatsoever. There's nothing I can tell you since I have no idea. It's a complete mystery. But I don't really tend to think about things in advance. I like to keep an instinctive element in my work, like the Surrealists did with automatic writing. In any case, I don't think about the future as a function of the past. You shouldn't think too much about the past. When I do something I'm mostly guided by interior images. I try to preserve my spontaneity. This way, the film remains open to a world of possibilities. The biggest problem is to avoid censorship in any form and especially the pre-censorship that one might inflict on oneself.

Earlier you mentioned the preparation of shots in *Muriel*. What happened? Why the shot of the fly? Maybe it was a sentence that suggested the idea of shot planning . . . but no, it was the character of Alphonse, this older man who's sitting there in a chair with his oversized overcoat. He's just arrived at the home of the woman he'd once loved, and he's feeling awkward and doesn't know what to say. Hence, his stiffness. So what does he do? He looks around to escape from his own thoughts, but that doesn't work. I'm thinking of a mosaic. A mosaic is also composed of lots of little pieces that are fixed and juxtaposed and are made of many colors. Yes, we needed to film in color, and I told my producer that if I couldn't shoot in color, I couldn't take responsibility for this film. A mosaic, or, if you will, the fly we were talking about just now.

ORA: You rarely talk about your own work and never about other people's work. Can you talk about your favorite directors and your favorite films?

AR: Godard, Truffaut, Agnès Varda, Chris Marker, Jacques Demy, Rozier, Allio . . . among French directors. We were accused of being a clique, but I don't think it was true. I love Truffaut's *La Peau douce* for its purity and the clarity of its mise en scène. In general I think of myself as a good film viewer, but I'm only a member of the audience when I watch others' films. The films I prefer are obviously those that are farthest from what I do.

ORA: So you can sometimes be a director and sometimes a spectator?

AR: Well, it's not really an alternative. You've just raised the question of creativity. I remember something Marcel L'Herbier once said: "A film director is simply the first spectator of the film," which comes down to saying that in the film there are things that the viewer should be able to connect—I mean, connect poetically—so I have to find the connection before he does. My motto would be to confess to the audience: "I'm not any more clever than you are and you're no dumber than I am!"

So, to continue with *Muriel* . . . This film was written during the Algerian War, but when we started to work on it, neither Cayrol nor I had thought about making any allusions to the war. It simply happened that the character of Bernard, the young man who's twenty to twenty-two years old, more or less dictated this direction of the film. What was a young man of his age doing at that time? He'd just returned from Algeria. So, almost as a result, the episode in the film of the amateur film that he'd brought back from there seemed to work itself quite naturally into the screenplay. I didn't go looking for this allusion to current events. But once it worked its way into the film, I had no reason to take it out either.

ORA: In *La Guerre est finie*, on the other hand, you constructed the entire film around a given political situation . . .

AR: Yes. The film's producer was even warned before we started shooting that the subject of the film risked having cuts imposed or that it might even be refused a visa for export. So Sofracima, the producer, knew that they were taking an enormous risk financially. Their attitude was very courageous: we went ahead and shot the film despite the risks, and we were rewarded, since the film in its entirety was given a visa without any difficulties.

ORA: But this film displeased a lot of people . . .

AR: Yes, the film provoked lots of discussion, but I wouldn't say it was attacked, except if you consider the fact that it was banned throughout Spain. But you always take a risk when you incorporate contemporary real events into a fiction film.

I confess that I prefer to run this risk rather than to have the feeling that I've taken refuge in a Greek allegory or in *science-fiction*. And yet, it's no accident that the entire film is focused on the character of Diégo, and his individual reactions. We have no pedagogical pretensions,: but I don't see why the burning questions of the day shouldn't appear on the screen. Moreover, that's the reason there's a sort of narrative voice in the film, so that we can make clear to our audience that we're not attempting to present the problem in its entirety, but rather the story of a man in a specific situation. Without wanting—or daring—to compare my film to Renoir's *Rules of the Game*, I think that in my film, almost all of the characters are right, and have earned the sympathy of the director and the screenwriter.

ORA: So each member of the audience has the right to understand the film as a function of their personal preferences?

AR: That's another way of asking what will happen after the end of the film, even though this question isn't part of the work as imagined by the authors of the film and so they can rule it out. After he's crossed the border into Spain, is Diègo going to get arrested? Personally, I'd extend the film as follows: Diègo and Marianne are going to become more and more involved with each other, and Diègo is going to settle in Spain and continue his struggle against the regime there. It's in some way in his vocation, and I think the film communicates this. And I believe the recent events in Spain, since the release of the film, lend credence to this hypothesis. There's the very significant fact than in July 1966, that is to say, after the release of the film, the expression "the war is over" was adopted by several militant organizations in their manifestos. Which would tend to prove that if you let yourself be guided by the character, his behavior will intersect at some point with reality.

Interview with Alain Resnais

Jacques Belmans / 1968

From *Etudes Cinématographiques*, nos. 67–68 (1968). Reprinted by permission. Translated by T. Jefferson Kline.

Jacques Belmans: A number of studies of the cinema have proclaimed to whoever would listen that the seventh art is incapable of capturing our interior life. But your work seems to me to offer a particularly strong refutation of this assertion. What do you think of this?

Alain Resnais: Indeed, I would like my films to stand as a contradiction of this assertion. I've always been faithful to André Breton, who refused to believe that our imaginary life is not an integral part of real life. If there is a realistic element in life as seen from the exterior, there is also an equally realistic element in the interior life of each one of us. But cinema is certainly equal to the task of describing this interior life and the interiority of the character. The challenge is to create an image capable of touching the audience's unconscious almost in spite of themselves. This creative process remains intuitive, so I don't have a theory about it. Obviously, I'm not against filmmakers who have a "message"! But as for me, I don't have the impression that I must operate in this way.

JB: I've been fascinated by the themes of forgetting, of memory, and of the effects of time's erosion on the characters you depict, all of which seem to constitute the leitmotifs of your work. Do you intend to continue in this vein? If so, why, and how will you do it?

AR: It's possible that I'll continue to treat these themes. I never decided consciously to do this . . . nor am I the only one to explore these subjects. You see, ultimately it's always a matter of wanting to counter death and the ravages of time, for example, when a photographer or a painter tries to fix the image of the face and body of the woman he loves. It's our way of protesting against the human condition imposed on us. A revolt against temporality. That's how it is presented in my films. Ultimately, this is a banal, popular theme . . . I think I'm afraid of analyzing this too closely. A film director has everything to gain by remaining solidly in the daily and concrete aspects of our life. It's the tinkering aspect of our profession.

JB: *Muriel* is the least well known of your films. But I find it an extremely important film and a success in every way. Is it a film that's very important in your eyes, and as important as your other work?

AR: I'm reluctant to make such comparisons. Like all directors, I'm always focused on my next film. The reasons for *Muriel*'s lack of success aren't so mysterious: it's a very melancholic film and a bit uncomfortable to watch. On the screen we are forced to watch our own flaws as average human beings. We don't really want to watch touching characters whom we don't find inspiring. The film's heroes confront seemingly minor problems that they don't seem to be able to resolve except by accident. They're too much like us. "We love drama but not unhappiness," Roger Vailland once said. *Muriel* is too full of termites and has no leopards or elephants. Nevertheless, this wretched film has been making a comeback among certain audiences.

JB: So you like treating ordinary people in ordinary situations? I'm thinking of *Muriel*, of *Hiroshima mon amour*, and of *La Guerre est finie*. They're not really about heroes, but, initially at least, just anonymous people.

AR: I think this phenomenon is common to all of modern—truly modern—cinema . . . Look at the work of Truffaut, Godard, and so many others. There are no more superheroes and supermen with lessons imposed on the audience. I think the reigning imperative of this generation is to make the behavior of our characters more understandable to our audience. In other words, we want to be more critical in our presentation of human behavior.

JB: Do you think it's always necessary to call on a well-known writer to create the screenplay for your films?

AR: I have always refused to film a completed book. If the book exists, then it doesn't interest me to film it. On the other hand, since I'm not what you'd call a film auteur, I don't see any other solution than to ask the people I like to work with me. For example, I'm very sensitive to the breath and to the role of oppression in Jean Cayrol's novels. I love the lyricism and the Edith Piaf side in Marguerite Duras. And, like Jacques Sternberg, I appreciate the work of Charles Addams, of Folon, and of Topor. I'd never read any of Robbe-Grillet's novels when our producers asked us to collaborate on something, but as soon as we began working together, I filled in the gaps and became a great fan of his novels. For me, he's almost an author of *Lieder*, a poet, very nearly operatic. *Jealousy* is no doubt his masterpiece.

JB: Would you be interested in doing a film of science-fiction? Do you think that this genre, so often done stupidly in film, can produce masterpieces as it does in literature, or, at least, interesting works such as Chris Marker's *La Jetée* or Truffaut's *Fahrenheit 451*? How might you go about such a subject?

AR: Every film director, or very nearly, has two dreams: to make a musical comedy and to do a film of science-fiction. Only, it's true that it's a very difficult enterprise. Not so much because of the technical means that the genre requires, but that it's a type of film in which you have to shoot every scene twice. First you have to see it on the screen, and then break down the entire set and start over. Your film must be a true expedition into unknown territory. It's tough to make that coincide with a preset working schedule. That said, at certain moments, Godard's *Alphaville* was very interesting. I really liked *La Jetée*. And I'm really looking forward to Vadim's *Barbarella* as well as the next film by Stanley Kubrick.

JB: Among the films you've seen most recently, which ones have most excited you?

AR: I've seen very few films recently. I've heard very good things about films like Miklos Jancso's *Silence and Cry*, *O Salto* by Christian de Chalonge, and *Terre en transe* by Glauber Rocha, but, alas, I haven't found the time to see them, since I'm so overwhelmed by work on the editing of *Je t'aime, je t'aime*...

I have a very positive memory of Bergman's *Persona* and Godard's *Week-end*.

JB: Do you think that film audiences have become differentiated as much as readers of literature? If so, is this a good thing?

AR: Certainly! Things have changed a lot since the time, ten years ago, when Claude Mauriac could write, in substance, "I never see a film that I have difficulty understanding." Film has caught up with the other arts; there are now films that you have to see several times to penetrate into their world. My friends will say, "I really loved such and such a film, but I didn't understand another!" Today's films require intelligence and perceptiveness together with a certain culture. Happily television eliminated certain categories of films just as photography did with regard to painting. But the cinema needs to attract a certain number of viewers, so . . .

That said, I wonder if the film industry is doing everything it can to attract audiences. I'm thinking as much about the physical comfort of the audience members (projection, reception, seats, and especially sound) as of their moral comfort (questions of publicity). When you see the efforts made by other industries . . .

JB: Do you think that critics can sometimes play a creative role? Do critics influence you? Do they influence the public?

AR: Critics play a major role. Their influence is very clear on certain types of films that wouldn't exist without them. There is no doubt that they sometimes fan our interest in difficult films. On the other hand, they can neither guarantee the success of a film nor ruin its success as things stand now. They sometimes let us down completely, as in the case of their dismissive treatment of an important work like *Umberto D*. More recently, however they got the public interested in *O Salto* . . . so, although contradictory at times, yes, they play an important role.

I prefer a didactic critic to an impassioned one. For example, André Bazin. A critic can be professorial by allowing us to see the work in context, in its author's filmography, for example. Obviously, that kind of criticism is more essay than review, and is most often found in publications that allow for a certain distance on the work and time to develop one's ideas.

JB: In the same line of thinking, are there books on film that are significantly important in your view?

AR: The essential books are the writings of André Bazin, *The Technique of Film Editing* by Karel Reisz, *The Intelligence of a Machine* by Jean Epstein, the theoretical writings of Pudovkin and Eisenstein, the essays of Jean Mitry, and *The Haunted Screen* by Lotte H. Eisner.

JB: Do you have a theory of mise en scène or are your ideas on that constantly evolving?

AR: You always hope to do the opposite of what you've just done!

JB: What do you think about the role of the actors? Do you consider them to be a malleable material, the way Antonioni does, or do you give them more importance as human personalities?

AR: I believe every film has three equal authors: the director, the screenwriter, and the actors.

The actors are an integral part of the film. The work they do is very important, and I refuse to consider them as simple instruments.

In general, I meet with my actors one or two months before the shoot. The conversations I've had with them often help advance our work on the screenplay and the dialogue.

The vocation of the actor is a very difficult one. In my eyes, the human quality of the actor is primordial.

JB: Are you conscious of the exceptional importance your work holds for the young generation of cinephiles? What would you tell them about the vocation of the director?

AR: I'm not at all conscious of my reputation! I would find that too overwhelming! I consider myself to be a student, a self-taught practitioner. Playing pope doesn't interest me.

Of course, I don't want to practice false modesty either. I'm well aware that my films have excited some interest, but that whole question remains pretty obscure to me. If I saw things more clearly, I might worry less about finding myself unemployed.

You can't let being a director be your second job. It's absolutely impossible. In literature, it's different: with rare exceptions, the novelist has another job, usually to make ends meet. Another difference is that a novelist works and lives entirely alone. The film director works in collaboration with others. I would find it too sad working alone! A question of temperament. In the cinema, the work of collaboration is primordial.

JB: One last thing: with the film *Far from Vietnam*, you took a very clear position regarding the unhappy problems of our times. I believe that violence plays a significant role in your work.

AR: Even the word "violence" evokes an unacceptable idea for me. Useless suffering, inflicted by men on other men. Oppression. We have enough problems with the normal accidents of nature without adding persecutions, wars, torture . . .

I cannot bring myself to accept violence, and I feel, as you do, powerless to resolve the problem in everyday life. Whence my defensive reaction: I am afraid; I try to defend myself with my own means. I participated in a film that is a means of playing with public opinion. With one grain of sand after another, maybe we'll succeed some day in throwing a wrench into that machine.

Memories of Resnais

Richard Roud / 1969

From *Sight and Sound* 38, no. 3 (summer 1969). Reprinted by permission.

Beginnings

Richard Roud: When did you first decide that you wanted to make films?

Alain Resnais: I can't give you an exact date because . . . Well, do you know the story of when I first visited Darius Milhaud, the composer? He began to tell me about the day Fernand Léger came up to his flat accompanied by a lion. Léger had rented the lion from a traveling circus that had set up on the Boulevard Clichy. And before Milhaud could finish his story, I said, "Oh, yes, and then you said to Léger . . ." "Oh, God!" said Milhaud. "I always forget that I told that story in my autobiography." It's the same with me. I always forget what I said in previous interviews. But whether I've told it already or not, this is how it began. I wanted (like everybody else) to be an actor. The results of my efforts to become one were not particularly encouraging, so I gave up. But, by then, I had grown so attached to the milieu that when IDHEC (L'Institut des Hautes Etudes Cinématographiques) opened, I signed on to learn how to be an editor. At that time, the very idea of a school to teach people how to make films was something startling and exciting. Anyhow, I said to myself, if I'm going to spend my whole life at a job, wouldn't it be better to be in the film world rather than among books? Until then, I had always wanted to be a bookseller. I *was* interested in editing; and more important, I would be able to earn my living without losing contact with the world of actors. That was the main thing: not to leave this milieu I found so fascinating. I would still be able to go backstage, as it were.

RR: Had you never thought before that time of going into the cinema?

AR: I never dreamed of being a film director when I was young, but when I saw the first Ginger Rogers/Fred Astaire dance numbers (or maybe it was even before, with Dick Powell and Ruby Keeler), I suddenly had a strong, even violent, desire to make films. Those dance numbers had a kind of sensual movement which really took hold of me, and I remember thinking I would like to make films that had the same effect on people, that I wondered if I could find the equivalent of that exhilaration.

RR: The strange thing is that one does find that sense of exhilaration in all of your films, even in *Muriel*, where the camera scarcely moves.

AR: My great hope in making *Muriel* was to save time by not having any camera movements, and when they asked me how many feet of track rails I was going to need, I said, "None at all." I wanted to see if I could make a film without using a single tracking shot. But in spite of this the shooting went more slowly than ever. Mind you, we did pan and tilt, but the camera didn't actually move until the final scene. *Harry Dickson*, on the other hand, would have been done in 70mm, with the actors always framed full length—head to toe—throughout the film. A little like Feuillade, perhaps. But I would have been able to take advantage of the high definition and absolute clarity as well as the absence of depth of field that only 70mm can give you. That way I would have been able to show the characters full length without sacrificing any details or facial expressions. In both cases, the formal structures were dictated by the subject matter. *Muriel* had to be a mosaic. I mean, Cayrol and I didn't just decide to make a film that would be shot this way or that. It all began with one idea: one day on the stairs, Cayrol said, "I've got an idea you might like, a film about provincial life. Wouldn't you like the idea of a movie about a kind of double city—prewar and postwar, with people who can't find their way any more because the new streets don't follow the lines of the old ones?" Of course, I was interested.

RR: Don't you think you were in some way influenced simply by the desire to make a film that would be, independently of the subject matter, different from *Marienbad*?

AR: No, no. That is, well, perhaps yes. I've always been tempted by the idea that *since* the last film was such and such, the next one should therefore be different. Therefore, since *Marienbad* was made up of only one shot, so to speak, why shouldn't I do a film that would have an enormous number of shots? Since I was always inside the characters' minds in *Marienbad*, therefore couldn't they in the next film always be seen from the outside? *Marienbad* was unchronological; *Muriel*, therefore, would be completely chronological.

RR: On the other hand, all of your films have taken place in the provinces, with the exception of *La Guerre est finie*.

AR: Oh, how I suffered precisely because that was made in Paris. First of all, there are practical problems when you shoot in Paris. Parking, traffic, things like that. And I don't like going home after a day's shooting. The crew had marvelous memories of the shooting of *Muriel*: we each left our respective hotels at five minutes to nine, and by nine we were all on the spot, ready to go. In Paris, it's always taxis; people are usually late, and you spend a fortune keeping parking spaces open . . . I have no desire to make another film in Paris. Nobody likes filming in Paris: it's so much easier for an actor to believe in his role if he doesn't go home to his family at night.

Mind you, we did get away a bit, since some scenes were shot in Stockholm [it was a Franco-Swedish co-production]. We had to construct Marianne's apartment, because we couldn't find one available in Paris. It may sound strange, but it's true. In any case, apartments are very expensive there: $200 per day. Geneviève Bujold's flat was also shot in Sweden; it was a reconstruction of Jean Vilar's apartment in Paris. The only important interior shot in Paris was the student meeting in the flat overlooking the Montparnasse cemetery, and that cost plenty.

Actually, there are people who have fitted out private houses in the suburbs as mini-studios, but they are never very good, because sound recording is too difficult; there's too much reverberation. Someone like Godard wouldn't mind, because he has been able to turn such a disadvantage into a positive style. He discovered that "bad" sound has a kind of charm, and he uses it. But you should never make the mistake of thinking that his kind of sound is in any way more realistic; the human ear selects, and the microphone doesn't. In conversation, we automatically block out traffic noises; a microphone will pick them up as loud as our voices. Godard may think his sound recording techniques are realistic, but actually the result is pure expressionism.

I don't think the French cinema as a whole pays nearly enough attention to sound. If I'm ever lucky enough to make another film, I'm going to try to have two or three sound boom operators instead of the usual one. If sound crews were only bigger, I am sure the results would be better. Post-synching is all right if you want to try for a special effect, but I think it's better to get the sound during shooting. Of course, the Italians—Fellini, in particular—do everything post-synch. That's his idea of making movies: it's not mine.

Feuillade

RR: Let's go back to your early filmgoing experiences. When did you see your first Feuillade film?

AR: My first? It must have been, yes, it was very late—in 1944, when Langlois showed *Fantômas* [at the Paris Cinémathèque]. Then there was that great evening with Musidora there in person at the Cinémathèque, when they showed *Les Vampires* and then *Barrabas*. I adore *Barrabas*.

RR: The guillotine scene at the beginning reminded me, because of the elliptical way in which it is edited, of some of your own films.

AR: Really? You know, the trouble with those films is that they are like dreams. If you don't write them down when you first wake up, it's hard to recall them later on: I just don't remember the guillotine sequence. In any case, Feuillade's cinema is very close to dreams—and therefore it's perhaps the most realistic kind of all. For me, *Les Vampires*, *Tih Minh*, and *Barrabas* are the best. *Judex*, on the other hand, was too much a film made to order. Even the book by Bernède was written purposely to try to correct any bad impressions left by *Les Vampires*. And this approach is as bad as trying to make a film with a very specific message. When Feuillade made *Fantômas* (and when Marcel Allain wrote the book), they let their imaginations run wild. But they pondered over *Judex*: they injected moral notes, comforting elements. Of course, there are moralizing bits in *Les Vampires*, but they seem quite natural. It was Feuillade's own morality that came out, but at the same time he was obviously fascinated by the diabolical nature of the characters. *Judex* was all too carefully worked out; there was none of that marvelously natural, easygoing quality of *Les Vampires*.

RR: Legend has it, however, that your connections with Feuillade went back much earlier than 1944.

AR: That's true. I must have told the story a hundred times, but it's true nonetheless. I was lucky enough as a child to have one of the first Kodak 8mm cameras—they had just been launched on the French market. I began to make an adaptation of one of the *Fantômas* stories, but as I had only little boys and girls to play the parts, I brought the camera up close to them, thinking that would make them seem bigger, like adults. But my critical faculties were already sufficiently developed for me to realize, once I saw the finished film, that somehow the dramatic atmosphere and tension I was trying for was just not there. It's too bad I noticed, because otherwise I would have gone on, and we would have had hours and hours of *Fantômas* played by school children, and what a document that would have been. One funny thing was that the only way I could think of linking shots was with dissolves (maybe this was the influence of Marcel L'Herbier); I also wanted to have iris shots, wipes, composite images, and no amateur camera could do any of these things. Except, of course, for the famous Cine-Kodak Special that I used to look at in the shop windows. It could do everything, and, of course, it was a 16mm camera! Really professional! Disney even used it for his documentaries later on. For a long time, it was the finest camera in the world, and it still remains a fascinating object. It had a rectangular shape like the 1925 Voisin automobiles—the art deco influence, I suppose.

L'Herbier and the Avant-Garde

RR: When Sadoul interviewed you for *Le Point*, he quoted you as saying, "What I like in Marcel L'Herbier is his sure taste in the popular novel, his attempts to remain in contact with the literary men and artistic movements of his time, and his definition of the director as 'the first spectator of a film . . .'"

AR: That's all true. Also, I think that the attacks on L'Herbier's films have been widely off the mark. What was it they reproached him for? For using sets, for not thinking writers were a separate race from scriptwriters, for therefore using Blaise Cendrars as his scenarist, for using Fernand Léger as his set designer. All of these seem like good ideas to me. And it's also true that I have a great feeling of nostalgia for the expressionist film. Although I don't know why I say "nostalgia"; such films are still being made, and as far as I'm concerned we can never go *beyond* expressionism. Bill Klein's *Mr. Freedom*, for example, is a completely expressionistic film. Maybe that's why it provoked such violent reactions: some people just can't accept having reality transposed to another level.

RR: Which of L'Herbier's films did you see when you were young?

AR: *Eldorado*, for one. The reason I spoke in that interview in *Le Point* about the popular novel (the *feuilleton*) is because when I was younger, I didn't understand its appeal or its value. The other films of L'Herbier I saw very much later, around 1946 at the Cinémathèque. I used to think that his *L'Inhumaine* must have been (for I hadn't seen it—in fact, I *still* haven't seen it) quite marvelous just because it was not adapted from a *feuilleton*. But *Eldorado*, my first contact with L'Herbier, certainly was *feuilleton*-esque. Later I learned to like the *feuilleton*; starting of course with *Fantômas*, which is the masterpiece of the genre. And then I understood much better why the young directors of the twenties used *feuilletons* as a basis for their films. I used to think it was purely as stylistic exercise, for I hadn't yet understood to what degree the subconscious, the surrealistic association of ideas, were present in a pure state in the *feuilleton*—more than in other forms of art. Now, you see, I understand Abel Gance much better.

I now feel both attracted to and repelled by L'Herbier: attracted by his principles, his ideas, his theoretical writing. And I'm quite prepared to believe that they had some influence on me. Jean Epstein, too: for I am convinced that one can be influenced by a man in other ways than through his films. The three lines about him in the Bardèche and Brasillach history, a still in *La Revue du cinéma*, an article by Brunius, a text by Breton: I'm convinced that all these had their effect. And the one book about the cinema that really fascinated me before I began to make films myself was by Epstein. I did in fact see some of Epstein's films when I was very young. He made some films in Brittany, and as these were the first talking Breton films, they were widely distributed in my province: *Mor*

Vran and *L'Or des mers*, for example. And I found them very, very disconcerting. I was only nine years old at the time, and they both frightened me and left a really deep impression. Then there were the texts of Delluc: I used to dream about what *Fièvre* must be like, but I never saw it, and, as a matter of fact, I still haven't. I did see *La Femme de nulle part*, however.

Germaine Dulac, on the other hand, I found very disappointing. Her attempt to apply musical time to pictorial time was a real disaster. (Mind you, I'm glad she tried it: somebody had to.) Her mistake was in confusing aural and visual perception and retention. I suppose she had to do her symphonies on flowers just to teach us all that it was a path not worth pursuing. And *La Coquille et le clergyman* was really proof that . . . well, that *Un chien andalou* was authentic. You would have thought the two films could be lumped together, but they can't because one is genuine and the other is sheer coquetry. Another example of the partly phoney film is Man Ray's *Etoile de mer*.

Cocteau, Bresson, Guitry

RR: When did you see your first German expressionist film?

AR: It was *Caligari*, in 1936. My goodness, how I admired that film! Of course, like Jacques Demy, I was a real provincial. There were a lot of films that just couldn't be seen in Brittany, so when I got to Paris and found them all there, wow! I remember reading a review of *Le Sang d'un poète* in a magazine called *Le Coup de patte*: I was really intrigued by the violence of the review—it said that this was a quite disgraceful film. As I read it in Vannes, I thought to myself, does this mean there is a kind of cinema that's really so different from the kind I had been used to? So the minute I got to Paris, I started to track down *Le Sang d'un poète*; when I finally did, I was extremely impressed. Actually, I still admire it very much.

RR: How did you feel about Cocteau's work as a whole?

AR: Oh, yes, yes. I was very moved by *Orphée*. I remember though, that when I first saw *La Belle et la bête*, I didn't really get it. Without knowing it, all through the Occupation, I was waiting for a film like *Citizen Kane*, a film that would overthrow all the established conventions. So when I heard Cocteau was making *La Belle et la bête*, I thought, "This must be it." Then I saw it and all I found was a very pretty Vermeer-like film, but not a revolutionary one. Only in 1955 did I understand that it wasn't trying to be revolutionary: that it wasn't trying to follow the line of *Le Sang d'un poète* or *Les Mariés de la Tour Eiffel*. So the second time around, I just sat back and fell under its spell.

RR: During the early forties, what films impressed you? Did you see [Robert Bresson's] *Les Dames du Bois de Boulogne* when it first came out?

AR: On the first day, and I was rather disconcerted. As Bazin said when he saw it first, it seemed to him like a total impasse for the cinema; only on a second viewing did he realize how easy it was for a critic to make a mistake. The first time I saw it, I loved it, except for the ending. It seemed to me that the vengeance of Hélène didn't make any sense in our time. The whole idea of a misalliance just didn't work, I thought, and only proved that you couldn't transpose Diderot into the twentieth century. I was very struck, however, with Cocteau's dialogue, its sheer musicality. Two days later, I saw it again.

Of course, I had already been fascinated by *Les Anges du péché*, Bresson's first film. For me it was a filmgoer's dream come true: someone had finally asked Giraudoux to write a film script. And in heaven's name, why not? I was—and still am—obsessed with the idea that it should be possible to create a soundtrack that will be just as beautiful, just as magical as, let's say, the language of Shakespeare. Just because there is an image, it doesn't mean that it has to replace all that words can create. I'm sure that if there were a twenty-year-old Giraudoux now—and perhaps there is—one could resolve the problem.

Furthermore, I am convinced that the quality of the sound can convey both the meaning and the emotional charge of a text. You see, an actor's performance can be modified for the spectator solely by the way the microphone is placed. I've verified this for myself and it is both true and terrifying; it shows to just what an extent the actor can be deprived of his natural resources in filmmaking. And he can do nothing about it: if the boom operator is clumsy, many of the subtler effects simply won't come through. And no one will understand why: they'll say, "Oh, he wasn't up to scratch in that scene"—and it will be just because of the placing of the sound boom. Progress is being made in sound recording, but a lot remains to be done. There is no standardization of loudspeaker equipment in theaters, for example. One day, we will get there, and then perhaps we'll be able to have on the screen the same kind of language we get in the theater. Some people say this is wrong: that the language of Shakespeare served to make up for the lack of sets. But I don't think that's a good enough argument.

RR: It may not be good enough, but there is always the danger of redundancy, of pleonasm.

AR: Of course, but it's only a question of balance. I like the story of Abel Gance's presentation of the sound version of *J'Accuse* at the Studio 28 cinema. There was a triple screen sequence, and in order to give the projectionists enough time to lace up, he had a five-minute sequence with no picture on the screen, only sound: it was supposed to be taking place in the dark underground tunnels at Verdun. So instead of an interval, the audience sat in the dark just listening: and it really worked, it was wonderful.

RR: Do you like those later films of Bresson which did not have scripts by an important writer?

AR: Let's say that working with Cocteau didn't in any way diminish Bresson. Furthermore, in *Diary of a Country Priest*, there is surely a great deal of Bernanos. *Pickpocket*? People say there's a lot of Dostoevsky there, but I'm not so sure about that. In any case, film is a matter of collective responsibility; not only the director and the writer, but the set designer and the actors.

RR: Was *Le Roman d'un tricheur* the only Guitry film you liked?

AR: Oh, no. If only one could find a print of *Bonne chance*—there doesn't seem to be one left. That for me was an excellent example of Guitry's genius. When I was a boy I always used to wonder: Why is it that I'm never bored by Guitry? The camera doesn't move very much, the shots don't change very often, and yet I'm not bored. It's only people sitting in chairs talking to each other, but it's never dull. You never long for a change of shot, you never get restless, whereas in other films, if there wasn't movement, I used to get very impatient. Is it simply because what they're saying is so interesting?

RR: Have you seen Chris Marker's *Le Mystère Koumiko*?

AR: A lovely film: now *there's* a Guitry-like movie. It infuriates Marker when I tell him he's in the Guitry tradition, and yet it's true. All he can see in Guitry is his bourgeois mentality, not the charm of the actors; so he always denies any idea of a connection.

RR: I suppose he prefers to think of himself as having been influenced by Giraudoux?

AR: Yes, but we should never forget that the first enthusiastic review of the Giraudoux-Bresson *Anges du péché* was in fact written by Guitry in *Comoedia*. It was on the front page, boxed, and it said, "Although I don't really like the cinema, I must admit that here is a great masterpiece. I take my hat off to it . . ." et cetera.

La Règle du Jeu

RR: Did you see *La Règle du jeu* when it came out?

AR: Not until 1944. But it remains, I think, the single most overwhelming experience I have ever had in the cinema. When I first came out of the theater, I remember I just had to sit down on the edge of the pavement; I sat there for a good five minutes, and then I walked the streets of Paris for a couple of hours. For me, everything had been turned upside down. All my ideas about the cinema had been challenged. While I was actually watching the film, my impressions were so strong physically that I thought that if this or that sequence had gone on for one shot more, I would have either burst into tears, or screamed, or something. Since then, of course, I've seen it at least fifteen times—like most film-makers of my generation. I even recorded the whole soundtrack on my tape-recorder, and it's amazing how well it stands up on its own.

RR: Did it already have its reputation in 1944, or did you see it by chance?

AR: It had a reputation all right, but that of a *film maudit*. I didn't know quite what I was letting myself in for. I knew it had been hissed at the Cinéma Madeleine when it first opened, and I believe it only ran for about a week. And the critics attacked it so violently! Nobody has ever understood why it was so fiercely attacked. Renoir himself said one of the strangest parts of the whole affair was the fact that when he had cut a scene that had been hissed at the previous performance (he spent most of that week in the projection box), the audience at the following show just hissed something else a few minutes later. The most surprising thing of all in 1939 was that Renoir's other films, like *La Grande illusion*, had had perfectly normal commercial careers; so why the fuss over this one?

Welles

RR: When did you first see *Citizen Kane*?

AR: When it opened at the Marbeuf in 1948, the very first performance. I had already seen *The Magnificent Ambersons*, though, which had come out on the film society circuit. I was rather bewildered by the violence of the audience's reaction to *Kane*. First of all, there were a number of professional filmmakers in the audience, and they were absolutely livid—you could feel it in the air. Once again it was a question of a mental block: here was a film which shook all their preconceptions. In the first place, they had the idea that America meant Westerns, perhaps comedies; otherwise it was a country of barbarians, a country in no way up to *thinking*. "What's all this?" they said. "We did it twenty years ago. Here are these Americans imagining they are intellectuals. Don't they know they're not, that they mustn't try to be: they're nothing but grown-up children, and that's their charm—their spontaneity, their liveliness. They should stick to that and not bore us to death with such complicated, confused stories."

That was one kind of reaction. The other was more subtle: "Really, that kind of photography went out twenty years ago; and, my dear, the editing, it's so old hat." Of course, in France at that time, we were plumb in the middle of that school of photography, which depended on lots of small spotlights. Hundreds of tiny ones, with filters, too. The most famous lighting man of the period was Roger Hubert, and he did in fact get some remarkable results with this method . . . but that didn't mean other solutions weren't possible as well. Like the short focal-length lenses which the audience objected to so strongly.

RR: When they said the French had done it all twenty years ago, whom did they mean?

AR: That's just it! I don't know, unless perhaps it was L'Herbier. Anyhow, the conversation always ended up with, "Welles, who is this Welles? He must be some kind of intellectual film-maker ..."

But one mustn't forget that it was Jean-Paul Sartre who had started the whole campaign against Welles. When he first came back from New York, he wrote a famous article about how he had been frightened out of his wits by Manhattan because, he said, it was the only city where you could see the horizon on all sides; and it had given him a real sense of nausea. In this same article, he said that he had seen *Citizen Kane*, the film by this new genius, who had come to the forefront during the war. And that although *Kane* might have been interesting for the Americans, it was completely *démodé* for us, because the whole film was based on a misconception of what cinema was all about. The film is in the past tense, whereas we all knew the cinema had to be in the present tense. "I *am* the man who *is* kissing. I *am* the girl who *is* being kissed. I *am* the Indian who is being pursued, I *am* the man pursuing the Indian." Any film in the past tense is the antithesis of cinema, said Sartre. Therefore, *Citizen Kane* is not cinema. It's literary and intellectual, but it's not cinema.

This article had appeared in *L'Ecran français* and was very widely read, so even the reception of *Ambersons* had been colored by the piece.

Antonioni, Visconti, Godard

AR: I was very impressed by the early Antonioni films. Not *Cronica di un amore*; I find it nice to look at, brilliant even, but a bit too much like sparkling water, Pérrier water. Furthermore, it had too much of the thriller about it; too much like some of those American things, the Hemingway short stories. But *La Signora senza Camelie*, with its marvelous sequence shots, that really impressed me. As for Visconti, I thought very highly of *Ossessione*, which I saw at the Cinémathèque in 1944. It seemed to me to have all the freedom of Renoir and yet its own formal qualities.

RR: In an interview with Bernard Pingaud in *L'Arc*, you said that of all Godard's films you particularly like *Deux ou trois choses que je sais d'elle* because of its total narrative dislocation. I think you said that if one examined the film closely, one might find new laws of progression. A spectacle has to be carried along by its own movement ...

AR: That's a problem which interests me because I am never sure how to resolve it. I realize dramatic construction has to evolve, but you can't dispense with it altogether. It's just a question of finding a new form for it. Many people argue that all the rules of dramatic construction are now outdated. But I can't imagine a film in which the contact with the audience is not achieved by some form of dramatic construction.

People say that Godard puts his films together any old which-way, but I don't believe it: I'm sure there is a kind of construction there. The trouble is that many younger directors use Godard as an excuse to string together a whole lot of images and then claim it's the new style. I'm very skeptical; I don't believe you can keep an audience in the theater without resorting to some form of order. Of course, this form has constantly to be reinvented—each time, in fact. But I wonder whether a really careful analysis of certain new techniques might not reveal that they are in essence still the same old rules which have applied for six thousand years. Mind you, I'd rather not think too much about this, because such a close examination tends to dry you up.

Robbe-Grillet and Duras

RR: How do you feel about the comparisons sometimes made between *Marienbad* and *L'Immortelle*?

AR: Of course, there are great similarities, but if anyone had the right to make a film along the same lines as *Marienbad*, that man was Robbe-Grillet. So many annoying things were written comparing the two films, that it almost makes me think there must be something disturbing for the critics in the fact that when the shooting of a film really goes well, it means there is no single author. Everybody is responsible for everything.

RR: And yet . . .

AR: And yet, yes, I know what you mean. But there is often a moment during the making of a film when a scene hasn't been written, or part of the script hasn't yet been delivered; the scene still has to be shot on the day, so somehow between us all, we manage. And I maintain that such a scene, even though it wasn't written by the scriptwriter, nevertheless belongs to him. During the shooting of a film, there is something stronger than any of us, something which takes possession of the whole crew, and that is the film itself. That is why it is difficult afterwards to know how much any one individual was responsible. And that's also why I got very angry when people said, "Oh, Robbe-Grillet copied *Marienbad*." It was a stupid thing to say because for one thing, *L'Immortelle* had been written before *Marienbad*. There were two producers, Raymond Froment and Pierre Courau, who thought that I ought to make a film with Robbe-Grillet. I said no, because going by what I had read about him in *L'Express* and elsewhere, he was apparently a very boring writer. But I had never read anything of his myself. They said, "Well, at least the two of you should meet." So I agreed, since I always like meeting people, and I took an immense liking to him. We talked about movies, the kinds of things—shots, sequence, set-ups—we wanted to do, for we both seemed interested in the same things.

At the end of the morning, he said he would try to think of a project for us. There was a film he wanted to make for himself—*L'Immortelle*—for which he had already done the treatment, but he wouldn't mind postponing it. "It might be more sensible," he said, "for you to make a film first so that I can get an idea of how it's done." He said he would 'phone me in a week with a few ideas. Meanwhile, I read all his books: I read one a day (there were only four then) and I remember being especially impressed by *La Jalousie* and *Dans le labyrinthe*, too. Each was better than the last. So by the time we met the following Sunday, I already felt much closer to him.

RR: Had he been to see your films during that week?

AR: No, he had seen them already; he goes to the movies a lot. Anyhow, on Sunday he gave me four possible subjects plus *L'Immortelle*. The choice was mine. It was, he said, all the same to him. We took about three days before deciding to do the *Marienbad* subject.

RR: I see, but nevertheless I was struck by the difference between what were roughly the same shots in both films. Just as Delphine Seyrig in *Marienbad* is always turning up wearing different clothes, so there is a sequence in *L'Immortelle* in which we see Françoise Brion head on, and then the camera does a 360 degree pan without a cut, coming back to her wearing a different dress. It always seemed to me that such a shot was a failure because all one could think of was, "How did she manage to change her clothes so fast?" And this is just an example of the difference between the realization (not the conception) of *Marienbad* and *L'Immortelle*.

AR: Yes . . . We did the same kind of thing in *Marienbad*: in the course of a single camera movement the same character appeared twice. But for one thing, he didn't turn up in the same spot. Also, we tried to distract the audience during the camera movement just to avoid making them think that Albertazzi must have been running around behind the sets.

RR: You certainly succeeded. What about *Trans-Europe Express*?

AR: Oh, it's funny, very funny indeed. The only criticism I could make would be about the way the film looks. It seems to me that the kind of sumptuous mise en scène Robbe-Grillet is after needs a lot of money to be realized properly, with every detail perfect. But the conditions in which he is obliged to work don't allow him this luxury. It's a shame: in his books, every comma, every full stop is in its place, but he can't afford to make his films as visually perfect, as *soigné*.

RR: Is it true that you once wanted to make a film of Marguérite Duras's *Moderato Cantabile*?

AR: I know that I have always said that I don't want to adapt novels, but just before *Hiroshima* I had thought about making a 16mm version of *Moderato*. I think the reason was the same one that impelled me to make my early shorts about painters: I just wanted to meet them. I admired Marguerite's novels so much that I conceived this fantasy that the only way I would get to meet her was to make a 16mm amateur film, and then write her a letter telling her about it and asking if she would like to see it.

That's why I was never able to have an opinion about the Peter Brook film; I had the whole mise en scène of the book in my head. I had imagined all the characters, for one thing. For another, unity of place seemed vital to me: the whole film—the whole of *my* film—was to have taken place in the café. So when I saw Brook's hero and heroine walking through the town, it seemed all wrong. I had thought of the hero as an older man, someone like Alain Cuny, so Belmondo seemed wrong too. This may sound silly to you, but I had such a clear picture of the film in my head. Of course, Belmondo was wonderful in the film, and Jeanne Moreau, too (I *had* thought of using her). For me, Brook's masterpiece, however, is the *Marat-Sade*. His solution of the problems of filming a play was totally convincing.

RR: The ritual last question: now that you have abandoned *Harry Dickson*, what are your plans?

AR: I just don't know; I'm looking. Maybe a comedy? Something different, in any case.

You know, I still find it hard to get used to the fact that what I have to say is of any great importance. I can talk about one of my films, but to talk about the oeuvre or the context—that still surprises me. What I mean is that I am still surprised when people ask *me* the same questions they ask Fellini or Bergman. And yet, when I look at the books written about me, they're the same as those written about Bergman or Fellini. The stills are the same size, the questions are often the same—though the answers aren't always. I suppose it all has to do with the fact that I don't feel any older now than I did twenty years ago. Except that time goes by much faster. You do less and less in a day; you have more and more little things to do, so the days seem to get shorter. I used to read three novels a week when I was eighteen; now I read one a month. Where's the difference?

Conversations with Resnais: There Isn't Enough Time

James Monaco / 1975

Film Comment XI, no. 4 (July–August 1975). Reprinted by permission.

Alain Resnais hadn't made a film for more than five years when he finally got behind a camera and started shooting *Stavisky* . . . . He had been busy all that time with a series of projects, none of which had proved attractive to financial backers. While he had a reputation as one of the most interesting directors of the sixties, his last film *Je t'aime, je t'aime* had not made any money. *Hiroshima mon amour*, *Last Year at Marienbad*, and *Muriel* had established Resnais's credentials as an intellectual, "difficult" director, but only *La Guerre est finie*, made in 1965, had been really popular with general audiences. At a time of tightened budgets in the film world, he did not seem like a "safe bet" to the moneymen.

Stavisky . . ., it turns out, is a lot more complicated and resonant than it first appears; it does have some of the density and irony that first endeared Resnais with critics ten or fifteen years ago; but it also has the kind of mythic qualities which up until now had been generally lacking in Resnais's movies and which are going to make it an unusually popular film (for him). The best of both worlds finally: a profitable movie *and* an interesting one.

Resnais, as one might expect from his films, is a kindly, thoughtful man who thinks hard before he answers questions about his work. He wants, above all, to make sense, to be understood. Having lived in New York for a year and a half several years ago, he speaks English well, but with a certain French reticence often—how you say?—*suggesting* a word modestly, rather than imposing it. Needless to say, it is always the precise word needed. We talked in English.

James Monaco: You work very closely with your screenwriters and I'm wondering if you ever make any changes during shooting, or do you follow the script very closely?

Alain Resnais: Making big changes is very awkward when you are shooting because it costs money. If a film did not cost too much money, I would love to improvise, and if I had the freedom, to shoot for six months and try different things. But as to make a film is to keep within a budget, I feel it's more important to be in complete agreement with the producer, with the screenwriter, with all the actors. That's why, beginning shooting, I always show the complete script to every actor, even if it's a small part, and I always talk with him about the *complete* product, and if there is something he says that is interesting I will ask the screenwriter to reword the script, to give the product the feeling that it has been made and criticized by *everyone.*

JM: Did much of that happen with *Stavisky*...?

AR: Oh, yes. Of course, Semprun did not have the time to fully complete every scene before we started shooting, but there wasn't any real improvisation. The time is too precious.

JM: You once said, I think, that you couldn't make a film about the present because by the time the film was released, it would be out of date...

AR: Yes, that's a big problem. When you decide that there is enough material to make a film of a certain subject, sometimes two years elapse between, and that's a lot. Even if it's not a film based in the present. I had a project on the life of the Marquis de Sade a few years ago and now, even if a producer would give me the money to shoot that film, it would have to be completely rewritten, because what we could say about the Marquis de Sade four years ago is now obsolete in a way.

JM: Do you feel that pressure a lot when you're filming?

AR: Yes. As *Stavisky*... was a period film, I was less anxious, but I was wrong. I discovered just one month before *Stavisky*... was completed that there were many films where the action was taking place in the thirties. And when I read in *Le Monde* four pages that were very violent and aggressive about films that were not made of the present time, I was afraid that the reception would not be too good. If *Stavisky*... had been completed three months earlier, I think that would have been better because I would have been on the crest of the wave instead of in the trough.

JM: I know a couple of projects that you've been working on for the last five or six years, but were you beginning to get worried that you'd never get back, that there was a curse?

AR: No, I did not have the feeling that there was a *curse,* but I was very worried because it's impossible to survive just asking friends to lend you money. It's very depressing. I didn't have the feeling that it was a curse because all the projects that weren't realized were very expensive. If I could have found a script that could have been made for less than half a million dollars and nobody cared to produce it, then I *would* have felt there was a curse.

JM: For the record, what were those projects?

AR: There was a project with Richard Seaver, the translator of Beckett and editor, who wrote for me a life of the Marquis de Sade which was called "Délivrez-nous du bien," and Dirk Bogarde said all right but his name was not powerful enough to raise two million dollars. I spent one year on that. After that there was Stan Lee's project and that took another year, with the same result—till now [*sic*]. I had a project of a documentary on the life of H. P. Lovecraft; and William Friedkin and Warner Brothers *seemed* to be the backers, but after all, nothing happened and William Friedkin had to begin the shooting of *The Exorcist*. I had another project with Penelope Mortimer called "Zero," but the producer gave—how you call a check when it bounces?—a bad check!

JM: You talk often of the real business of filmmaking being in the editing process.

AR: It's true that I am very proud when I can say I did not throw away much material. I think for *Stavisky* . . . maybe thirty seconds were thrown away. But the editing must be in the shooting script.

JM: You must save a lot of money in film stock!

AR: Yes. No. Well, I don't save a lot of money because I like to work without much speed. I have exactly the François Truffaut speed. Where other directors could make a film in five weeks, I need ten or twelve. But I don't throw away much. I think it's important for me to have the feeling that I haven't shot too much.

JM: You've mentioned several times the "process"—that you want everyone who makes the film to feel he has a part in it, that there was a kind of biological relationship between you and Jorge Semprun and the character—I don't know whether we could call it dialectics. . . .

AR: We *could* call it dialectics!

JM: Well, this is what fascinates me about your films. Do you feel yourself in this dialectical relationship with your films?

AR: In a way, yes.

JM: I think the structure of your films, because they deal with time, so often makes people think this way, of contrasts, and balance, and so forth.

AR: I work like that, but it's very difficult to talk about because it's not completely conscious and I am sure I don't want it to become too conscious for me because when I try to write the shooting script, I try to just let the images come to my mind, and not to have any second thoughts.

JM: Do you think about this film in relation to your other films? Do you bother to think that way?

AR: I never think about that. I guess I've decided not to think about that too much because that would be dangerous. That would be contemplating oneself as a kind of monument!

JM: I ask because *Stavisky...* is not as consciously intellectually complex as, say, *Last Year at Marienbad* or *Je t'aime, je t'aime*.

AR: Yes, but *La Guerre est finie* was not complex. My idea is that the complexity of the structure of the film comes—*must* come—from the characters of the story. If in *Muriel*, the characters are *very* complex, everybody is thinking a lot, and so it leads to a very complicated structure. But in *La Guerre est finie*, Diègo is a kind of—not too simple—but not very subtle character. He has two or three motivations, but he is not a mysterious character at all. Yves Montand as Diègo is clear, so it would have been silly to impose a kind of complicated structure with *La Guerre est finie*. In a way, maybe the same thing with *Stavisky...*, I don't know.

JM: How do you react to all the complicated theories that people work up about your films?

AR: I don't know. I don't think they are so complicated, do you? My reaction would be that I am "flabbergasted" to see that *everything* you do during the shooting is always perceived by somebody! Now I know that *every* detail will be understood by somebody, and I am very surprised. That's why I'm so "fastidious" or meticulous when I am shooting. I have understood that even the title of a book in a library behind Yves Montand or "Claude Ridder" [in *Je t'aime, je t'aime*] will be "debated." (That's Stan Lee's vocabulary.) And so I have to have the right book that he could have read and many little details like that, and it's the same thing with camera movements, the lighting. Really, I can't complain because a lot of people have understood what have I tried to convey. But it's a big surprise.

JM: So you're saying that for you it always comes from the character while a lot of people prefer to regard you as a theorist—complicated ideas about time and memory—and write about your films that way, almost ignoring the character.

AR: Yes, the flashforward in *La Guerre est finie*, for example, was for me the simplest way to give the feeling of premonition that that life implied. I did not go to Semprun telling him, "I want you to write something with flashforwards." But when Diégo's character began to emerge, I said I think we should use the flashforward for Diégo because he seems to be the kind of guy who has that kind of image in his mind. Maybe we should have used it more! We were a little too shy, I think. But for Stavisky it's different because Stavisky is always thinking about the money he has. He's anxious about death in general, but he's not anxious about what will happen to him. Stavisky could never imagine that he'd be put in jail a second time.

JM: In the other films I think it's more the way the people in the films saw their lives, while in *Stavisky...*, it's more the way we saw him.

AR: Yes, I think in *Stavisky...* we are looking at people, and in *La Guerre est finie*, we were "walking" with Diégo and all of the film is seen by Diégo himself. *Except* the last five minutes. But I have not made a fade-out, fade-in and I made a mistake with *La Guerre est finie*. I should have made one at the end, just to show that we were leaving Diégo and we were changing our point of view.

JM: Do you have any second thoughts about *Je t'aime, je t'aime*?

AR: Well, it was not at all a commercial success, but I have the feeling that it is better than we thought!

JM: Well, I like it very much! The only thing I don't like was that you thought it necessary to have the science-fiction framework.

AR: Maybe it was because I like pulp literature and so I thought it was fun to have the film begin as a "B" movie or a "Z" movie! Like a kind of bad serial, but maybe that was a little too perverted.

JM: Yes, well that's the kind of narrative irony that's in *Stavisky* . . . .

AR: Yes, that's because for me, *Je t'aime, je t'aime* is a very ironical film—with a lot of sadness, that's true, but I would have preferred to hear people laugh more.

JM: I want to ask you a particular question about *Muriel*, too, which still fascinates me now, ten years after it was made. The color is astonishing. That was a period of time when people were just beginning to do interesting things with color. The technology was developing. How did you get that liquescent, transparent color?

AR: In the simplest way. We decided with Sasha Vierny that we would stick with realistic light and that we would shoot the film exactly where the action would have taken place in Boulogne-sur-mer and we would not try to change the slightest thing for the color. If it was raining there would be rain. If there was sun there would be sun. We wouldn't pay any attention to that. That's very simple.

JM: No special treatment for the film stock?

AR: Absolutely not. No filters, nothing. Just complete simplicity. But it was in a way too because we had the feeling that in real life there are a lot of colors that we don't perceive and that in *Muriel* because of the editing (there are a lot of shots, nearly a thousand) we would get some kind of effect. I wasn't sure what, but I had the feeling that the color would become sometimes very aggressive, and so on.

JM: If you had to pick another film for color at that time, it would be *Red Desert* and there was Antonioni going around painting the leaves and then painting the film!

AR: Yes, it was exactly the opposite. And the same thing with the sets, too, because when I was in Boulogne-sur-mer I visited an apartment and I decided that it would be *that* apartment that Hélène Aughain would live in; it was in the real building you see when we were shooting in the street. And so our set designer rebuilt *exactly* that empty apartment in the studio, and he painted the walls as white as they were in reality. For color, it's very difficult to shoot white, but Sasha Vierny, who also photographed *Stavisky* . . ., said, "I enjoy the challenge.

I want it to be white and see what happens." But nothing with the laboratory, to get back to your question.

JM: Let's shift to politics. You have a reputation for being political; that is, you've made films that always seem to have some political content.

AR: Well, at the same time, a lot of people have been "shocked" that there was never a clear political message in my films. I think maybe you can try to have that in a documentary, but if you deal with fiction, it's very difficult, because if you have some respect for character, the character very often takes over. In *Hiroshima mon amour*, for example, there were three or four lines that were more clear politically, and which Marguerite Duras (the author) and myself enjoyed. But when they were spoken by the actor, it did not fit with the character; it became silly because we had the feeling that it was like a commentary and it did not work. We discovered that a character becomes a real character when he begins to do things we don't approve. So that's a big problem. Especially in *Muriel*, it's true that I don't approve of the characters but Jean Cayrol, the screenwriter, and I could not make them act differently—and I think we have to accept that. I have nothing against very politically oriented pictures, but I think it has to come from the script. But at the same time, when you are not shooting a documentary, I am slightly skeptical. I think you have TV, you have newspapers, you have books, and sometimes when you feel that the thing you have to say would be more effective in a book or a newspaper, you have to admit it.

JM: Truffaut said in 1961 or 1962, at the time a lot of you were being criticized for not being political enough, that he, for instance, could never make a film about Hitler because he would become fascinated by the fact that he seldom slept or that he had trouble with his stomach—the character would take over. Did you feel close to the people who worked for *Cahiers du cinéma* and then went on to make films?

AR: Well, I did not know them, but I felt close to what they were writing. Especially the way they were thinking that American directors were not barbarians. Because that was a very strong idea in France, that if there was something beautiful in an American film, it was just by sheer luck. And thanks to *Cahiers du cinéma*, we learned that American directors were just human beings and that maybe Vincente Minnelli knew more about art than any French director who was so proud of his culture! I knew François Truffaut, I had met him, but I don't remember us discussing film very seriously.

JM: Didn't you work on one of his short films?

AR: Oh, there's a kind of legend about that! The first time François Truffaut made a film—it was about ten minutes—he showed it to me and maybe for one afternoon I just said maybe we could make the cut here instead of there—

I spent a very good afternoon! And after that Truffaut said, "Resnais has given me fantastic advice!"

JM: He even put your name in the credits. Did you ever write any criticism yourself?

AR: No, never. I've never written anything.

JM: Godard once identified you and Demy and Varda and Marker as "left-bank" new wave, because you were more literary.

AR: I admire Godard a lot but I think I have only met him twice in my life. But it's true I'm a friend of Jacques Demy, of Chris Marker, and of Agnès Varda. We see each other. Sometimes we talk about our films, but I think we talk more about food or books or painting. I think in a way we are a little bit afraid to speak about film when we get together.

JM: Critics seldom talk about the people who influenced you. Was there anyone in particular?

AR: Oh, a lot of them. I discovered Jean Epstein's book just before the war and I am sure that I was very stimulated by his writings. And Griffith, of course, and Pudovkin and Eisenstein and their theories about editing. Also, Karel Reisz's book *The Technique of Film Editing*—I am sure that Karel Reisz was my real teacher. I took a lot of things from his book. I am not ashamed to say that.

JM: Now, on the other hand, there have been quite a few people influenced by you. You almost have a "school," so many of your screenwriters have later become filmmakers, directors.

AR: Well, I think that's because I was not choosing those screenwriters because they were writers, but because they had a hidden desire to make films! So I enjoyed seeing them make films after, because that was the proof for me that I was right.

JM: Would you have made more films if you could? I suppose that's a stupid question.

AR: Yes, I am very disappointed by the fact that I have made only six films in fifteen years. I don't know what it is, whether it's the traffic, or because I spent too much time *trying* to answer mail, or else because it's that if you live in a big city, nobody has enough time. That's the big problem with screenwriters, if you need them. They are not available seven days a week. It's necessary for them to do another thing and screenwriting can only be secondary. So they work only on Saturday and Sunday, something like that.

JM: Did you ever try to write a script yourself?

AR: No, I never did. Of course, it would be more practical, but to write a script myself I would need maybe three or four years. I don't enjoy very much to direct something I've written. I don't know why, but it's no fun for me. It bores me a little. Or maybe it's because I'm hiding from responsibility, who knows?

JM: What are you working on right now?

AR: It's a very ambitious project and I'm afraid that it's a little too ambitious. It deals with the way the brain works. A third of the picture would be a lecture by a French biologist named Henri Laborit; his books have very interesting ideas about how our mind works—and does *not* work, especially. And this would be interwoven with the other two thirds of the film, which would be fiction.

JM: What do you do when you aren't making films?

AR: It's very difficult to answer, because I have the feeling that if there was no problem with money, I could very easily spend my life without making any films. But maybe I'm wrong; maybe I would miss it. I hate the preparation work. I hate the writing period. But I enjoy very much the shooting. Even the editing period. But every day is too short for me. I never manage to do what I want in one day, so sometimes I have the feeling that moviemaking is taking too much of my time. I also think that if I want to read or listen to all the music I do before I die, my time is full! Eh? If you consider that Josef Haydn wrote one hundred symphonies and about thirty quartets and about fifty concertos for different instruments, and I just discovered Haydn a month ago, you see that just listening to two symphonies a day, my year would be full till December! I had a friend who once looked at his diary and discovered that even if he stopped completely filmmaking—he was a filmmaker too—and just decided to read all the books he had in his library, it would take him until he was one hundred years old. He was a little bit panicked. But he was courageous. He went out of his house. He went to the bookstore. And he bought ten books!

Facts into Fiction: An Interview with Alain Resnais

Richard Seaver / 1975

Film Comment XI, no. 4 (July–August 1975). Reprinted by permission.

Wherever Alain Resnais's *Stavisky* . . . has opened outside the director's native France, it has been received with generally rave reviews and excellent public reaction. In France itself, although the film had perhaps the best box office of any Resnais film, it was received with mixed reviews. We asked the director of *Hiroshima mon amour* and *Last Year at Marienbad* if he knew any reason for this disparity.

Alain Resnais: I think the answer is really very simple. In France, the name "Stavisky" still evoked memories for many people. Even though the scandal went back forty years, there are a great number of people who still react emotionally to the name, who perhaps were hurt financially by the affair, who were involved politically on one side or the other. For them, any film on Stavisky would have to deal with the realities of the affair, present the facts as they occurred.

Richard Seaver: Didn't you present the facts?

AR: Any film is a fiction, at least for me. Unless, of course, one sets out to make a documentary, such as Jean-Michel Charrier made on the same subject for French TV. That was an excellent documentary, but its concept and goal were totally different from ours. But going on the premise that the length of a film is from an hour and a half to two hours, it's absolutely absurd to think that in that space of time one can properly present the historical reality of such a complex event. This said, the facts in our *Stavisky* are all historically exact as far as I know. But they were the bases for our "fiction" point of departure rather than ends in themselves.

RS: If your film was so clearly fiction, why did Stavisky's son try to get an injunction against it?

AR: On the grounds that it was defamatory, that it slandered his mother's name.

RS: Arlette Stavisky is still alive?

AR: I believe so. In fact, I seem to remember that she's living in America.

RS: I take it the injunction was not granted.

AR: No. In fact, the tribunal stated that, far from defaming the Stavisky name, the film constituted "a veritable rehabilitation" of that admittedly dubious character.

RS: Was that your intent, to rehabilitate Stavisky?

AR: Not really. Neither Jorge Semprun nor I set out to whitewash Stavisky any more than we wanted to blacken his name. What did interest us was the man's personality: on the one hand, an enormous generosity, a theatricality, a strong life impulse; and on the other, an almost inexorable thrust toward death. I'm always interested in what goes on inside our brain, especially when I see two parts of the brain that seem to be out of synch, as in the case of Serge Alexandre. But the period, the historical situation in which Stavisky lived also fascinated us: there were clearly strong parallels between his time and our own. It was a time of political instability, a time when societies were living beyond their means. We were also interested in exploring the mechanisms of that society, how it "uses" at the same time as it is being "used." Stavisky took good advantage of his opportunities, but the world in which he operated flattered and encouraged him, until such time as it judged he had exceeded the limits, at which point it coldly suppressed him.

RS: You're implying he was murdered by the police sent to capture him in Chamonix?

AR: Whether Stavisky was shot by the police or killed himself remains unsolved to this day. What we do know is that when the police went up to the Vieux Logis they made no effort to conceal their presence. It's a small three-bedroom chalet, with a cellar beneath.

RS: Is that the real Vieux Logis we see in the film?

AR: Absolutely, with its little red curtains that you see and say to yourself, "you can't use those, they're too red to be true." But the fact is, when reality has the air of a stage set, it doesn't bother me to use it, as in this case . . . But, about the question of murder, the police took a good hour to search this rather small house, during which time Stavisky was locked in one of the bedrooms. They knew full well he was suicidally inclined. So whether Sacha put the bullet in his head, or the police did, seems rather academic: either way, it's murder. What was more, after he was shot, they waited two full hours before taking him to the hospital. There are those who maintain that if he had been taken immediately, he might have been saved.

RS: The point being that under no circumstances was he to be saved, simply because he knew too much.

AR: That's the clear implication, and the basis for much of the resulting scandal. Cover-up: it's not a new story.

RS: I seem to remember your once having declared that you were incapable of making a "historical" film, one that requires reconstituting the past in any way. And yet with *Stavisky...* you have, for it is nonetheless a film of the thirties.

AR: The problem for me in making a film that isn't contemporary is that it seems to call for a suspension of belief: the creation of an illusion you know is false. But Semprun and I were in agreement right from the start that *Stavisky...* would be an anti-illusionist film.

RS: By which you mean?

AR: Simply that we didn't for one moment set out to try and make people believe that, since we were using actors, they were anything *but* actors. I was, I won't say inspired by, but certainly had in the back of my mind, the way in which Sacha Guitry played Louis XV—or Louis XIV or XVI. He always made the spectator aware that it was he—Sacha Guitry—playing the king.

RS: Could you tell us a little about the genesis of the project? Whose idea was it to make a film on Stavisky? Was it yours?

AR: No, I was in the States at the time. Semprun and his producer had talked about the idea but in a vague way. When I came back to Paris, Semprun and I had dinner one night, during which we brought each other up to date. Semprun, of course, had already written one film I made, *La Guerre est finie*, and had said that he wanted to be the first writer to collaborate a second time with me. He mentioned Stavisky as a possible future project that he might do after he had finished the two films he was working on—one his own documentary on Spain, and the other entitled *L'Attentat*, another rather documentary film on the kidnapping of Ben Barka. But I don't think he had me in mind as director at that point. Since, however, no director had been decided on, I told him the subject intrigued me, as long as it was clear we would treat it as fiction.

When, a few days later Semprun's agent, Gérard Lebovici, called me to ask if I was serious about directing the Stavisky, I told him I was, but reiterated my concerns about any historical film. If Georges [Jorge] could give me a short first draft, I said, I could get a much better idea whether or not it was feasible. As soon as he did, I knew it was something I could do.

RS: I note that the French edition of the script published by Gallimard bears the title *Alain Resnais's Stavisky*. Does that mean that you wrote the script with Semprun, or that it's more yours than his?

AR: Not at all. That's Georges's way of saying, I suppose, the vision was mine, if you will. But I've never, never written a script, nor provided a subject. What I can bring is a kind of abstract form, a structure.

RS: How long was it from the time you saw the first draft until you had a finished script?

AR (laughing): About a year. Georges had figured he could write it in about three months, but I knew that was unrealistic, for several reasons. For one thing, he badly underestimated the editing time he would need on his own film, *Les Deux mémoires*. He expected to be finished in a couple of weeks. And for months I would receive phone calls from Georges, from the editing room, saying, "I'm still here, but we should be finished next Sunday. Let's meet on Monday." Then Monday another call. "I'm still here, Alain, but it should be only a few more days." Also, I mentioned that however much the film is fiction, it is grounded in strict reality. There are about ten books on the Stavisky affair, all of which we read and assimilated. The best of them from our point of view was Joseph Kessel's *Stavisky, l'homme que j'ai connu*, published in 1934, at the height of the scandal. Kessel had known Stavisky, and unlike most of his contemporaries who, as soon as the bubble burst, acted as though they had never laid eyes on the man, had the courage to come out and paint a fair portrait. "I knew him, I wined and dined with him," Kessel proclaimed, adding, "and for those whose memories are short, I would like to remind the world that Sacha Stavisky was an uncommonly charming man." I might add, parenthetically, that after the script was finished we showed it to Kessel, to see whether he felt we'd been unfair in any way to the subject, and his response was: "That's it, that's the way he was. You've really captured the essence of the man." And while most of the press and some professional colleagues raised their eyebrows over our choice of Belmondo to play the lead, when Kessel heard it he said, "An excellent choice."

RS: What about the commission's records? Did you use them for source material?

AR: Oh, yes. Semprun steeped himself in them, and considering the thousands of pages involved, it is understandable why it took longer to write the script than we had envisaged.

RS: You mentioned Belmondo. How did you decide on him?

AR: The same way I try to decide on all my actors. I have a mental file of the possibilities for each part. Then, when I have a finished script, I read each scene, trying to visualize who among them best works for it. Then I add up the totals. In the case of Stavisky, the Belmondo total was overwhelming.

RS: What was his reaction when you contacted him about it?

AR: Cautious. I might say understandably cautious.

RS: Why?

AR: For the simple reason that Belmondo is the most sought-after actor in France. He must receive two or three scripts a day. So he is naturally wary. "Does

Resnais want me because he thinks I'm the best person for the role, or because of what my name will mean to the film?" But the fact is, he was the actor I wanted.

RS: What about the fact of using a "name" actor?

AR: That doesn't bother me. In fact, since we were dealing with a public figure—Stavisky—the notion of superimposing another public figure—Belmondo—rather intrigued me. But once having settled on that concept, I wanted to buttress his presence with other "name" actors. I feel it's better to have all unknowns or the contrary; that is, if you have Belmondo, then it makes sense to have Charles Boyer, François Perier, for example. It's in a way less shocking, more natural.

RS: How did you get Boyer?

AR: I've always wanted to do a film with Boyer, whom I greatly admire. In fact, Semprun said, "All Resnais wants to do is make a film starring Belmondo and Boyer with music by Stephen Sondheim. He couldn't care less what the subject is, so long as he has those three elements in it." He's exaggerating of course, but there's a kernel of truth there . . . In any case, Boyer is semi-retired, living in Switzerland. But when I contacted him, he agreed to come to Paris to discuss the project. I spent three hours trying to convince him.

RS: How about François Perier? He certainly ranks as one of France's leading actors. How did you persuade him to play Borelli?

AR: Perier is a great actor, and I was very lucky to have him in that role. With him, it wasn't a question of persuading; he *wanted* the part. It's all the more remarkable because when you read the script, Borelli seems to be a non-role. But he read and liked the script, and that was enough. I've found, at least in Europe, that when actors really like a film, or a part, they'll do almost anything to play in it.

RS: And Anny Duperey?

AR: I remembered her in Godard's *Two or Three Things I Know about Her*, where I thought she was very good. Then I went to see her in a play, Molière's *The Misanthrope*. Her Célimène impressed me greatly, especially the way she could magnetize the public. It was a matinee, and the theater was filled with school kids who were not exactly models of decorum. But whenever they would begin to get out of hand, she would turn a withering gaze out at them, and within seconds the theater would be totally quiet. Arlette was a beautiful, liberated, magnetic personality—anyone who could mesmerize Stavisky had to be magnetic—and Anny Duperey struck me as perfect for the role.

RS: Speaking of mesmerizing, one senses that you, or Semprun, or doubtless both of you, were rather mesmerized by the subject.

AR: By the subject matter, or the person of Stavisky?

RS: By Stavisky himself.

AR: No question. It's not as though we planned it that way, however. I think what intrigued both Georges and me initially was what I might term the "mechanism of fraud," how it worked and how society, including some of its most powerful—and presumably upstanding—members, could not only condone it, but become inextricably involved in it. But the deeper we went into it, the more I found myself captivated by the character. Originally Stavisky did not occupy as preponderant a place in the script as he ultimately did. All I can say is that his proliferation in the film happened naturally, and in a way might be considered the cinematic equivalent of what had happened forty years earlier in Stavisky's life. The fact is, neither Semprun nor I was able to resist Stavisky's charm, and if we have been criticized for making him too sympathetic, can't it also be looked on as the same kind of "fraud" he perpetrated so well in reality? In any case, since it did happen organically, we thought we ought to respect it.

RS: Was that the major criticism of the film in France?

AR: That, plus the fact that we hadn't dealt with the heart of the matter, namely the scandal itself. For most French people, the Stavisky affair begins where our film ends, that is, with Stavisky's death. What they wanted to see were the repercussions, the riots in the Place de la Concorde, the behind-the-scenes political intrigues trying to keep the government from falling, the attempt of the Right to capitalize on the situation. All of which is of course a totally different film, which I'm incapable of making.

RS: Speaking of politics, where did the idea of juxtaposing the Trotsky subplot originate?

AR: We were looking for a subplot, parallel plot, call it what you will, which would help situate the time and the world in which Stavisky's actions were taking place. We considered any number of possibilities—we could have used Mistingette or Maurice Chevalier, to name but two—and Semprun came up with the Trotsky idea. Semprun's novel, *The Second Life of Ramon Mercader*, dealt with Trotsky in exile, so he was especially familiar with the details of Trotsky's sojourn in France, which coincided with Stavisky's rise and fall. But even so, it was only one among several possibilities until one day, in reading the investigating commission's report—as Semprun says, "in Volume 6, on page 4,749 to be exact,"—Georges discovered that a Chief Inspector Gagneux of the Sûreté, who in 1933 had been urgently requested by the Ministry of Foreign Affairs to make a thorough report on one Serge Alexandre, alias Sacha Stavisky, was the same man who had been assigned to keep a close watch on Trotsky during part of his stay in France. That was the link that clinched it, and Gagneux became our inspector Gardet. But there were other buttressing parallels that we liked: both Trotsky and Stavisky were Russian Jews, both were, in different ways, exiles; both magnetic; both lost. In the eyes of the French, both were "métèques"—lousy foreigners, and one of the feelings we were trying to convey—and which the Trotsky subplot helped illustrate—was the scope and depth of xenophobia then prevalent in

France. In the thirties, the French seemed convinced that whatever misfortunes they were suffering could be blamed on outside forces and influences. The two most common prejudices were anti-Semitism, on one hand, and Anglophobia on the other. I think Ophuls's *The Sorrow and the Pity* was the first post-war film to document forcefully the depth of that double prejudice. If the Germans "succeeded," if one can use the term, so well in their Occupation of France, it was because so many French people felt that way. After Dunkirk, the average Frenchman figured that between the German "enemy" and the English "enemy" there was really very little choice. And if, in the waning days of Stavisky's life, the Trotskys and the Erna Wolfgangs could still find refuge in France, the threads of the future were beginning to come together, and the brutal truth to which Borelli gives voice at the *Théâtre de l'Empire*, toward the end of the film, is what lay in the hearts and minds of most French people at the time.

RS: Is Baron Raoul the spokesman of that sentiment?

AR: In a sense, because it is also true that most of the people who had those admittedly base feelings were not really evil, or bad. I remember a cousin of mine, a decent well-meaning Breton, who in 1949 or '50, when he learned that I was breaking into films, came up to me and said with a comforting air, "I really feel sorry for you. I know how hard it must be for you to break into the movie business." I asked him what he meant. "Well," he said, "with all those Jews who control everything, it must be impossible to break in." And when I said to him, "Thank God for the Jewish producers, without whom it would be impossible for me to break through," I suspect he thought I had lost my marbles. And my cousin, I hasten to repeat, was not a bad man, simply ignorant . . . But to come back to Raoul, he is obviously a composite portrait, at once the symbol of French smugness and also the typical kind of person that Stavisky loved to have around him: impeccable credentials and lineage, perhaps dubious motives and reasons for orbiting in Stavisky's circle, but ultimately the epitome of respectability. Also, the symbol of the person who is overwhelmed by the circumstances, who understands only imperfectly what is happening to him.

RS: Earlier you mentioned Stephen Sondheim. Can we talk a little bit about the music? How you decided on Sondheim, and why?

AR: That's a question the film's producer, Alexandre Mnouchkine, asked me more than once: "Alain, why make things more complicated than they already are? Why do you have to have an American composer for a French film? And, to boot, someone who has never written any music for films before? . . ."

RS: What made you think he should?

AR: I knew all Sondheim's music, but the deeper I got into the Stavisky, the more I knew his music was perfect. I remembered in particular one scene in *Follies* that has always remained with me: a scene that begins in gaiety and high spirits, with John MacMartin in white tuxedo and top hat singing and dancing, a scene full of joy and hope, when all of a sudden the music deteriorates, the lighting turns funereal, the girls collapse and dissolve, and he, MacMartin, can no longer remember the words or music. It's devastating, a scene I've never forgotten. The worm in the apple, death in the midst of life. For essentially, that's the story of Stavisky: a man condemned to death, fully aware of it, yet madly in love with life. In the middle of preparing the shooting script, I picked up the phone in Paris and called Sondheim in New York.

To give you an idea how important Sondheim's music was to me, when writing the shooting script, I conceived certain key scenes rhythmically, in terms of his music. And on the first day of shooting, I had my tape recorder handy, with key passages of *A Little Night Music* constantly in my ear, to make sure that the rhythm of the scene coincided with Sondheim's music. That involved the speed with which the actors walked, Baron Raoul's gestures, the whole scene with the white airplane outside Biarritz . . .

RS: Can we talk about the technique for a moment? Some American critics have compared *Stavisky* to *The Great Gatsby*—I realize the comparison is superficial—and found that you captured the feel of the time the way *Gatsby* didn't. Forgetting the comparison, one does get from *Stavisky* a real feeling of the thirties, and especially of the films of the thirties. How did you achieve that feeling?

AR: I decided from the outset that we would make *Stavisky . . .*, from a technical viewpoint, as though it were being made in the thirties. By that I mean that our set-ups and our shot angles would be those that, technically, could have been made with equipment available to thirties directors. With the colors too: I felt to convey the feeling of 1934 I couldn't use realistic 1974 colors. Sacha Vierny [director of photography] and I decided to take the risk—and it was a calculated risk—to try to simulate the style and colors of the Pathéorama films of the thirties, limited ourselves to a minimum of colors. Ideally, we would have liked to make a bi-chrome film, that is, one in which the only two colors would have been dark brown and red. That proved technically impossible, but we nonetheless worked in that direction. What we also did was steep ourselves in the pictorial magazines of the period, which helped us orient our characters' pace and positions. By the way, the issue of the *Petit Journal* you see in the picture, the one whose cover depicts Stavisky's arrest at Marly, is the actual 1936 issue. And, obviously, our filmed depiction of that scene, and Sacha's arrest, were influenced by those thirties graphics.

RS: Are colors symbolic for you? One can't help remarking the almost postcard summer warmth of the opening scene, moving to the browns and grays of fall at Barbizon and the deathly white of Chamonix. But the colors red, black-and-white predominate.

AR: Their use is intentional, of course, though my goal was to make them inobtrusive. What I am striving for in a film is to try to construct a kind of compact object in which all the pieces or elements interrelate, but in isolation seem irrational. What I'm trying to create are different kinds of harmonics, which taken together, will make an emotional impact.

RS: One final question: could you tell us what the small stone pyramid is that recurs, I believe, twice in the film?

AR: It's one of those irrational but not meaningless elements I just mentioned. The pyramid is located in the Parc Monceau in Paris, and no one, including the guidebooks, seems to be able to account for its origin. All they seem to know is that it was there as early as the eighteenth century. Then too, Stavisky lived near the Parc Monceau—another irrational but interesting coincidence, and as Dr. Mezy notes at one point, Alexandre's youth is full of mysteries. So one can dream of the young Sacha walking in the park, passing that mysterious pyramid. There's something funereal about that pyramid, and *Stavisky* . . . is ultimately about death. And there is as well, as I suggested, something mysterious and enigmatic about it, just as the life—and death—of Stavisky were mysterious and enigmatic.

Interview with Alain Resnais: On *Mon Oncle d'Amérique*

Robert Benayoun / 1980

From *Positif*, no. 231 (June 1980). Reprinted by permission. Translated by T. Jefferson Kline.

Robert Benayoun: How would you define this film and how do you see it today?

Alain Resnais: You could say that it's a film about the central nervous system and behavior, accompanying those words with a laugh, since my response could be seen as so wildly pretentious. I'm looking at it from the perspective of its dramatic structure. I wanted to see if one could make a film using deductive scientific reasoning (in the same sense that you find in detective novels), mixing two types of storytelling: the scientific and the novelistic, to see if this combination would make an interesting dramatic universe. I wanted to see if, by introducing a scientist like Henri Laborit, I could offer him complete freedom, without locking the characters of the story into a demonstration. The characters were created out of Laborit's ideas, but from the moment they were born, we gave them complete autonomy. You could say that, at their birth, Laborit is their father, but that he bears no responsibility for their education. He may or may not recognize them, and may propose his system to them, but they won't necessarily do what he would have wanted.

RB: You have been talking for a very long time about your interest in biology and the mechanisms of brainwork, notably since the time of *Marienbad*. From what period would you date these preoccupations?

AR: From roughly 1953, when I was an assistant to Nicole Vedrès for the film *At the Frontiers of Man*, and we interviewed, among other people, Rostand on the notion of acquired heredity. It was much later than I met Professor Henri Laborit, when a pharmaceutical laboratory proposed that he do a short film on a product that would increase one's capacity to remember. Laborit had seen *Marienbad* and liked it a lot. He talked about it from a biological viewpoint, and considered that it was a film that perfectly reproduced the mechanism of thought. As for me, at the time, I thought that it was a dilated reproduction of the mechanism of romantic love, a terrain that my collaborator, Alain Robbe-Grillet, found very suspect; he didn't agree with me on the play of feelings. He laughed at me for having "introduced psychology" where there wasn't supposed to be any. To make a long story short, Laborit asked to work with me on this short subject, which we never in fact made because of the lack of financing. So I told him that if we couldn't find the money to fund a short subject, perhaps we could find enough to do a full-length feature film, and I found a producer willing to have Jean Gruault write a screenplay based on Laborit's theories. It was at that point that the project ceased to be a documentary and merged with fiction. I had read Laborit's *The Inhibition of Aggression* along with *Man Imagining, Structure and Biology*, and *Man and the City*. But after we agreed to make a film together, I read all his other books, including *Behaviors*, an enormous work of 500 pages.

RB: Also, when you were doing *Muriel*, a completely behaviorist film, you effaced yourself behind the behavior of your characters without trying to explain their behavior.

AR: Yes, the camera watched them without making any attempt to interpret their actions. I tried to display their behavior objectively. I looked at them from the outside.

RB: Even in *Providence*, there was a biological side in its fascination with the visceral and corporeal aspects.

AR: In any case, I felt a certain stupefaction at the phenomena of biological life. You know, it wasn't so much about memory that Laborit and I wanted to collaborate on that short film that never got made. It was about biology. Despite everything that's been written on the subject, I'm not obsessed with memory. In any case, I find this word too limited. I prefer to talk about imagination or consciousness. What interests me in the brain is this extraordinary faculty we have of imagining in our head what is going to happen, to remember what has happened, and to see to what degree all that is so much a part of our life, that it transforms our body's reactions.

RB: This film contains, perhaps for the first time, some personal notations and memories of childhood. Did you know this island that appears in the opening images? Did you watch your grandfather grilling crabs like the scene in the film?

AR: The island we see in the film is in the Gulf of Morbihan, it's one of the 400 islands in the gulf, and legend has it that there are as many islands there as days in the year. I went there as a child and never told my family. I had to go secretly since I wasn't allowed to take the dinghy out on the open sea. I was about eight or ten years old, and I waited until my family was away to go out there. I never saw my grandfather grilling crabs but I grilled a bunch myself. I loved doing it! With my pals we played great games on the sand and even tried to roast sand, because we'd heard that the Egyptians made glass that way. But we never succeeded in doing it ourselves.

So I knew this island, and when we began looking for sites, I went back there, but only after trying others first. I didn't really want to go back to Brittany. I would have rather gone to islands that I didn't know, and I visited a lot of them, but none in Brittany. I tried going to the Mediterranean but that didn't work because all the islands there are much too big. Gruault's screenplay mentioned a little island. And it had to be small so that one would know that it was an island at first glance. So, I came back to that one. It felt a bit as though it were predestined, since my family hasn't lived in Brittany for a long time. My life in Paris cut me off from this region after I grew up.

RB: Was it Gruault or you who had the idea of the three parallel lives and the excerpts from films?

AR: That was Gruault's idea. We asked ourselves: how can we use Laborit's theories and still make a film with a robust storyline? And Gruault invented these three lives without either of us being specifically identified with any of them. The films were my idea. I wanted a group of very well known actors to furnish us perfect examples of behaviors. But we needed actors who had rich professional lives stretching out over several generations. Which gave them an immortal quality. But ultimately there aren't that many stars at that level. So Grauault decided we'd use Jean Marais, Danielle Darrieux, and Jean Gabin, not because they were his or my personal choices, but because they represented the most likely candidates for each of our three heroes: Jean Le Gall, Janine Garnier, and René Ragueneau.

RB: If you yourself had had the choice, which actors would you have identified with?

AR: If it had been up to me, I'd have chosen Ronald Coleman or someone like Gary Cooper. Inevitably foreignness is a factor there. I very much admire Darrieux and Gabin, but they're French, so they have less of an aura than someone like Katharine Hepburn. But I really admired Charles Boyer. He was one of my great heroes—the European Boyer before the American one. The one who played in Siodmak's *Tumults* or Lang's *Liliom* or *The Hawk*. It was his voice I loved, and obviously one of my great joys was to have met him when doing *Stavisky* . . . . That said, I have to add that I've never identified with him in the least. Of course, when we were choosing the excerpts of Marais, Darrieux, and Gabin, we found ourselves discussing the range of their "mythology," especially in the minds of our three heroes, and that provided some distance on them. At one point, we played with the idea of making a film without shooting a single frame, by using only excerpts from other films. Of course, we quickly realized that not only would it be expensive, but also we'd have to devote two or three years of our lives to the project. I had an experience of that kind of work when I was assisting Nicole Vedrès, and I have to confess it's a bit austere. Spending one's life in cinemathèques might be fun, but it's not very stimulating! So we gave up on the idea.

RB: This was the film in which you focused the most on the theater, which has played an important role in your life. Not only is your principal character an actress, but all the families have very theatrical attitudes, that make me think of certain paintings by Greuze, *The Village Bride*, or *The Prodigal Son*.

AR: I wanted these scenes to be very inspired by Epinal. But I hadn't thought of Greuze. Certain situations are meant to make us laugh, with a nuance of pity. The idea is that certain clichéd images are the ones we love. As for the theater, we wanted it to be an experimental theater rather than a repertory theater, a little left-bank theater, like the Lutèce or the Théâtre de Poche or the Théâtre National Populaire. Although not consciously so. We chose Roger-Pierre because we wanted him to play dramatically but still make use of his more fantastical side. The actors from the music halls can do absolutely anything you ask them to. They know instinctively from their first line how to impose their rhythm on the spectators, and I'm surprised we don't make more use of them in our films. But then I'm not the only one in this business to have been an actor. Gruault was also an actor, and I didn't have to push him to do anything. He's played quite a gamut of roles in both repertory and traveling theaters. As for Jean's renal colic, I did some serious research. I went to see a doctor and asked him for a consultation. I'd known a couple of people who suffered from such ailments, and Jean Gruault had himself suffered from them. In fact, our work on the screenplay was interrupted by a bout of it. There's a bit of acting in such disturbances and in the case of Jean Gruault, I wouldn't swear that there wasn't a bit of fiction mixed in with his great outbreaks. My only health problem has been asthma, and I never had an ulcer. It's funny that people think my asthma is responsible for having taken an interest in Proust. But that's totally ridiculous, because I read Proust at age twenty for fifteen days in a row, fifteen days without interruption, and then I never reread him. I've reread and still read Giraudoux or Huxley *Eyeless in Gaza* or *Point Counterpoint* but never Proust. It's really silly because I didn't even have the same kind of asthma as Proust; mine disappeared when I moved to Paris far from my birthplace. It's like Bergson, that one of my biographers identifies as a direct source for my work, whereas I've absolutely never read Bergson. I don't know anything about his work except for having tried like everyone else to read his book on laughter, but only because of the subject. And yet still today, people label me as Proustian or Bergsonian!

RB: We knew you liked certain comic strips, but not *The Golden King*, which is not very well known.

AR: Yes, *The Golden King* by A. Pujo is a strip I read as a kid. But I couldn't remember it very well, so I had my prop person do some research to find a copy, rue Bayard. It was published in 1920 and I had five or six albums of the original series. What I really liked about it was that the hero, Samuel Night, embodied the dream of absolutely every child, which is to be both a millionaire and an orphan!

Of Mice and Men: An Interview with Alain Resnais

Tom Milne / 1980

From *Monthly Film Bulletin*, no. 47 (December 1980). Reprinted with permission.

Tom Milne: *Mon Oncle d'Amérique* is an unusual film for you, given your other work over the past twenty or so years. How did the film fare in France?

Alain Resnais: To my great surprise, *Mon Oncle d'Amérique* was a huge success in France, my first real popular success. It may be my most directly accessible film, but this was something we couldn't have foreseen while actually making it. We were very worried. I think my producer was glad to have done the film because he liked the subject, but he didn't really expect to get his money back. And he did. There's a moral there somewhere!

TM: Why do you think the audiences like it?

AR: I don't really know why people like it. Perhaps they feel a certain malaise in their lives, have the impression that they should be looking for something else, and for a few seconds, the film gives them the hope that there *is* another direction. Or so I hope: that's the optimistic solution, if you like, as against the pessimistic one that they are liking the film for the wrong reasons.

TM: The film is based to some extent on the work of Henri Laborit. Do you subscribe to his theories?

AR: I can't really say I subscribe to Laborit's theories, but then I wasn't making a thesis film. My idea was, primarily, to make a film from the standpoint of dramatic construction; and what I enjoyed was putting the thesis not into the characters' mouths, but squarely into the mouth of the person responsible for it, and then mixing it all up in the editing to see what would happen.

TM: How did you work this all out with Laborit?

AR: Well, we couldn't know exactly what Laborit was going to say, because I left him entirely free to improvise and then used what he said, *after* having shot all the rest of the film. Laborit never saw the film itself: he was very generous and agreed to play himself without knowing how he was to fit into the film.

TM: So you didn't supply him with a script?

AR: Well, he'd read the draft script a year before, and what he was to say may have been outlined, but it wasn't scripted. So *Mon Oncle d'Amérique* is, in effect, a collage, in which Laborit's contributions were shot only after the film had been fully edited, leaving gaps in the rough cut where he was to talk or appear. No additional scenes were filmed.

TM: Was he given any freedom to cut or edit the film?

AR: Laborit only saw the film after the whole thing was finished with some of the things he said he rejected, others placed where they seemed most relevant to what was going on. This was a day of anguish for us, because if he hadn't liked it, it would have been catastrophic. We'd have had to start all over again, facing another two or three months' work with no money left to pay for it. But there again, he was very generous: he was much amused, saying "Of course it's incomplete, but it's a *film*, not a film about me.'" And he gave us his blessing.

TM: So how closely did the story of the film follow his theories?

AR: Well, Laborit merely outlines the result of forty years of research, in a tone that is, I hope, not at all dogmatic, a conversational tone. Basically, what he says about the consequences of inaction, inhibition and so forth, is plain common sense. He isn't the only biologist to have talked about such ideas, they don't *belong* to him. They may be proved true or false, but they are ideas at least worth investigating.

TM: For instance?

AR: For instance, one that isn't in the film but which I find very interesting concerns madmen or lunatics or what-have-you. Words I don't like much using, but it seems that when one has retreated totally into madness, one becomes effectively immunized against all infectious diseases, and maybe even immune to cancer. This may be true or false: I'm no biologist. But statistics being prepared in asylums may show whether Laborit was right or wrong in his intuition.

TM: So the film presents a kind of laboratory for his most accessible thoughts.

AR: To my mind, *Mon Oncle d'Amérique* is a bit like that. It may present ideas resembling what has been common knowledge for fifty years: after all, it wouldn't make sense, especially in what is first and foremost an entertainment, to present the average filmgoer with the more difficult aspects of Laborit's work. But if, by chance, thanks to the film, attitudes change and people become interested, and begin to read Laborit's books and wonder about the questions they pose—as has happened: his books are being reprinted—then I think that's interesting.

TM: But not everything in the film conforms to Laborit's theories. . . .

AR: Of course, as you say, some of the scenes escape the net of Laborit's theories. The funny thing about the film is that it's based on a complete contradiction. We wanted our characters to illustrate what Laborit says; but at the same time we were very careful, Gruault and I, to leave them entirely free, once they had been chosen, artificially at the outset, to fit the three categories. After that, we forgot Laborit, and would say of a character, no, I don't think he would do that in the circumstances, or yes, I think she might say that. And, of course, since we didn't know exactly what Laborit was going to say, we couldn't predict anything exactly in terms of the theories.

TM: Several people have commented that the Nicole Garcia character in the film emerges as much stronger than either of the two men.

AR: I agree, although this wasn't something we had consciously planned, but which developed in the narrative. It was during shooting, towards the end, that I realized she was always acting, always taking action, unlike the two men, contradicting the inhibition theory in a way. The men are both sick, both develop psychosomatic illnesses if you like, but not her. When I had realized this, I telephoned Jean Gruault to ask if we had deliberately avoided providing her with an illness. "No," he said, "but good God, we can't have another one getting sick!"

But to return to your earlier question whether Laborit's theories were the starting point of the film. Well, yes and no. There are always several reasons for anything. It all began with a pharmaceutical laboratory that was marketing a product designed to develop the memory. This laboratory asked Laborit to write a script for a short film intended for use in publicizing this product. Jokingly, to get them off his back more than anything else, Laborit said, "All right, but you must get someone like Resnais to make it." An editor friend made the connection, telling me that Henri Laborit wanted to talk to me.

TM: How did you know who he was?

AR: I'd read a couple of his books, plus interviews and odds and ends about him in magazines. He uses very simple language in expressing his ideas, which suits someone like me who finds it hard going reading abstract or difficult ideas. So I was interested, and pleased at the prospect of meeting him. He explained what it was all about; we talked it over; and very soon discovered that the laboratory had enough money to invite us to lunch, but no funds available for producing a film. So, of course, the short never materialized, but a sort of regret was left hanging between Laborit and myself. Because we had got on well together, he'd invited me to his home, and we'd spent several Sundays dreaming about making a film together, a feature, since there's really no market for shorts, any more than there was for the laboratory's product: a film about the history of humanity, perhaps, or the history of the planet, or the way the human brain is constructed. But nothing came of it. Just conversation on a Sunday.

TM: So how did the project ever get off the ground?

AR: Well, my wife, Florence, who had been Truffaut's assistant on *Jules et Jim*, knew Jean Gruault very well and said I really ought to meet him. So she set up a meeting with Gruault, who showed me some Griffith films, some old John Barrymores, things like that, which he had in 8 or 9.5 mm. We got on well together, thanks to these old films. So one day I told him about a film I'd never got round to making, and asked if he would be interested in a film where—to come full circle—the thesis would not be expressed by a character, but by the scientist or scholar who would appear in the film with the fiction on one side, the didactic theories on the other, and then seeing what the montage would produce. Grauault thought it sounded impossible but he wanted to try. So he started to write, and one day I took a first draft along to Laborit, wondering if we should go on or not. Laborit said it was all a bit unexpected, that he wasn't qualified to judge a script, but that as far as he was concerned, we could go ahead and he would do whatever we wanted. For a period of about ten days then, I thought we might do the film just with Laborit and clips from old films, certain that with a little patience, in seventy years of cinema history, film could be unearthed illustrating all the variant forms of behavior.

TM: Clearly, from the film I've seen, this approach didn't work. What happened?

AR: Well, I am no saint and life is short, so I very soon realized that it would take ten years of my life to bring the idea off. Not so much to choose the films or the excerpts, but to find copies, and then buy the rights for each of them. The hellish thing is that for every film, there are five or six people whose consent must be obtained. I could see myself never getting the rights to the excerpts I wanted. But this first version of the film probably lingers on in the use made of Gabin, Darrieux, and Marais. As my producer would tell you, it was easier for him to set up the film and finance it than to tie up the rights to use those wretched thirty-odd shots from other films. Even after three months, letters were still going back and forth: "Was it twelve seconds you wanted to use, or seven seconds?" I did eventually get more or less what I wanted, though not entirely, because some clips were too expensive.

TM: I'm fascinated in particular by the shot of Jean Marais falling down a staircase.

AR: The shot of Jean Marais falling backwards down the staircase is one I find intensely moving. I hadn't seen it before. We were working very quickly towards the end, and it was my editor who suddenly said, "Look, I've something to show you. I'd like to know what you think?" When I saw the shot for the first time, there, in its place in the film, I was intensely moved, and of course kept it in. I find it very realistic. When you suddenly realize that your life can be judged in a totally different light, you get that icy sense of falling, for which the Jean Marais shot is an exact *realistic* equivalent. I worried in the planning stage that the danger of using such shots would be that people would find them funny and they'd lose their more serious aspect. But this shot of Marais worked perfectly.

TM: Some people find the film somewhat flat.

AR: Well, for me *Mon Oncle d'Amérique* is first and foremost a montage film: that's what we enjoyed the most. So, yes, some people might ask why the mise en scène is so flat. But I hope it isn't that—*sober*, let's say, instead. Given the acrobatics we were going to try in the montage, I felt that the images themselves couldn't stand further fireworks, like the tracking shots or elaborate camera movements I used in *Stavisky . . .*, otherwise the montage would have been obscured.

TM: And what would you respond to people who say the film is reductive to a theory?

AR: Well, to see the film as reductive, or rather the theories as reductive, trying to fit the characters into a fixed pattern, seems to me possible only for a passive spectator. A spectator, in other words, who thinks to himself, right, the man is telling me this, therefore this is what I must believe. Now, I've never made a film like that in my life, even my documentaries. They were always interrogations. And Laborit in fact hesitates, stammers a bit; I don't think his tone is in any way definitive.

Interview with Alain Resnais: on *L'Amour à mort*

Alain Masson and François Thomas / 1984

From *Positif*, no. 284 (October 1984). Reprinted by permission. Translated by T. Jefferson Kline.

This interview was given a few days after the release of *L'Amour à mort*. Noting that it was the first interview that he'd given, Alain Resnais explains the difficulty of speaking about one of his works without himself having seen the film "in the light of the reactions of a fairly large number of people." But, this time, the projections that usually allow him to have access to such reactions didn't take place because of the selection of the film by the Venice Film Festival. "But," Resnais adds, "it's also fun to begin this way."

Alain Masson and François Thomas: What was the point of departure for *L'Amour à mort*?

Alain Resnais: The point of departure was first of all the temptation to use music as a dramatic element; to see, during the editing of *Life Is a Bed of Roses*, whether we could organize a film and a story by using music as a kind of fifth character, by considering that ultimately music was a piece of the story. There's always this pendulum effect. You try to do the opposite of what you've just done. After a film with lots of characters, I wanted to do a film with just a few characters. I wanted to continue my research—I don't like this word "research" because it sounds a bit like "experimental"—to see if we could use music not as background, but completely in the foreground, and in a different way than I'd done in *Life Is a Bed of Roses*. We started with this idea: can we construct a film never using music as accompaniment, or as support for the actors, but using it openly in such a way as to develop the story, explain the story, taking up the baton from the actors and from the dialogue? There are certain films where I tried to use dialogue a bit like music, to try to achieve a kind of incantatory side with words, in the sonority of words, in the sonority of voices. This time I kept the sonority of the voices but tried to put the musicality in the music and no longer in the words. It's in this vein that Gruault and I tried to work: to make music intervene to express what images and words didn't say. I'm not saying "couldn't say" since I think we might have also said certain things, but it seems to me that in attempting that, we'd have to do a three- or three-and-a-half-hour film. I wanted to make a short film, which was another reason for using music. So that was the point of departure, this desire to use music in a way that was very different from my other films. The characters came second, as usual. We took lots of notes in a very unsystematic way. Then Gruault and I talked and tried to put some order into all these characters and scenes, and then using the bits we liked and tossing out the rest. But that's always the way I work.

AM and FT: Was it also the desire to make a film with more narrative continuity than you usually do?

AR: Perhaps, to link the story more with the music so that the unfolding of the musical themes should be more directly perceptible. We had to try not to interfere with the music. We also tried to do something that was very concentrated in terms not only of the numbers of actors, but also the timbre of their voices, using a very limited budget, which was certainly desirable if we hoped to be able to edit the film, and from the point of view of the story to make a kind of "Kammerspiel" or chamber cinema. But I have no set principles as to whether a film should be linear or discontinuous. It just happens the way it happens, and I try ultimately to be faithful to my first impressions. When the images, the scenes, and the characters have begun to appear, then you have to try to stick with the first intentions you'd had, if they've lasted more than two or three days. Sometimes, of an afternoon, something just won't make sense, but if, two or three nights later, the image or the situation or the dialogue are still there, then it's up to us to use them. There's an enormous contradiction between respecting a kind of automatic writing and then using the material to create a coherent storyboard, develop a working plan, and shoot. I've never made a film out of five lines of story—the famous story, the great idea for a screenplay—then ten pages, thirty pages, then adding dialogues and getting to 150 pages by developing the same story. For me, it's always been fragments, pieces, discussions with the screenwriters where you say: "Couldn't we make a film in which there'd be this scene, where we'd use this particular form at this particular moment? We could add a particular effect and then put it all together." So, with me, it's often the middle of the film that's written first, and then we try to add a beginning and an ending around this middle piece. Because there's always a desire to begin and end a film. You can't just leave things to chance. The primary material always comes to me in a disordered way, so the work consists in using this raw material to make something organized.

AM and FT: We were struck by some anomalies in the film's continuity, for example, the moment right at the beginning, when Sabine Azéma's telephone conversation is interrupted by the resurrection of Pierre Arditi, and we don't hear the click on the telephone signaling the end of the conversation.

AR: That was intentional. We were trying to avoid, perhaps wrongly so, a certain naturalism or realism. This is what I might term an "anti-illusionism." I never try to make people believe that that they're not in a darkened theater in front of a screen and that these aren't actors, or that the photography is life itself. But, of course, that depends on the subject. And, indeed, there are films where I'd take the opposite approach if I felt that the subject demanded it, but in this case, I was trying to achieve a form of lyricism in the acting, in the image, and in the desire to erase any sounds that distracted from the image. I wanted an extremely clean soundtrack, and in a very large number of scenes, we tried to suppress all the natural sounds and leave only the actors' voices. So when I heard the sound of the telephone being hung up, I found it very jolting. So I took it out and left the sense of continuity. I wanted the viewer to focus on Elizabeth's surprise, not on the sound. When you're filming in direct sound, the noises of plates and silverware sound automatically very prominent. In this case, I tried to put the viewers in the most comfortable situation possible, so that they can move from the voice to the music: voice, music, voice, music. When there's music, I eliminate all the natural sounds. I never mix music and sounds, but I will mix music and voices. This time, however, I went further and wanted only voices and music and then voices again. So that justified this tendency to eliminate a certain number of sounds, like that of the telephone. We had the impression, before taking the sound out, that she thought first of hanging up and then of looking, but there was something there that didn't work for me. After having tried a dozen times to make it work, we ended up making the decision when we were mixing the sound, and told ourselves it was very daring. We were a little scared, but it worked best that way.

AM and FT: We wondered how the shots which were, in a sense "fades to black" but weren't really black, were shot.

AR: I call them particles. For the moment, I'd rather not go into this. I'd rather wait a bit. All I can say is that I was trying for a maximum of simplicity: not to use electronic tricks—I tried some, I watched, but they seemed very artificial. Instead, I wanted something without intervention of lab work or trick photography. Obviously, I know that these particles are problematic for a certain number of viewers, but a fade to black raises another problem and that, for the moment, the perfect solution is difficult to achieve on film, since we're not accustomed to listening to music with that degree of concentration and intensity. What I tried to obtain with these particles was a non-figurative image that would allow the viewer to better follow the music, to be as little distracted as possible by the ambiance of cinema itself, and especially not to push the audience to get up, go protest to the usher, and ask to see the projectionist to tell him that the projector had broken down. I'm sure that if I'd started at the beginning of the film with fade to complete black, there would have been this sort of reaction. After these interpretations—I don't want to call them a misunderstanding (that would be pretentious, first of all)—I suspected that some people would interpret them as a voyage to the dead or something like that. In my mind, there was no symbolism. It was just a matter of helping people relax. That's the ideal. So when it functions in the way I'd like it to, I have the same reactions as the audience does: which is to say, the first time, it's OK, the second and third, I get anxious and am afraid that it's becoming systematic, and then after the fourth intervention, I get in the rhythm of it and it works all the way to the end. I knew when I started the film, since that was the point of departure (and the producers were very courageous), that it would be dangerous to make fifty-five to seventy musical interventions in the film.[1] It wasn't going to be easy, and it hasn't been easy.

AM and FT: The distribution of these fades to black wasn't random?

AR: The editing of them wasn't random; the order in which they were shot was. We had a lot of footage, and had a stock of particles and, according to what Jurgenson and I were feeling, we'd choose one or another of them depending on the rhythm they provided. The particles were shot . . . was it before or after the film was recorded?

AM and FT: That's the question we were going to ask you!

AR: In any case, I'd told Henze that there would be some non-figurative images, sort of reflections, and that the dominant tone would be black, but he didn't know how they'd be used. What's more, we simply felt our way along. But we had only forty-eight hours to succeed or fail. We didn't have enough money to make experiments, consider them, and start over. So the whole thing was done at top speed, but maybe it wasn't so bad to be rushed like that, to have your back against the wall: if we'd had two years to work it out, it might have been a bit cold.

AM and FT: So it's the spacing of the musical interventions that wasn't random . . .

AR: Working with Henze, I had already proposed a certain number of seconds for each, and also what should be said for each interlude, but indicating to him, which is interesting for a musician, that he wasn't forced to respect what I proposed. If he felt that to develop his musical phrase, he needed fifteen seconds rather than the seven I proposed, he could do that. But in the end our two times were, curiously, only a minute different than what I'd proposed to him in the editing room.

AM and FT: What guided you in the choice of placement?

AR: Instinct. Desire. When I felt like adding them. When I had the impression that we could use a certain intonation. That was fascinating to me and to Henze too.

AM and FT: So that happened when you saw the film again and added new interludes?

AR: Yes. But first of all to be able to hire a musician like Henze you have to contact him a year in advance. We had to fit into his calendar. So he arrived exactly on the date we'd fixed; he saw the film several times and then we worked together for about two or three days in all. But he already knew from the screenplay the gamble that the project represented from a musical standpoint. (Only the film was, of course, a bit different from the screenplay.) So, right from the beginning, he understood the challenge that the film represented and, at the same time, it was, I believe, pretty exciting for a musician. More often than not, they're not even mentioned by the critics, and at this we would often laugh a diabolical laugh and say to ourselves: this time they're damned well going to be forced to talk about the score, whether they like it or not, they cannot omit the music from their remarks. And, indeed, from this point of view it's working better than usual. In any case, there are reactions in the press. I notice that the music has been called "deafening," "prehistoric," "electro-acoustic," "cacophonic," and even sometimes "superb" and "moving." People's reaction to the music is a problem: as soon as one moves away from tonal language, it's certain that many viewers lose their footing. I conceived the film as having this kind of music, so one can't escape it, but people do indeed have expectations about film music. They might tolerate this kind of music in a concert hall, but they're not used to making this kind of effort in a theater. In this film, the music is much more dense than usual. There's no filling or padding.

AM and FT: Did Henze compose the music as an ensemble of twenty minutes that he subsequently fragmented, or did he have to write these separate fragments from the outset?

AR: He wrote it respecting each of the separate fragments while also trying to make a construction that would allow film viewers/hearers to connect the present fragment with a memory of the preceding one—in some unconscious way, of course—to fit each piece into a form which is developing gradually. The film was in three movements and indeed, he enjoyed respecting each of the three movements. Each of the fragments is ultimately attached to the following one and to the preceding one. He didn't work by making each of them isolated, impressionistic things. One could no doubt qualify the work as post-serial, and indeed there is a serial effect that is soldered to emotions—to love, to Elizabeth's anguish—to which is superposed, mixed in, and counterpointed a series that is

Simon's attraction to death, this kind of slow and disquieting aspiration—at least in the first movement.

AM and FT: So ultimately there are two forms that are developed in the film: the linear one of the story, and the parallel one of the music.

AR: Exactly.

AM and FT: Why does Henry-Louis de la Grange receive thanks in the credits?

AR: Because Henry-Louis de la Grange knows contemporary music very well. So does Maurice Fleuret, and I had conversations with both of them. They were gracious enough to receive me and answer a great number of my questions. I had already chosen Henze since I'd worked with him on *Muriel*, but I wanted to be sure that he was the one best suited for the kind of story we had to tell. I don't know how to read a score. It's very useful to have a conversation with competent people. And since I think that these two, with Marc Vignal, are the three most interesting music critics, I was really very touched that they would agree to spend a few hours with me and talk about all the musicians who might be interested in such a film.

AM and FT: Marc Vignal and de la Grange are both Mahler specialists, and it feels like there are echoes of Mahler's *Song of the Earth* in the film score.

AR: There's no direct echo of Mahler in the film score, in my view, but in certain "feelings" of the film, absolutely. I'm delighted that you mentioned *Song of the Earth*. And the actors will be even more so since they know that work very, very well.

AM and FT: You mean you had them listen to *Song of the Earth*, and that it was the basis of a discussion?

AR: Yes. We worked harder on the musical sensitivity of the characters, using certain names of composers we loved—and sometimes discovered during the filming—than on the psychology or logic or things like that. This said, don't misunderstand me! I'm not saying that the film is not psychological; there's a principle according to which you must never be psychological, whereas I find it amusing to say that the film is 110 percent psychological. But anyway, we worked a lot on feelings through our discussions of the music, since all four really love music. I had them listen to a huge amount of Henze's music, so that they ended up knowing his symphonies, *Voices* and *Tristan*, and so that by listening to them they would be maximally prepared for Herze's interventions (as much as I would be, since I couldn't predict what he'd compose). In a certain way, for certain intonations, they knew perfectly after one phrase or one syllable that it was Herze's music. And Herze carried a cassette of the film's soundtrack with him and worked while listening to this cassette, writing the music to follow from the previous sequence, the previous word, the previous sound, the previous silence.

We tried to do this as precisely as possible, but a film is never anything but an approximation of what one wanted to do, and as there are so many people involved, it is the sum of those approximations. This is not a bad thing: it often happens that unexpected results are better than what we'd planned. But it's impossible to achieve 100 percent of the possible perfection. You can reach that degree of perfection, perhaps in painting, in poetry, in literature.

AM and FT: At certain moments, we noticed a connection between the noise that ends a sequence, and Henze's music, for example, when Simon and Elizabeth's car starts and sets the music in motion.

AR: Well, we certainly tried to organize such effects as much as possible, not on paper, but during the editing. What Jurgenson and I tried very hard to achieve was, for example, to let the music follow the movements of the actors, by cutting a musical segment in synch with the turn of a head, for example, so that when the music stopped, the film might cause real uneasiness. The viewer would feel that we'd cut too soon.

AM and FT: You often praise your collaborators, but no one ever asks you about Albert Jurgenson who, however, was the editor of every one of your films since *Je t'aime, je t'aime*. What's kept you together so long?

AR: Well, as I often say, you should change your team with every new film so that you don't develop sclerosis, so that you don't start doing things out of habit. But you should also do the opposite of what you say. It's true that I get along very, very well with Jurgenson. We've never been in disagreement at the end of our work on a film. It's a well-justified collaboration. He's played a very great role in my work, for sure.

AM and FT: What does he bring you? Has he changed your conceptions about editing?

AR: We try things. We try every possible combination until we're satisfied. We never consider that the mise en scène is finished with the shooting. If we change things in the editing room, it's simply a continuation of the mise en scène. The material we bring to the editing room must be considered as perfectible; we mustn't remain stuck in the paths made during the shooting. And Jurgenson has an extraordinary mind because he is capable of putting everything in question, of trying everything, and yet making decisions very rapidly, always within twenty-four hours. We'll work at it all night until we feel we can breathe—yes, it's really a sensation of respiration. Whenever a shot comes onto the editing screen and our breath stops, we know something is wrong and we try something else.

You people make the director talk a lot, the author of the screenplay already a bit less, sometimes the cameraman, but almost never the director of production or the dolly grip. And as a reader, I'd find it very interesting to read an interview with the grip, for example. His role in pushing the dolly around, following the actors is very important. If we made the actors rehearse to the nearest millimeter, we'd end up with completely stiff scenes: so you have to give the actors and technicians a lot of freedom of movement, especially at the moment of the take. So the grip must be immersed in the story, in the dialogues, and in what might happen with a given actor. His work is extremely delicate. A film can be completely derailed by a grip who isn't in synch with the actors. And while I'm at it, I could mention Gamet, my sound engineer, a very important role. The sound in this film is 95 percent direct; there was no post-synchronization this time. He, too, had an instinct for following the timbre of the actors and anticipating what was going to change. Sometimes when we did a retake, I'd stupidly forget to go warn Gamet. Afterwards, covered with shame, I'd go say, "Excuse-me, Pierre, I didn't tell you I'd asked for that," and he'd reply, "No, no, I thought that's what you'd do, so I wasn't surprised." Moreover, if you watch Gamet while he's recording a scene, it's absolutely fantastic: he's so focused on what's happening that his face is practically miming the story. His hands are working the mixer like a pianist, and he's completely consumed by the interior workings of the actors. It's very moving to watch. And he has a boom operator who's an ace: Bernard [Chomeil] is really someone.

AM and FT: This is your third film in CinemaScope.

AR: It's thoughtful of you to include the first one.[2] It's a format that interests me a lot. It allows great close-ups. Right from the start, we knew that it would be a film about faces, and CinemaScope lets me to get much closer to my actors without losing the sense of space. In 1.33, if I frame a shot at the neck, I often have the impression that the actor is in a photography studio and that he's sitting for a portrait, whereas with 'Scope, even if I do an extreme close-up, there's enough space around him that I don't have the impression he's been separated from the action of the story. I'm very happy in this format. I couldn't have made the film if we hadn't been able to use CinemaScope. It's harder to do films in 'Scope today because the producers always hope to sell the film to foreign TV (not just in France), so that becomes an additional risk.

AM and FT: How much of the décor did you have to construct?

AR: Nothing was built, but the dining room/office/living room in the parsonage was rearranged. As for the house itself, obviously we did some rearranging, but otherwise it's as is. We worked in natural decors throughout the film. We didn't build anything.

AM and FT: Was the choice of Uzès determined by its Protestantism, or was the choice of Protestantism determined by Uzès?

AR: As always, it was through associations of ideas: from the moment we decided on a love story, a death, and a man who comes back to life, I wanted to have rhymes. There are people who believe in an afterlife; clearly this is typical of religious people. I remembered a Protestant church in Nice. It seemed to me that there was a kind of—I don't want to say dissonance—an intersection with this memory of the Protestant milieus in Nice that interested me. Next I went looking for Protestant churches in this region and discovered they were mostly to be found in Cevennes; there was a very concentrated Protestant community there, with more established traditions than in many other places in France. So I went to look at Uzès: all the Protestant locales were grouped, and that's very important in a film. You don't want widely scattered locales. You want backups, so that if there's rain or sun when you don't want it, you have another place to shoot. And there, in a space of about 3 to 6 kilometers, we found everything we needed. That's what decided me to stay in Uzès. It was a good place to work. Of course, some people had reactions, like, "Why didn't you show more of the town of Uzès?" The answer is that you can't do everything. I wanted to make a relatively short film and not go over one and a half hours, so I'm very proud of having kept it to 1:32. And then, it's true, I was a little afraid that it would be too picturesque. We could have accentuated this aspect, but to do so would have seemed to me to go too far outside the subject, and I needed to remain within the general theme suggested by the music. For me, music renders feelings . . . international, even interplanetary! To be too precisely connected to a recognizable space would have been a distraction, I think.

AM and FT: Is the play on words between the names Simon Roche and Simon Pierre intentional?[3]

AR: No! I didn't notice it until you just said it! You always discover very alarming things. When I did a short subject called *Van Gogh*, I had him say, "I'm always on the move, going somewhere!" So I was told the audience would end up saying, "Van go!" But no, there's no attempt at punning here. When we discovered intimate jokes like that we'd strike them from the film. There may still be some that remain, but we did our best to avoid them.

AM and FT: You could have invoked Catholicism, Brahmanism, Islam, or even other cults of the dead. Why Protestantism?

AR: Maybe because when you're making a film you always want to learn something you didn't know. I was brought up Catholic, so that doesn't interest me much because it's too familiar. But the Protestants intrigue me a lot. It was also an opportunity to travel to a part of France that wasn't so invaded by tourists. But the film isn't meant to be a description of Protestantism. Quite simply, these are people who are all thinking about what might happen after death. These are associations that I would qualify as plastic or acoustic. I have the impression that I'm frequently criticized for making didactic films. But I don't see that didacticism. But if there's such a misunderstanding then there must be reasons for it.[4]

AM and FT: Didn't you find the rigorous side of the Protestant mentality somewhat seductive given its contrast with a more passionate side?

AR: Of course! That's why I talk so much about contrasts in timbre and contrasts in theme.

AM and FT: We were very struck by the fact that the dialogue is written in very precise, almost intellectual language, but the subject is passion. Isn't there a kind of dissonance there, where most of our contemporaries would see an implausibility in the subject of the film?

AR: We wanted the dialogue to be a bit dry, but also very literary. Whenever words that were too familiar or slangy cropped up, we felt obliged to remove them. The idea wasn't to be elegant, but the film just didn't allow for such words, and the actors couldn't pronounce them! There would be an immediate reaction. We wanted a written effect, but as un-lyrical as possible, so as not to seem redundant with the music. Deliberate, yes, of course, but intellectual, I'm not so sure. It's a strange word, "intellectual."

AM and FT: Let's say "conscious," then.

AR: "Conscious," yes. They're analyzing each other.

AM and FT: And in very precise terms.

AR: In a love dialogue, in a dialogue on passion, we're always scrutinizing and analyzing things. We could even push this tendency to the extreme . . . Passion can do without words, but it can also develop a very lyrical vocabulary. Of course, these are two people who are very culturally evolved, they have a large vocabulary at their disposal, but that doesn't strike me as an obstacle to passion. The idea lurking in this film is precisely that anyone could die of love. You don't have to be a Tristan or an Isolde for that to happen to you.

AM and FT: Didn't this very explicit side pose problems for the actors?

AR: No. We always tried for maximum economy: our rehearsals, reading and staging were always pretty free, we tried to eliminate anything that wasn't useful or that could be replaced by a gesture. It wasn't because of the linguistic difficulty of a phrase but out of interest for the enterprise. There wasn't a single sentence pronounced by any of the four actors that they didn't actively approve of. I can say that this did not pose any problems.

AM and FT: Was the film shot in continuity?

AR: Each sequence was shot in continuity. I absolutely do not know how to shoot the last shot of a sequence before the first one. I find that such an approach is torture for the actors. It's also dangerous since, if you've already recorded the last shots, you can no longer improvise in the slightest, you only think about how to prepare the last shot, and you end up losing all spontaneity. This approach takes longer, obviously. So, every sequence is shot in order, but, everything else depended as usual on the weather. So that upsets the continuity sometimes.

What was special in this film was that the four actors were co-producers of the film, which is very moving.

AM and FT: Were they more involved in the conception of their roles than in your earlier films?

AR: No, it was pretty much the same. I think I always work the same way, that is, I attach enormous importance to the reactions of the actors. I think they have an important stake in the creation of the film, and I've never worked with an actor who didn't have something interesting to say about the film. Every chance I have to use their observations, I take. I've never shot a film saying, "Hello, sir, hello, madam! Here's the script. We begin shooting tomorrow." I have always enjoyed an exchange among the actors, me, and the screenwriter. That way, we succeed in finding what seems to all of us as the best solution. That's what makes it fun, otherwise people get bored and annoyed. This is not a matter of principle, but of pleasure.

AM and FT: Did anything unforeseen happen during the shooting?

AR: Nothing very notable. In the first movement, or the first act, if you prefer, we switched around a couple of scenes. We shortened the film by about two minutes, that's all. We always discuss what we're going to do, and then we improvise as much as possible before the takes, in order to keep most closely to the work schedule, which is obviously of great concern to all.

AM and FT: Why did you choose this particular quartet of actors that you had already used in *Life Is a Bed of Roses*?

AR: I was very happy when filming *Life Is a Bed of Roses*, and I didn't want to leave them, I wanted to continue the film. The shoot was very difficult because we didn't have enough money, even though conditions were pretty luxurious compared to the little productions I'd done. Things were pretty tense from this perspective, but, on the other hand, the ambiance of the shoot was extremely upbeat, warm, and, I think, no one wanted to part company at the end. The role I'd given to Dussollier was a bit limited, a few cries, a few moans. We could have done a bit more with it. There was also the meeting of these four voices, and these four personalities. Why is it that we want to associate a bassoon with a flute or a piano? What pushes a musician to choose certain timbres? I don't know, but that's what happened.

AM and FT: It isn't just actors that you've used from one film to the next, but also characters, or rather couples. You re-engaged Fanny Ardant and Dussollier, and in *Life Is a Bed of Roses*, Elisabeth is confronted with a choice: Vittorio Gassman or Pierre Arditi, a bit like the heads or tails of *L'Amour à mort*. In *Life Is a Bed of Roses*, she chooses Gassman, and you kept the other solution for the film that followed.

AR: Well there, a miracle of the unconscious! You've proved that you're a psychoanalyst and are helping me to discover the simplicity of my interior schemas.

I'll talk to Gruault, but I don't think I ever thought about that. We never spoke about it or paid attention to it! A good thing, too, since it might have scared us. Yes, it's true: we've brought together the two different periods.

AM and FT: In your view, is *L'Amour à mort* the most provocative or the most accessible of your films?

AR: Well, until the film is released and I've heard reactions to it, it would be difficult to say. Curiously, up until now, my films have provoked such contradictory reactions that I have trouble orienting myself. I was once amused to note that if we cut out of a given film everything that people didn't like about it, since there were such divergent views, the entire film would have disappeared. So it's a question that I don't ask in those terms: we'll see in three years. Alas, I have the impression that it takes almost three years to know roughly what a film is worth, which is dangerous because the economics of the situation demand that you know right away. But the second law is to see whether negative reactions lose value, including economic value, over time. So you definitely need a bit of distance.

AM and FT: At the release of each of your films, some of the critics wrote that Resnais has finally made a simple film that's easier to understand.

AR: Generally, when the film is released, we do try to say, "This time you're going to understand." But I wonder if this doesn't backfire and make people mistrust us. If we say to them: "You're going to understand this time," it really means that it's going to be hard. What's funny is that ultimately I do try to be clear.

AM and FT: But in *Marienbad* also, no doubt.

AR: Yes, I really wanted to clarify things. We could have complicated *Marienbad* enormously. Moreover, this is problematic since *Marienbad* provoked more opposition from very cultivated people than from people who just let themselves go with the rhythm of the construction. *Marienbad* is made up of two or three themes that recur and keep developing. If you pay attention to the imagery, it's entirely musical.

Notes

1. Besides the opening film titles and the ending credits, there are fifty-two musical interventions.
2. *Le Chant du styrène*, no less.
3. "Roche" means "rock" in French, and "pierre" means "stone."
4. After the film, Alain Resnais clarified that he had nothing against didactic films as artistic forms on condition that they be integrated into a dramatic construction.

Tracking Some Angles: A Talk with Alain Resnais

Frederic Tuten / 1984

© Artforum, no. 23 (November 1984). Reprinted by permission.

We were intending to meet for days, but Alain Resnais was caught up in the final postproduction touches on his most recent film, *L'Amour à mort*. This would have been one of the many talks we have had over the years of our friendship. In the summer of 1980, Resnais and I spent at least two hours a day for two months drinking coffee and talking casually in an apartment in Paris across from the Luxembourg gardens. At the time, I often thought about taping our conversations— I even may have taken notes, especially when Resnais talked about Paris before the war (the Paris he was sure I really would have loved), or about a composer he was studying, or about Claude-Nicolas Ledoux, the eighteenth-century architect whose work fascinated him and whose building in the Parc Monceau he once took me to see—but I felt shy about it, fearing it would rupture the naturalness and fluidity of our words and make him uneasy. Yet, over the years, I have blamed myself for not keeping a record of those talks. So, this past August, I proposed a formal interview. When Resnais returned my call, we joked in our usual vein, he in his dry, precise tone of well-mannered irony, the dramatistic elegance of Racine with a twist of Jack Benny, me in my bursting Bronxese—all punch lines and no story. But, for reasons I don't recall, I soon turned to my customary complaining about the world at large and about the miserable polluted condition of the Mediterranean. "Years ago you could drive there for fresh oysters. And now it's finished, glunk and devastation; nothing can live in it." "Ah yes, I remember," Resnais interjected, "in the years just after the war, I once rode a train for twenty hours and arrived on the Riviera early in the morning and we walked down to the empty beach and saw a crab moving in the sand. It was wonderful to see that crab." He said that with the same excitement and awe he must have felt on that beach that morning years ago, and I could not help but think of the scene in *Mon Oncle d'Amerique* [1980] when the grandfather grills for his grandson a little crab freshly caught from the waters of Brittany—the region where Resnais was born and raised. And I could not help but feel a renewed desire to record Resnais's voice, his thoughts, before they slipped away from me. We made our appointment, we met, Resnais on time as always.

Frederic Tuten: There are thematic patterns in your work that can be traced from one time to another. Are you aware of them?

Alain Resnais: They're unconscious and I'd prefer to leave them that way.

FT: And not know why or how they happen?

AR: Yes. I think a person making a film should try not to control what it says, except on the level of dramatic pleasure. One should let things happen, through a kind of "écriture automatique." A film is like a plant—you have to let it grow by itself, you have to respect that kind of biological rhythm.

FT: I've often thought the storyline in your films was a pretext for the complete abstraction of imagery. That what is really important in your work is this fabulous motion and musical pacing of visual and auditory images; that what you're doing is making the purest cinema possible within the confines of the marketplace.

AR: It's true that the first thing that comes to my mind when I start a picture is a kind of abstract figure. After that, I try to find a title, and after that I try to discover characters, sometimes with the screenwriters, or maybe sometimes I bring in images. It's always a structure that's the point of departure. Sometimes we abandon it when the story begins to be developed, but sometimes we keep it—it's not a fixed decision. I am always ready to change things. We never start with a plot. We always start with some fuzzy ideas and then a scene is written, a scene which could come, say, from the middle of the film, and little by little, the thing becomes a screenplay. That's why it's difficult to get backing from a producer for a "good idea," because there are no good ideas at the beginning. Regarding the issue of pure cinema, within the confines of the marketplace, as you called it—it's not only the question of selling a film, but it's also the conviction that a film is something that must be shared with an audience. I can't imagine a film for ten people, or a film just made for us directors. Some directors say, "I need to express myself." I don't feel that need at all, but if I did I think I would use essays or maybe paintings, maybe music, but not film. You have to keep in mind that the audience must stay in a dark room for ninety minutes or two hours. That's an interesting challenge, but it does not prevent you from using scenes from your life and the lives of your friends. I like the quotation of Douglas Sirk that we put in the pressbook [for *L'Amour à mort*]: "One cannot make films about something, one can only make films with something."

FT: It's always so vague when we speak about expressing ourselves because it usually implies the pejorative sense, the expression of a self-centered autobiography. It usually means this happened to me, I did this, I lived this, like the worst of Walt Whitman, "I am the man, I suffer'd, I was there." I was thinking about your work and that made me think of the paintings of Poussin. Poussin is the most seemingly impersonal of artists, the most classical. His work is built on the belief that there are principles that endure for the ages—a metaphysical science of space and composition. It isn't based on the inspiration of a unique artist, as it was thought of in the nineteenth century; it isn't like Van Gogh painting a landscape that really is an interior of himself.

AR: I have to agree that between the Dionysian and Apollonian, I am on the Apollonian side—not on purpose, but I feel fraternity with people like Joseph Haydn, Alban Berg, Anton von Webern, and Igor Stravinsky; and Poussin, yes. You know that statue in *Marienbad* as described in the script by Alain Robbe-Grillet? The source is Poussin. I asked a sculptor to make the statue using the feeling, the gestures, of the characters in his paintings.

FT: Was this from one particular painting?

AR: I don't think so. But in his work there was something that attracted me. It would be impossible to change the location of a sculpture that would weigh tons, so we had to build something very light, in papier-maché, so that it could be moved each time it was necessary. And it was necessary to do this quite often, since my script breakdown implied that the location was changing for every shot.

FT: Are there any other painters you are interested in? Cézanne?

AR: Yes, Cézanne, of course. Max Ernst, René Magritte, but he is so well known now.

FT: He's like a fresh cliché.

AR: Yes, but remember the trouble he has had in being considered a real painter, because the work is so intellectual. I've always been a fan of his and of the Belgian, Paul Delvaux. Each time it is possible, I try to shoot in Belgium because I think there is a kind of fragrance there that I enjoy. I am sure it is not a coincidence that Surrealism has had so many disciples in Belgium.

FT: Because we talk about you as the classicist of images, and see your impersonal parade of exquisite images, I sometimes forget the Surrealist side of Resnais. But when you go underneath the pictures, they're filled with waves of absolute passion and mystery, and when you speak of Surrealism, I think, "Of course!" I forget, for example, that it was you who told me to read *Le Paysan de Paris*, the Louis Aragon book; it was you who brought me to see the Park Buttes Chaumont and talked about the Surrealists walking there at night. And I remember that marvelous evening when we went off to find *L'Allée des Brouillards*, Fog Alley. But we did not find it.

AR: We didn't have a map with us.

FT: Exactly my point. There is a kind of irony to this Surrealist side of yours. In fact, it's the irony I find in your films. I say "irony," you use the word "dissonance" to describe it, but I think we mean the same thing. I mean dissonance as a structure and irony as an emotional standstill, where we are never certain of what the emotional tone is, because at the moment we think we understand it, you undercut it and make it something else; sometimes by humor.

AR: I think sometimes it is interesting to bring to the screen a kind of conflict of ideas because conflict is basic to drama.

FT: I'm thinking of that scene in *Mon Oncle d'Amérique* where the husband is leaving the house, he has packed up his bags and he leaves. It's a tearful scene. The children are crying, and then you cut to an image of a giant white rat in distress and flight. When I called you perverse recently, I meant that in your work there's much more of both humor and detachment than I think people realize. What is becoming clearer to me is how you can change a scene with immense emotion, to the brink of it being a kind of cliché—for example, that scene of the husband leaving, which is something out of a soap opera—and how you can turn it around, by cutting to the rat, and take such an Olympian view of the experience. While we are in the middle of our most anguished moments, we are also in the middle of our comedy.

AR: That's why some people resent my films. They say that my characters are too unstable, and they wonder whether they are idiots or courageous or cowards. People who don't like my work say it makes them uneasy and bored at the same time, because they are never sure of my point of view, if I have a serious moral judgment to make. I am just fascinated by human beings, by all the contradictions I can feel even inside myself. That's what unconsciously could be—may be—reproduced on the screen. I am not sure of what I am telling you, but I can feel in a kind of fuzzy way, a foggy way, that we are nearing something that could be exact.

FT: Of course, this brings to mind Flaubert and the notion of the artist as the impersonal observer whose obligation is the creation of artwork. Here it's Resnais in the tradition of the artist whose religion is art.

AR: I have no faith in myself. I don't believe in anything. I mean anything religious; in things like that I have no faith. But I have to admit that I have a total faith in art and beauty. I could say that all my films, especially the last ones, are a kind of critique of faith. But, as I said, even though I imagine myself an unbeliever, I believe in art and in love too.

FT: I guess life is what it is, we can't ask for something that it's not. This morning I thought about how prominent love is in your films. No matter how much we talk about detachment, the impersonality, the coolness of the films, there seem to be, time and again not just figures and places in space and time, not just abstract forms against the composition of music which compose these events—but there are stories in which there's disappointment in love. Almost all the films have situations where people are thwarted, disappointed, in love or by love. Almost all are triangles. It starts with *Hiroshima mon Amour* [1959], where, you would say there's a triangle. The war is what has brought the lovers together, but it is also what separates them. It is as if there's a third person there, the painful memory of the war. In another sense, in *Marienbad*, there's always something that prevents love from being achieved, except through violence. There's either memory or there's action.

AR: I disagree. In *Marienbad*, the problem is just one of conquest. I would say that usually love does not come to people who are completely free and have no links to anything. Except when you are in high school. Yes, you mean a triangle stretched in that way. I think in *Marienbad* there is a triangle. But the woman has to make her choice, and that's the end of it. A kind of happy end. A man makes her leave her husband and takes her with him. The husband is not a stupid, ridiculous guy, so it's not an easy decision, but it just comes to that, so I would not say that in *Marienbad* the story is one of frustrated love. You can also look at the film in a symbolic way, as a kind of legend—the story of Death who has given the young woman one year to live. When we had finished the screenplay, Robbe-Grillet discovered that his description of the garden could well have been a perfect description of a cemetery. He was quite surprised. Of course, he enjoyed the idea, so we worked out the film—not with a thousand solutions as has been written; that's totally untrue—but with at least five or six different levels.

FT: That's enough.

AR: All the stuff that has been written saying that Robbe-Grillet had a completely different way of seeing the story than mine is rubbish. We discussed three or four different interpretations together, and after that maybe Robbe-Grillet made some public statements just for fun. That's the way he works; he's very tongue in cheek. He has a lot of humor, but when he works he is very serious. He does not joke at all about his work. It is difficult to say that my films are more about love than other films. After all, this is the material of 90 percent of all films. It would be pretentious to think that mine are different.

FT: But you chose these subjects; you didn't choose comedies. This is your preoccupation.

AR: Yes, but not by choice or by any kind of decision.

FT: OK, let's say, Alain, that love and disappointment in love are *my* preoccupation and that I'm always seeking an aesthetic format in which to frame them, all the same, for any given work of art in which there is a love story the structure of drama dictates a conflict and for there to be conflict there must be a disappointment in love.

AR: Yes, but not especially in my work.

FT: Well, the aesthetic problem would be how to create a work in which love stays alive for years, without conflict, without a rupture. I mean, Alain, a work where a couple meet, fall in love, and fall more deeply in love, and remain in love throughout the entire cozy thing. In fact, I can't imagine a novel or opera or film in which that happens.

AR: Well, it shows how illiterate you are. There was a French writer, Paul Guth, who published at least twenty books. A lot of them sold very well. I remember that he wrote a novel twenty or thirty years ago. It was just a man and a woman, married, I think, who enjoyed life for more than 200 pages. There is another example that is more interesting for my taste, a play by Sacha Guitry called *Je t'aime* [1920]. It's in five acts. In the first act, the boy meets the girl and they fall in love; in the second act they are in love; in the third act they are in love; in the fourth act they are in love and of course in the fifth act, they are still in love. This is a challenge. I took an excerpt of it for *Stavisky . . .* [1974].

FT: Is this where the title of *Je t'aime, je t'aime* [1968] comes from?

AR: No and yes. Jacques Sternberg wrote the script for that; the title came from thinking about a satellite that is lost and goes beep, beep, beep. My hero, my character was lost in a kind of space-time continuum, and I had the feeling that he was saying, "Je t'aime, je t'aime, je t'aime," like beep, beep, beep. After that idea emerged, I was a little bit worried because of the play by Guitry with the same title, but then I realized that it was a homage to him, and that Guitry would not have minded, so I kept the title.

FT: You're right, I'm illiterate (laughs). But I'm also a monomaniac of persistency. I still maintain that there are triangles of thwarted love in your films—the triangle need not be with a third person, but there's some interference that deflects love.

AR: I don't think there's a triangle in *La Guerre est finie* [1966].

FT: The triangle is the Spanish Civil War.

AR: In that way, yes. But I think there is no real triangle in *Je t'aime, je t'aime*.

FT: Except for the morass of time.

AR: In *Stavisky . . .*, there's no triangle except that of the crook's work, if you call what a crook does work—being a crook takes a lot of work, takes more work than for an honest man.

FT: You know, I've always wondered about that film. You've placed your work in historical contexts before—*Hiroshima* and *La Guerre est finie*—and you have made documentaries of artists, like *Gauguin* [1950] and *Van Gogh* [1948], but you've never based a fiction film on a direct biography.

AR: I think it would have been better not to use real names; it was the producer who asked us to use "Stavisky" as the title of the film. I felt it was a bad idea, because in France, Stavisky is a kind of historical figure, and people resented him being played by an actor. But the distributor said that if we didn't call it *Stavisky*, he wouldn't buy it. This was at the end of the shooting, and we had no choice. All I tried to get as consolation was to add three dots after the name, to give it the feeling that there's something more, the feeling that it's a kind of ballad about Stavisky.

FT: How do you mean that, Alain?

AR: I mean a popular lament.

FT: You mean in the "Mack the Knife" tradition? Alain, I know nothing about music, therefore 80 percent of what I need to ask you I can't. It has to do with the relationship of your films to music. I don't think I know a director who is so immersed in the musicality of his films.

AR: I don't know much about music either. All I can say is that I am sure there is a relationship between tempo and editing. I find it easy to work with composers. We feel at home immediately.

FT: It's obvious how much you're concerned about the music, that you don't see it just as decoration.

AR: Thanks to the music you can say many more things, you can get emotions in one minute that might have taken ten minutes of dialogue.

FT: Do you know while you're shooting where you will have music? Is that already in your mind?

AR: Yes, of course. When I'm shooting I know where the music will be put. It is necessary.

FT: How does it work? Has the music been composed at that point?

AR: No, but I know where I'm going to use it. I think every director does that, except the director who doesn't think music is important. I do not say that I can hear the music, but I know where I will ask the composer to write it for. Plus, I make special shots for the music.

FT: Do you think this happens with American directors?

AR: With somebody like Alfred Hitchcock, I am quite sure, yes, and Martin Scorsese, especially in *Taxi Driver* [1976].

FT: What ideas do you have for future work? What would you like to do? What are your plans?

AR: I'm working with Milan Kundera on the screenplay for my next film. Then there are two American projects that I've wanted to do for at least fifteen years. One's with Stan Lee, who created the characters Spider-Man and the Incredible Hulk. The other is with Harlan Ellison, who began writing his fantasy fictions in the '50s. Years ago, when the producer discovered that Ellison, who was working like a beaver, wanted what the producer felt was too much money, he said, "We have a better writer than Ellison." I asked, who? He said he could get a better deal with somebody who would be better. I told them to call me when they found that man. They never called. So I consider my project with Ellison still on. But you know how it is in the film business. There are hundreds of undone projects every year.

FT: You must know that Steven Spielberg has bought the rights to Tintin.

AR: Yes, I was a little bit surprised.

FT: It's strange, isn't it? Spielberg?

AR: Yes.

FT: Several months before he died, Georges Hergé, the creator of the Tintin comics, told me he was hoping to come to America for a big project he wanted to do. This was obviously the one. To my mind, it should have been you. You should have made that film of his book *L'Ile noire* [*Black Island*, 1956] that you once planned. I still remember how you were going to have all those characters wear masks.

AR: If somebody can do something with *Tintin*, it's Spielberg. It's interesting how we're both attracted to the same subjects. In fact, we even have a friend in common, James Steranko. Of course, I've long been interested in that kind of material. Years ago, I proposed a Conan film to a producer who said it was impossible, just a subject for students.

FT: You're mysterious. I knew you loved all this freaky popular stuff, but not Conan. You proposed to do a Conan film?

AR: I would have loved to make not only that one, but to make at least one kind of crazy adventure film.

FT: So why don't you make one? It would have all the intellectual and aesthetic substance of a Resnais film plus all the fluidity allowed by a supertechnology of special effects.

AR: I don't think I'd enjoy it very much. You have to wait too long for each shot. I would not like to direct a film where the emphasis is on special effects. Adventures, all right, but special effects, that's very boring. The actors have less importance: you just shoot in front of black drapes, making sure that things work well.

FT: Then again, what would it mean? Everyone wants to do these kinds of films—Superman, Popeye. What was once a radical notion, an iconoclastic strategy, is now a schlocky would-be formula for success.

AR: Yes, this is the kind of project that producers talk about over after-dinner drinks, and so often nothing comes of it. There's been a project to do a Mandrake the Magician film for some twenty years now. I was once contacted about it, but I said no. I had a film to shoot first and needed some time. "But that's impossible, we have to start shooting in two weeks, we have start shooting in one month," they said. I've waited, but I still haven't seen any Mandrake film.

FT: Would you have worked on a commission like that?

AR: With Mandrake, yes, but only under the condition that Lee Falk, who is the creator of Mandrake, would write and have absolute control over the script. I would never have accepted an assignment to do an adaptation, or anything like that. I remember one adaptation—the opening scene was in a nightclub, with the corpse of a girl with a knife in her chest—it's the very opposite of the spirit of Mandrake, which is never gory, always elegant, and sweet in a way. Lee Falk actually started a screenplay. The villain was to be a man obsessed by an idea. The film opened in a building in Washington, where there were two big clocks—one showing births, the other deaths. And the villain wanted to regulate the world so the two would be in perfect balance, so that the whole world would be in perfect balance. From that starting point, all bad things follow. I think he fell in love with Mandrake's companion, Nadra—maybe you would say that is a kind of triangle!

FT: I would say everything's a triangle!

AR: There's yet another Mandrake saga. It seems someone bought the rights and asked Paul Newman to play Mandrake. He said he would accept if I were the director. I think that was very nice of him. But the producer said, "It's not a good combination. For Mandrake, I'm afraid of Alain Resnais. I need a commercial director." So Newman said, "I'm out of the deal. I'm not interested." And that was that. This story may be a legend; I have no proof that it happened. But that's the way it was told to me. I think it could have been right. Paul Newman is an actor I admire very much. He could have given to Mandrake his appropriate charm and elegance. My American projects seem to go to pieces because of money.

FT: I can never understand how anyone would not find the money to do a film with you.

AR: American films especially are produced by a kind of conglomerate. Even when an American producer wants to make a deal with me, he has to go and get, say, seven other people to agree. That's very difficult, to have eight different people agreeing on the same project before it's made. Most of my films have not been great commercial successes, so it's logical that a conglomerate would be cautious. It's not something to be bitter or complain about. In a way, it's logical; I am not complaining.

FT: I'm complaining! I'm always shocked that beauty is treated so crudely. I know it's an absurd feeling to hold in today's world, at my age, but I can't bear to think that vulgarity triumphs everywhere—the more vulgar, more sleazy, more debased, the better. That mediocrity wins, that while millions of dollars are pumped into making witless junk films, which turn us into capons—you have to worry about finding an amount a twentieth of what it costs to make our usual steroidal idiocies. It also astonishes me that you can't find producers to back you when I always meet people in Paris who say they would do anything to make a film with you.

AR: Yes, but that's just talk. A recent example went like this: "You have a project?" "Yes." "I want to see you on Wednesday. What is the budget?" I said it would be between 10 and 12 million francs. "Oh, that's nothing to me. I will give you a call within two days. But, don't worry, it's a deal." After one week, he made a phone call to the producer and they made an appointment, then his secretary called and said the appointment was canceled, but that he would call again. He never called again, and he says we did not have an agreement.

FT: Ten million francs by American standards is absolutely nothing. A little more than a million dollars is a cheap movie.

AR: Yes, but for France, it's a whole lot. It would be impossible to produce *Last Year in Marienbad* or *Providence* [1977] now. *Providence* would cost, say 25 million francs. *Last Year in Marienbad* would be 30 million. I have been very lucky to have been able to do films of that sort.

FT: We've talked about various projects that have not materialized, but it seems to me you've done exactly what you've wanted in the films you've made. It's always been on your terms. Obviously, a producer who works with you wants to do so.

AR: I consider the producer somebody who helps the film, not an adversary. For example, I've never had an actor in my films who I haven't admired, almost never someone who wasn't chosen by mutual agreement.

FT: When I was sixteen or seventeen, there was always the question of Hemingway. Whenever I thought of writing a sentence, it came out of Hemingway. I couldn't express a great deal of experience unless I visualized it with a Hemingway sentence. Over the years, when I've thought of cinema, I've thought of Alain Resnais's cinema and sometimes I've framed an experience through the filter of your films. It's very strange. There are actual moments when I feel like I'm living in a scene in one of your films, living in a static, operatic hold of *Marienbad*, or in a gliding, tracking, skidding swoop of *Toute la mémoire du monde* [1956]; a woman places her hand on her shoulder and I conceive it more from your film *Muriel* [1963] than from the woman beside me. It's like my earlier experience of Hemingway again. It's the essential truth of your undecorated grammar that stays with me after the house lights have gone back on. Alain, I've always wondered what led you to become a director.

AR: I never dreamed of becoming a director; it happened, but I did not do anything to become one. I just tried to be an editor. Then one thing led to another.

FT: When you talk to people about art, they have such strange ideas about how things are done. They think it's some kind of work in which people come to aesthetic decisions, and then everything just moves along. They have no idea of the ordinariness of it, how realistic the solutions are. Let's run away from it all and make a Western together.

AR: No.

FT: No Westerns, eh? Horses don't appeal to you?

AR: I am not very attracted to mysteries or Westerns. Adventure, that's all right.

FT: But adventure with mystery.

AR: Yes, fantastic adventures.

FT: Science-fiction?

AR: Science-fiction, no, speculative fiction yes, as my friend Ellison, whose work I admire, would say.

FT: Like the ones of *Fantômas*.

AR: But that was a possible project. They asked me, but I knew it was the dream of another director to do *Fantômas*, and I could not accept.

FT: So there are two forbidden qualities in your life—the forbidden subject and the forbidden triangle. By the way, is there one in your newest film, *L'Amour à mort?*

AR: No. Not one. But there may be many.

When the Cinema Emerged from Its Shell: An Interview with Alain Resnais

Jean-Daniel Roob / 1986

In *Alain Resnais* (Lyon: La Manufacture, 1986), 103ff. Reprinted by permission. Translated by T. Jefferson Kline.

AR: If cinema didn't "speak" from its inception, it was only because of a set of economic and technical circumstances. I'm entirely convinced that the first idea that its inventors had was the possibility of connecting words and images. There's a story that when Thomas Edison returned from a trip he'd made, he was met by his students in his office with an image projected on a screen of one of his students saying, "Hello, Mr. Edison!" I imagine that the students had succeeded in synchronizing the film projection with a roll of wax on which his voice had been recorded. Why didn't the cinema from its very invention develop in this way? It seems to me that these things should work in the same way nature does. Why, for example, out of the thousand upon thousands of possible combinations did the hermit crab emerge as a kind of lobster without a shell? That's a very perverse kind of tinkering! Well, this hermit crab had the intelligence to see that if there was an empty shell around, he could take up residence in it and therein be protected. And so he survived! So should we say that he was handicapped? He must now be in his nth year of existence and he's still here. That's all I have to say about that. Now let's take film directors, cameramen, and actors; they made such a beautiful thing of silent film that it served their needs quite beautifully.

If we wanted to playfully rewrite history, we could say that the talkies arrived ten years too early, since by 1929, they'd so perfected their audience's perceptions and appreciation of their "language" that it was a shame to abandon it! But it was inevitable.

J-DR: I sense in your delightful way of evoking silent films that not only did you love them, but that you would have wanted to make some. You only missed this opportunity by a few years, as you say.

AR: Well, I hadn't really expected to make any films at all . . . I really didn't anticipate doing so.

J-DR: But I thought you shot a version of *Fantômas* in 8mm film when you were thirteen, with the kids from Vannes as actors. Or is that a myth?

AR: No, it's true. But my critical faculties forbade me from continuing such an experiment. It's really too bad since I could have produced some monstrosities that would have been fun to look at now. Yes, it could have been quite funny . . .

J-DR: So here's Alain Renais, whom nothing destined to be a film director, except his solitary rise toward a career he found irresistible. Resnais, whose career describes an exemplary journey of love and respect for his art, never imagined making films! That's pretty surprising.

How does he explain that he was able to develop simultaneously his love of silent films and his love of theatrical language?

AR: Well, it's this way . . . What I want to say is . . . I always feel quite awkward in these interviews. Milan Kundera, with whom I'm working at the moment, told me, "In any case, Alain, you can't avoid it. Either you begin by saying, 'I've already said this in an interview' and that's very pretentious because it assumes that people have read everything you've said, and remember it, or else you say nothing and you repeat the same broken record ten times and they'll say, 'Oh, he's gone senile.'" And then it's not good to treat oneself as an object. As for me, if I stop to look at what I'm doing, I can't go on. When I'm shooting, it's very difficult for me to accept a presence . . . it's very mysterious!

J-DR: I would have liked to penetrate this mystery a bit.

AR: I'm always afraid of violating a film by speaking about it before it's finished. For example, as a filmgoer, I hate 99 percent of the previews that are shown for new films. When I see them come up in a movie theater, I try to close my eyes and block my ears in order to keep them from ruining the pleasure that I'll look forward to when I see the film. I think movie directors ought to be able to keep these previews to a minimum. I loved the time when movie directors were satisfied just to make films. Before the war, there were no declarations by . . . I don't know . . . Jean Renoir, Carné, Duvivier, René Clair, Grémillion . . . just to mention some French directors.

J-DR: But even the ones you mention made up for it later.

AR: Yes, and how! Mind you, we shouldn't get all nostalgic about the prewar years, when you consider that movies were made mostly for illiterates. No one thought that these people could be considered normal human beings. Especially the Americans. Everyone thought that American directors were barbarians. Someone once told me, "You know, they have Impressionist paintings on their walls." What? Paintings? They know what paintings are? I remember that at the Cannes festival in 1948 or 1949 you could count on creating a laugh riot if you claimed that Gene Kelly or Stanley Donen were cultivated people and had good taste. This prejudice lasted a long time. But now, happily, it's over.

My love of the theater came later, because I grew up in Brittany and I saw only horrible plays that were "classics." I even developed a furious hatred for classic scenery.

J-DR: But there must have been theater festivals or tours by companies like Kessenty's.

AR: Well, Barret's company did tours, but I didn't go to see them. They were for kids. And in any case, they didn't come to Vannes. The theater in Vannes was in such ruins that people brought garden chairs to sit in, and took the precaution to bring covers and umbrellas since the roof was so bad that rain fell directly into the hall. The entrance was very strange. In this little street, there were two porches that, from the outside, appeared to be identical; one led to the theater, the other to the urinals.

J-DR: In such conditions, these aren't the light perfumes of your nascent vocation that dominate. So you had to wait until you could visit your grandfather in Paris to go to the theater and discover the power of Giraudoux's *The Trojan War Will Not Take Place*, with Jouvet in the leading role, *The Sea Gull* starring Pitoëff, and such actors as Dullin, Guitry, and Claude Dauphin in Bernstein's *Hope*.

AR: It was a shocking discovery. I immediately became a fanatical theatergoer, but by this time, the cinema had become the talkies. It had happened. I'd accepted it as soon as I saw René Clair's *Le Million* and *A Nous la Liberté*.

J-DR: That is, from the moment René Clair accepted sound film.

AR: Yes. Chaplin was the only holdout. But I was already 100 percent enthusiastic about it. I didn't miss the piano player who accompanied the images or the pot-pourri of an orchestra, or the ridiculous records that were played.

J-DR: But if my math is right, you were still pretty young at that point: Clair's *Le Million* was released in 1931, so you were only nine . . .

AR: You know, Brittany is a kind of island, at kind of the ends of the Earth from Paris, so we didn't see any sound films until four or five years after they were introduced.

J-DR: You were a great fan of the ciné-clubs in your adolescence, and that's where you learned to watch films before undertaking them yourself, if we exclude your first childish attempts at it. If filmmakers had refused to discuss their films, they would have rendered the ciné-clubs orphans, abandoned to various speculators. You would have been very disappointed . . .

AR: Not really. The filmmakers didn't come as far as Brittany. The ciné-clubs belonged to amateurs. Then, in Paris, I went to the Ursulines and discovered another kind of film, as Cocteau's articles on film invited us to do. Langlois did a few minutes of introduction to each showing. It was particularly enthralling, moreover, since he never finished his sentences and . . . it was amazing! But at that time, we never saw any filmmakers. I'm not saying I approve of their silence. It was a question of equilibrium.

J-DR: And to what do you attribute the erosion of this equilibrium?

AR: I think it was essentially a question of economics. The price of film tickets never followed the rate of inflation. A ticket should cost 120 FF, but it's only 30 to 35 FF. To take out an ad in *France-Soir* or another paper would cost I don't know how many thousands of francs. You simply couldn't make it if you risked this kind of money on publicity even if you sell lots of 30-franc tickets. So you send the director and some actors to the theater.

J-DR: Well, I guess that's what's called after-sale services!

AR: Sure, because that way you get two or three columns of free publicity. The producers tell us: "Don't worry about what you're going to say, it's not important. People will see the name of the film. That replaces the advertising I'd have had to put in *Le Figaro, Le Matin, Libération* . . . I don't have other means of promoting the film." OK, but now we're running in circles. We all say the same thing. Evidently, François Truffaut gave wonderful interviews, but that's very rare.

J-DR: As for me, I'm not convinced—that's a euphemism—that one of Alain Resnais's presentations on TV would be so bad. But he wouldn't like doing it, so that's good enough reason not to do it. So what do you think about the evolution of publicity of the type that we see emerging now?

AR: Well, you can't help noticing that today's ads have taken a very aggressive turn. They don't brag about their products any more; they unsettle us, and want to engage us in a dialogue, no matter what the product. They try to surprise us, to amuse us and to speak in very familiar tones to the passers-by.

J-DR: A typical example of what you're describing is the advertising that accompanied Bertrand Blier's film *Tenue de soirée* [*Ménage*, 1986]. Almost as large as the print of the film's title, we see at the top of the poster, the hook, "Bitchin' Film!" But good taste no longer seems to be a criterion for doing publicity.

AR: I think, based on what I've heard, that Bertrand Blier wasn't very happy about this promotion. But there was nothing he could do about it. In the film director's contract, it is generally specified that he has no right of veto. You can ask that they show you the publicity, but you can't stop it.

J-DR: So how do you feel about this?

AR: Well, it's pretty complicated. Because if the director had this right, he would be able, in certain cases, to block the release of his film. He could blackmail his producer. You see, that wouldn't be good. So you can always say, "If you're not happy, produce your films yourself." It's stupid to beat up on producers blindly.

J-DR: Did that job ever interest you?

AR: To be a producer? It's a colossal amount of work. It already takes a huge amount of time to take care of the scenario, the actors, the shooting, the editing, et cetera. So if on top of all that, you had, after you left the set, to have dinner with foreign distributors, which happens a lot, and then do your accounting when you got home . . . You'd have to have the courage and taste for it.

J-DR: So you never thought of being a producer, but did you ever want to be an actor?

AR: An actor? Yes, I've done some acting, like everybody else. At eighteen . . . It was more the smell of the stage and the taste for spectacle that attracted me. It wasn't so much the acting itself, but being a member of the troupe. I really didn't have the true vocation. But speaking objectively, I wasn't always bad. The drama of it was that I didn't seem to have the instinct for which button to push. But when I was bad, it was abominable, and I really felt it. Afterwards I'd experience nights of despair and anguish. It was horrible. When you know you're going to have to do a scene, even in a theater course, after 11 a.m. you get into a crazy state. Stage fright takes over. You don't know if it's going to turn out well or badly, and you don't really know what you need to do to make it work. Maybe if I'd found some way of helping myself . . . But no, I don't think I had the temperament for it, in any case.

J-DR: Florence Malraux once said, "Alain an actor? I can't imagine that he'd ever have been good at it. He has neither the qualities nor the defects necessary for it. He's horrified of appearing in public. He's very uneasy if has to stand up and speak into a microphone. He can't stand being in front of a camera. He's never accepted to appear on television because of that. You see, this is not exactly the behavior of a man who was destined to be an actor." So you hate appearing on TV, but have you ever been tempted to work for television?

AR: Working for television comes down to making a film, but four times faster.

J-DR: Yes, but I was thinking about your project for *The Adventures of Harry Dickson* that required a three hour projection, what Americans call a miniseries. Television was the only way you could produce it.

AR: I got some proposals for it, but the budgets were so much lower than film budgets that I wouldn't have been able to pull it off. When I was in America, I proposed a film of *Conan* to a producer. He told me it was madness; that it would never succeed. But he was thinking of it as a low-budget series and I wanted to do a big-budget production. Because that was the only way to attract a large audience. At that time, Spielberg hadn't yet made his first film. If you made a film in fifteen days using painted sets, there's not much chance you're going to attract an audience.

J-DR: So, do you watch TV?

AR: Yes, occasionally. I like productions that are specifically made for TV, but I can't watch movies on television. After half an hour, I lose interest.

J-DR: Godard once said on the Apostrophes program that seeing a film on TV was like looking at a reproduction of a painting in relation to the original.

AR: Yes, Godard once said that when you see a postcard of a painting, you know it's just a postcard. When you watch a film on television, you think you're seeing the film. I really feel strongly that this is unjust. And this eternal conversation you have with people who tell you, "I saw or re-saw such and such a film on TV and I was really disappointed!" Yes, that's really unfortunate. Everyone has had the experience of gathering a few friends to watch a film they like on TV. After about ten minutes, the conversation drowns out the dialogue of the actors. There's just something wrong with it. But curiously, if you project the same film in 16mm or even 9.5mm in front of the same group of friends, they'll be quiet. I think it must be because you do it in darkness. With television you can't do it in total darkness, so your library is part of the scenery.

J-DR: That's a very severe condemnation of television as a way of accessing films.

AR: Take the problem of the ads that interrupt the film, which we would call "salami-slicing." It's terrible. But "salami-slicing" also happens when the telephone rings. Do you not answer if you're watching a film? So "salami-slicing" already existed with or without advertising. From the moment you accept that films should be shown on television, the rest . . .

J-DR: Can't you refuse to allow it for your films?

AR: Absolutely not! No contract gives this power to the director. And yet, for promotion that could be a good tactic: "The film that you'll never get to see on television!" That could be pretty shocking. Know what? I'm going to suggest it for *Mélo*. On second thought, since I'm financed by television . . . Antenne 2 has very graciously agreed to co-produce the film.

J-DR: And doesn't that happen more and more often?

AR: Yes, you have to begin by buying back the rights to your film. There's a chance they'd accept. But television is going to change. Some day things will be different. The conditions of reception, the size of the screens, the quality of the images and colors, the three-dimensionality, all the channels in the world. It's going to change everything.

J-DR: So you're predicting a revolution in this domain. When do you think it will happen? In ten years? In fifty years?

AR: There's a proverb—Chinese I think—that says, "You should never try to foresee anything, especially the future." But still, I have the impression that this spectacle made of sounds and images that is already being transformed before our eyes will evolve much more. Maybe the cinema is just one state in this transition.

Holograms, for example, if we master the science, could change everything. No, these are things that couldn't happen in ten years. It'll take half a century. We can imagine that in fifty years, apartments will have an entire wall dedicated to spectacles and audiovisual news. In this case the equilibrium wouldn't be the same as it is today.

J-DR: Will there still be movie theaters? Maybe not . . .

AR: We have to be careful not to have a negative attitude about this. For instance, when they began to record music, it was predicted that these recordings would put an end to live concerts. They also said that the cinema, when the talkies came in, would kill the theater. And, of course, they said that television meant the death of the cinema. But that's not what's happened. All these things manage to coexist for better or for worse. But it *is* true that television killed movie newsreels. It was the end of the filmed press.

J-DR: Natural selection?

AR: I don't know, but I'm amused by the sentimental use of the idea of ecology that reflects a very cruel equilibrium. Especially when you think of the insect world. So it remains to be seen whether the cinema, scarcely emerged from its chrysalis, is going to be swallowed up by television.

J-DR: Let's go back to the most determining point of impact for a career that has been constructed out of exceptions. Of every film Alain Resnais makes, you always want to say that it's exceptional. Every time a new title is announced, there's always a critic who will say, "This time it's really different!" But with the advantage of hindsight, we can make a fairer assessment. If, in some ways, one of your films seems, dare I say, more "exceptional" that the others, it would be *Last Year at Marienbad*. After the success of *Hiroshima mon amour*, the film was a lightning bolt in the world cinema. Twenty-five years later, this bold strike seems to have a patina of classicism. Today it has all the inalterable elegance of a painting by Magritte. A lot has been written about *Marienbad*. Indeed, each time one of your films is released, you see two opposing schools of critics, and beyond them, of spectators: those who say, "This one was different from anything Resnais has done so far." And those who affirm that, beneath genuinely new aspects, there reappear the major themes that animate you. How do you explain this contradiction which happened so early in your career, opposing *Marienbad* to *Hiroshima*, *Muriel* to *Marienbad*, *La Guerre est finie* to everything that preceded it, and so on. We can predict that *Mélo* is not going to escape from this pattern.

AR: I'm not looking for continuity. At least not consciously. Unconsciously, I can't say. I don't feel under any obligation to be an auteur, and I have only one fear, that of repeating myself.

J-DR: Don't you think that we all harbor fundamental motives in us that act no matter what we do or think?

AR: I can't answer this question, but something necessarily happens once we begin work on the screenplay, not under my direction—it would be pretentious to say that—but in close collaboration with the author. Moreover, this method is absolutely the classical one in America, and in England. Screenplay writers and directors get together for several days. It's often exhausting. In Los Angeles, there are even special apartment buildings specially fitted out for such meetings. With a table furnished with paper and pencils, couches for relaxing from time to time . . . After *Marienbad*, which was the translation, 100 percent, of emotion and the imagination, notions that are obviously important in our daily lives, it's true that it was exciting to do just the opposite in *Muriel ou le temps d'un retour*. To listen and watch the characters without ever penetrating into their thoughts. That's what Jean Cayrol and I were attempting to do.

J-DR: It's also clear that you wanted to renew the technical language of film.

AR: What was fun, after the great enveloping sensual movements—I hope!— of *Marienbad*, was to make a film in which there wasn't a single tracking shot or a change of position of the camera.

J-DR: Do you make changes in rhythm and tone only because it's fun, or are there other motivations?

AR: I'm not sure. It's just a need to try something new. But it can cause problems. I remember that the American distributor wanted to launch *Muriel* as a kind of sequel to *Marienbad*. To announce this film, which would be even more mysterious, he used photos of the characters in *Muriel*, and Photoshopped them into the scenery of *Marienbad* with a pink and blue background. So the American critics naturally thought that the characters in *Muriel* were imaginary . . . What a catastrophe! I think the film lasted only five days in New York. Less than a week in any case. A colossal flop!

J-DR: Well, maybe its failure was also because it treated problems that New Yorkers couldn't identify with.

AR: They have what they call "cult films" there. And I've been told that there's an association of the friends of *Muriel* that was created at one the universities there. So, some people at least were very touched by the film. But the launch of the film was botched. It's complicated, but it's a detail.

J-DR: If you look at your career in directing all these films that you feel are quite different, one from the next, viewed from another perspective, the ensemble of characters and the tonalities that you wanted to be different give the sense of being composed in the manner of several of your films, that is, of parallel stories and themes, advancing at uneven speeds but converging on a common horizon, or goal.

AR: Perhaps, but that isn't planned or intentional. What interests me is with each film to try a different way of telling a story. This time, with *Mélo*, I devised a completely linear story. I had fun elaborating a story that makes a single line, as though the pen never left the paper.

J-DR: Indeed, you didn't modify either the structure or the dialogues.

AR: Exactly. What I wanted to do was to bare the spinal column, the dramatic backbone.

J-DR: So is that why you had a curtain painted red that made brief appearances at the essential turning points.

AR: Yes, to give a sense of rhythm. Moreover, this curtain undergoes two changes in form to match the dramatic line of the film. I wonder if we shouldn't add some subtitles—"Three months later . . ." "Three years later . . ."—so that the audience would understand.

J-DR: Like in the silent films . . .

AR: You're not saying that to upset me . . .

J-DR: But isn't it sufficiently explicit as is? They say it in the dialogue.

AR: Yes, but does the audience pay attention?

J-DR: I think it's a film people pay attention to.

AR: I was so moved by this theater. Bernstein's reputation for being unplayable is solidly established. I've never met anyone who claimed the opposite. Except, perhaps, Jean Grauault. He brought me back from Italy a beautifully bound volume containing Bernstein's plays from his youth. There were several I'd never read. Thanks to him I was able to fill in the gaps in my reading of Bernstein.

J-DR: And beyond the challenge of his plays?

AR: I wanted to bring out Bernstein's musicality, his way of constructing characters and watching them evolve. His work is very comparable to that of a musician in his way of choosing a motif, of repeating it, inverting it, playing it backwards, developing it and contracting it. This is all very characteristic of his work. And yet Bernstein had no musical training. It makes you think that the movements that composers use must be profoundly ingrained in our brains. Even if you modify things as important as the laws of tonality, the laws of general construction are revealed in another way. In Bernstein's work, it's very impressive. That is, by the way, why I didn't put any music in *Mélo*. It's my first film without music.

J-DR: Except for the sonatas of Brahms and Bach.

AR: Yes, but those are quotations, it's not music that accompanies the images.

J-DR: So that accentuates the musicality of the dialogues.

AR: Yes, at least that's what I wanted. I don't know how it's received by the audience. As for me, I feel these rhythms are very interesting, but grammatically, maybe it's not impeccable.

J-DR: What struck me, in addition to the desired and intentional theatricality, it is, on the one hand, an affirmation of the time, with no ambiguity either in the scenery or in the language, all the while trying to avoid seeming to be a reconstitution of the times. On the other hand, we have a very strong sense of modernity. By which I mean that the characters and the feelings are very contemporary in their depth. Nothing that excites our emotions seems outdated.

AR: That's very interesting what you're saying. Because I've heard no echo, no reaction, other than that the *attaché de presse* and the producer tell me that the people who come to see the film are very happy and cry copiously. But I've heard nothing precise.

J-DR: Is this an experiment that you'd like to push further?

AR: I don't know. I think that when we started out on this adventure, I had developed a hatred of the adaptations of plays that the French cinema had often displayed. I would always leave the theater all steamed up. So, in this case, I finally made the film that I would have wanted to see before the war. In a word, I would have wanted to see *Mélo* like that.

J-DR: You mean an entirely faithful rendition?

AR: Yes, but the word "faithful" has a pejorative meaning for me. This is funny! Someone said to me, "You're so interested in the actors' performances that you've basically turned your back on mise en scène. I hope it isn't so obvious to the audience!

J-DR: There's another element of cinematic syntax that has practically disappeared, but that you've renewed in this film: lap dissolves. Are you satisfied with the way they work?

AR: Yes, in and of themselves. But the shots that follow suffer from their use. You know, in a general way, there's been a fantastic degradation in the technical quality of films there are in theaters these days. It comes from the need to make numerous copies. It has jumped from eighty to eight hundred copies. They used to be content to make about thirty copies from the original negative. Now they make about ten, and the rest are countertypes. The American films we received in France are often of deplorable quality. I don't know if you've seen Scorsese's *After Hours*, but it's shameful to show such things. The image is completely unstable. The first reel looks overexposed. That certainly isn't the cameraman's fault. They just say that it's good enough for Europe . . . That kind of thing is very serious and turns people off to the cinema. A beautiful copy is a dream. It was easier to obtain good copies in black-and-white, but color complicates everything.

J-DR: Let's go back to theatricality.

AR: I was speaking recently with Marin Karmitz, my producer who, as you know, is also a director. We were wondering—and you'd need time to verify this—if a large percentage of our favorite films weren't originally plays. More or less adapted, of course. Instead of seeing the two genres as completely separate, we realized that they have the same roots. Let's not forget that Lubitsch, now recognized as an inspired director, was entirely neglected for twenty or thirty years. There weren't many of us who admired his work. Now everyone says, "Ah! Lubitsch, he's wonderful . . ." But the majority of Lubitsch's films are adaptations, often very faithful, of plays. There's no question of his theatricality. But don't get me wrong, I'm not comparing myself to him.

J-DR: It seems to me that, beyond the question of the theatricality that you have enjoyed and employed in *Mélo*, you've come back to the themes of love and death that are dear to you.

AR: Well, there's certainly the theme of separation. But that's something you find in almost all films. Roland Barthes once remarked—I should find the exact quote—something like this: "What Satan created both love and death at the same time?"

J-DR: This seems to be very fundamental in your work.

AR: But it's fundamental in everyone's work. I don't know if there are thirty-two dramatic situations, but if there are three, this enters into all three.

J-DR: Even so, I have the impression that meetings in your films are always followed by separation.

AR: I don't know if "separation" is the right word. But I believe that man's dream is that his passions last for a hundred years. It doesn't seem as though things work out that way most of the time.

J-DR: Do the adjectives "optimistic" and "pessimistic" have a special meaning for you?

AR: Not really, no. From the moment you know you are going to die, that sickness has entered your body and will destroy you, your life can be happy only as long as one manages to forget the sickness. There are several ways you can succeed at this, but a lucid man cannot detach himself from this tragedy. Indeed, the only way to defeat this tragic sense of life is to understand that the fact that everything is limited and passing and ephemeral gives extraordinary force to our passions. This attitude also allows us to tolerate some pains. This is, of course, an infinite subject of reflexion, that men have debated for millions of years, or at the very least, for the last six thousand.

J-DR: Alain Renais's cinema—an example of coherence if there ever was one—is never inhabited by any god. His films are those of a man who has no response to the fundamental mystery of existence. An unbeliever—as he puts it—in any great organizer.

AR: Very early on, I had the feeling that, since the human brain is incapable of conceiving or apprehending the unknown, he invented dreams to reassure himself. On the personal level, faith might be able to bring happiness, but its consequences when applied to humanity as a whole seem, most of the time, to be negative. Faith has often served to justify the worst actions against those who don't share it. Actions produced by. . . . good faith.

J-DR: There is a comedian of the black humor variety, Pierre Desproges, who entitled one of his books *Let's Be Happy as We Wait for Death*. It seems to me that the most dramatic thing about the tragedy of our immutable destiny is man's awful tendency to ruin life's pleasures.

AR: That's the entire problem of the depressive state. In my own way, I incarnate a sort of Bouvard et Pecuchet Incorporated! We know that our moods depend entirely on the clinical phenomena that are going on in our brains. If one had a sufficiently intense power of concentration, one could activate endomorphines—is that right?—that are inside us that would permit us to master our thoughts sufficiently to forget the larger tragedy and to focus our passions on very precise little problems, such as driving a nail straight or painting the Sistine Chapel. I know our brain possesses the faculty—is slave to it?—that, once we've begun something, we have a hard time not pursuing it to the end. I think that's called Fechner's law. If you begin to repair a faucet, you run the risk of not being able to tear yourself away from this work even it you have to spend an entire night at it. You end up canceling meetings and obligations of all sorts in order to continue this work. I think that's what happens when one devotes oneself to a work of art.

J-DR: Perhaps this impulse is reinforced in your case by a sense of responsibility you feel towards other people.

AR: Yes, that's what happens in the cinema. You have to go all out to the end, and you make the effort because others ask you to do it. I suppose that when you're a writer it's different. I remember having begun a play about Katherine Mansfield when I was sixteen. I never finished it: no one was waiting for it.

J-DR: When one looks back over your career, Alain Resnais, one has, at first glance, the impression that a great many of your projects capsized in mid-stream, sometimes when they were very near completion. As for example, *The Adventures of Harry Dickson*, based on a scenario of Frederic de Towarnicki, after a serial novel by Jean Ray.

AR: Well, there were some projects that were stillborn but not an enormous number. If you compare my career with that of Joseph Losey—though there isn't a huge comparison to be made—you notice that the director of *The Servant* had a total of something like thirty or forty aborted projects. *Harry Dickson* remained viable for a long time mostly because the producer, Anatole Dauman, whose idea it was, didn't want to give up on the idea until he'd exhausted every possible solution. I was more ambivalent, since I had the impression we were going to build something based on material already written. That bothered me a lot. But Anatole Dauman was very persuasive. I hadn't really followed all of the stories, but the film was to have been a kind of huge melting pot, a documentary on the life of the great imaginary detective of popular Belgian novels. In the beginning, the idea was to make a three- or three-and-a half-hour-long film to combat the growing power of television. But *Lawrence of Arabia* having failed, the tendency was reversed and the keyword is now not to go over an hour and a half. So the project ended up no longer being viable.

We tried writing another, shorter version that would involve Dirk Bogarde. Bogarde would have lent the character a really disturbing and exciting aspect. Using him would have been very, very interesting. Bogarde told me immediately, "I'm your man without the slightest hesitation, but you'll discover that because of me you won't get the film off the ground." And, indeed, as soon as we mentioned his name to the producers, we discovered he was "box-office poison."

J-DR: Sometimes an apparently fruitless activity can turn out to be worthwhile. Without the failure of the *Harry Dickson* project, Alain Resnais wouldn't have thought of Dirk Bogarde for the role of Claude Langham in *Providence*. This theme of the happy consequences of failure recalls another memory: After the failure of *Je t'aime, je t'aime*, that had the "good fortune" to be obscured by the events of May 1968 in Paris. Even if people had wanted to go to the movies at such a moment, they would have had to scale the barricades to try to get into the Salle des Ursulines, in the middle of the Latin Quarter. After this long tumultuous parenthesis, silence.

AR: I didn't receive any proposals of any kind. Nothing. I went for two weeks to New York. There I received some offers. So I stayed almost two years, from 1969–1971 to work on several projects that never panned out. But during this time, I was paid, because the Americans pay for the writing of scenarios. It's a very healthy system. And then afterwards the difficulties start. "No we can't do it because it's too expensive, or because of the weather, of the shooting site, because of the unions that force us to use their services and their prices, because of this, because of that." But ultimately it was an adventure. And I'm sure that this stay in America allowed me to be completely at ease in *Providence*. I certainly wouldn't have ever dared do a film entirely in English without this period in the States. So, you see, I have no regrets.

J-DR: When critics talk about Alain Resnais, they often define him as *the* filmmaker of memory. On the occasion of a showing of *Providence* nearly ten years after its release, Henri-François Rey wrote an article in *Le Figaro* entitled "Resnais, the Artist of Memory." After having stated that ordinarily, the cinema loves to play with time, that it breaks "into pieces that are then carefully glued back together," he states, "Resnais disdains this procedure, he doesn't break up time, he smashes it to pieces." In this critic's mind, this "smashing" seemed to be a compliment, given that the article ended with this sentence: "No one has ever gone so far in his examination of the relationship between time, creation, reality, and appearance." What do you think of this idea?

AR: I wouldn't argue with this reference to memory, but I find that you could include all films, all songs, probably even all paintings, all music and I don't know what all else as an expression of memory. What I mean is that this isn't limited to my work.

J-DR: Yes, but the way you manipulate time in your own particular way, by confusing chronology, focusing on its most destructive effects on your characters, on their consciousness and the environment, memory plays a particularly acute role.

AR: But rather than memory, I'd say the imagination, since we are all unconsciously navigating between what has happened, what will happen, what could happen; without thinking too much about the differences between them.

J-DR: In *Providence*, for example, it would seem that time exercises a pressure and displays a rough unevenness that determine the thoughts of Clive Langham and condition his imagination. Are you yourself personally sensitive to the flow of time?

AR: Well, since I'm always anxious to accomplish lots of things, I find that there's never enough hours in a day. Yes, I would like to learn, to do, to enjoy everything there is to learn, do and enjoy, and it upsets me that time just continues to fly by. I'm also disturbed by time's inherent degradation. It's unfortunate. Cats seem to be able to escape this problem. They have a relatively short life, but don't seem to submit as much as we do to the destructive effects of age . . . But I'm not the only one who's preoccupied by time. In Guitry's work, the theme recurs in every one of his plays, even back when he was twenty years old. It's very present in Beckett's work as well. That may be the first time that I've ever associated Guitry and Beckett, but both of them want to make you laugh. That's important too.

J-DR: So, to recapitulate, you prefer the imagination but you don't refuse the notion of memory?

AR: I don't refuse it. I just don't think it belongs specifically to me. If you're telling me that I'm trying to make films in which various stories intersect, and that I use editing to give structure and rhythm to this theme, then yes, it's true. I remember a very dear old friend who had no use for the cinema. He loved literature and theater, but he considered me a dabbler, who spent my time in dark movie theaters. One evening, in the metro, he suddenly blurted out: "It's not an art, your cinema! The camera records, and you're standing behind it doing nothing. The product produces itself!" Once my provocative friend had left, I was left feeling at a total loss, but then I said to myself, "Okay, let's suppose that I could have no effect on the image. But I can have an effect on the succession of images and of sequences, and that changes everything! It's from this specific aspect of film that we can speak of the specificity of the art—a word we didn't use back then. But if this work has consumed my interest for the better part of forty years, it's not just because it has given me a lot of pleasure personally, but because I imagined that it captivated my audiences, that I could move people and that they'd be more eager to remain in their seats."

J-DR: Since we're talking about prejudices and false conceptions, what other label have people generally given you that you reject?

AR: I think the most tenacious misunderstanding that's haunted my work concerns the literary influences that are said to have governed my work, and the choice of screenplay authors according to their success as novelists. First of all, people who claim this forget one very simple thing: that I began by finding producers, just as Chabrol had done before me, who had their own screenplay writers. But after that, I tried to find screenwriters who had not done films before. It seemed like a good way to renew the cinema.

J-DR: And it seems that a good number of them ended up becoming filmmakers themselves.

AR: Yes, that proves that it wasn't uniquely novelists that I was looking for. Indeed, if I was lucky enough to convince Marguerite Duras to write for me, it wasn't only because I liked what she'd written, but because I'd seen *Le Square* at the Mathurins Theater and been very struck by its sonority.

J-DR: And what about Robbe-Grillet?

AR: Same thing. I was looking for a particular sonority. Robbe-Grillet's language is magnificent and haunting. It's truly musical. I think there are about forty minutes of dialogue in *Marienbad*. It could almost be sung. It's like the libretto of an opera with very beautiful and simple words that the characters keep repeating.

J-DR: Is it merely accidental that you display throughout your work a defense of humanistic values against oppression. I'm thinking of *Guernica, La Guerre est finie, Nuit et brouillard* (*Night and Fog*), and *Hiroshima* . . .

AR: Yes, it is among other aspects of my work, purely by chance. Pierre Braumberger asked me to make some short films, it wasn't me who asked him. Perhaps there are other reasons? Inevitably, we have tastes and distastes that simply influence us. Let's say that I never set out to organize things this way. I let myself be carried along like the proverbial cork on the crest of a wave. That's not very laudable, is it . . .

J-DR: Throughout your work, there seem to be negative characters. Perhaps it would be more nuanced to say that they doubt . . . They're tormented, they hesitate to act.

AR: Yes, I think I have a lot of trouble showing heroes whom one would label positive. That would seem to me to be disloyal. Since, in the screenplays I shoot, there are scenes that I ask the writer to redo several times, so it's possible that some part of my tastes do end up penetrating into the scenario.

J-DR: Aren't what you call "your tastes" more deeply grounded in you? I read a declaration you'd written years before you made *Mon Oncle d'Amérique*, well before your first encounter with Laborit. I was struck by the fact that you were already interested in the psychological motivations of behavior.

AR: Ok, yes, you're right! I'm laughing because as recently as yesterday I was listening to a tape recording from 1971 of Stan Lee, with whom I almost made a film—a very good memory.[1] On this tape, Stan Lee was summing up our preceding conversation. "So," Alain said, "we could establish parallels between the way certain animals and certain characters act, and we could edit these parallels into the film." And I said to myself, "That's funny! It's *Mon Oncle d'Amérique!*" This idea was not kept in the scenario we wrote, but it certainly corresponds to an obsession that I had.

J-DR: And you weren't aware of it at the time?

AR: I think it's better not to know such things. I'm not pressed like that to say to myself, I must write such and such a scenario. Once a psychiatrist told me that the fact that I didn't write my own scenarios was a flight from reality. I answered: "No, no! Why suffer for three or four years like that? It doesn't interest me." And also, it's sad when one is alone.

J-DR: Coming back to your work: do you always rehearse scenes before shooting them?

AR: Yes, always, but sometimes in a somewhat disorganized way. There are some production directors who don't like having rehearsals since they claim it's a waste of time and money—extra hotel stays, for example. They think that if one is a good actor, the talent ought to come out in the first try. If not, they're not worth their salt.

J-DR: So what do you think?

AR: I don't think that's true. Not at all. But obviously it depends on the kind of film you're doing. I'm not in favor of the method of rehearsing something thirty times and then doing the shoot. That's awful. Rehearse two weeks, stop for two weeks and then do the shoot, that's the way I like to work. What the actors have digested is the important thing.

J-DR: There are other methods.

AR: Of course! Godard would give the actors their script thirty seconds before they began the shoot, so that's pretty awesome as well. He didn't think there was anything to be gained by rehearsing. The essential thing, I believe, is to have a consistent method throughout the film. Of course, afterwards, one can modify it.

J-DR: Would you be interested in shooting an opera!

AR: Of course. But every director will tell you the same thing. It's a dream. Moreover, you'd have to have an opera specially written for the occasion, following the process that I've used to construct all of my films.

J-DR: That would be much more difficult.

AR: Yes, but Jacques Demy has already done it, so I wouldn't be the first.

J-DR: So you've actually thought about it, not just dreamed about it.

AR: Well, if you don't want your actors singing in front of painted sets, the financial requirements would be considerable for such a limited audience that I don't think it could be done in today's film market.

J-DR: Given the way you choose your screenwriters, and the requisite that they possess the rarest virtues, don't you fear running out of possibilities?

AR: Yes, it could happen. In my view, I've always been in a certain impasse. I look for a particular sonority in my texts and need to work with someone who has a strong personality, a particular style of writing, and who's interested in the theater or the cinema. That's fairly rare.

J-DR: Are you still working with Milan Kundera?

AR: We're going to start up again soon. But I think it's going to take a lot of time.

J-DR: When a film director arrives at his greatest strength as an artist, tranquilly assumes a hegemonic power, controls all of the various currents that are running through the film, as well as the power that is derived from the work, and also the drives that subvert it, he ends up becoming a sort of demiurge. Perhaps this explains why your films bear your indelible mark.

AR: A film director is like a gardener who takes an interest in the growth of the scenario; he never thinks about his personality or his lack thereof.

Note

1. Stan Lee was a well-known author of comic books and he and Resnais had discussed making films of *The Monster Maker* (1970) and *The Inmates* (1971).

Interview with Alain Resnais: On *Mélo*

François Thomas / 1986

From *Positif*, no. 307 (September 1986). Reprinted by permission. Translated by T. Jefferson Kline.

FT: What made you want to make a film of *Mélo*, Henry Bernstein's play?

AR: At the time, I was working with Milan Kundera on a film project. The producers told us that, if we wanted to shoot it, we'd have to do it for under ten million, which isn't very much, since what I'd call a "normal" film usually costs thirty-five to forty million. Kundera and I spent a lot of time cutting things and shortening scenes to try to remain within this budgeted amount, but after a couple of months, we just said, "Enough! We're just going to write the film we want to do and we'll see what happens." The project we ended up with, having done a thirty-page treatment of it, became a film costing thirty-five to forty million. We had no illusions about what we'd done. You can't say that it's impossible to make, but it can only be done in precise circumstances: for example, if a producer suddenly needs to reinvest his recent profits. So you can't count on finding resources within twenty-four hours; you have to figure that it may take twenty months to come up with financing—and even that might be optimistic. I realized that it would be very unhealthy to go three years without work, and I was speaking with Fanny Ardant when she suddenly said, "Why don't you stage a play with us?" And I answered that I'd be interested only if we were writing the play, but she insisted: "No, no! Let's do a play by Henry Bernstein. You're always talking about his work, but no one knows much about it and it would be an excellent opportunity to get to know it better." So, I reread Bernstein, and I was struck by the fact that, the minute I opened any of his plays, I was captivated and had to read the whole thing in one sitting. And since everyone agrees that his plays are impossible to stage, I thought it would be interesting to take the risk, to see if we could produce one. I had trouble choosing between *Le Venin* and *Mélo*, and ultimately chose the latter. Curiously, we found ourselves with the four actors who'd just done *L'Amour à mort* with me. But the idea of producing a play suddenly seemed very solemn and, in addition, the actors we wanted weren't available since they were all already playing on other shows. So we would have had to wait for months, but the enterprise would have interested me only if we could have started right away, so that my work with Kundera wouldn't be delayed. So I explained to my friend and agent, Jean-Louis Livi, that, after considering the possibility of putting on a play, I'd decided against it. I laughingly added that if we filmed it, it would have been possible to do since the actors would be free to work afternoons, but that evidently it wasn't going to happen since we'd never find a producer who'd agree to film a play by Bernstein. Jean-Louis Livi then said, "Give me twenty-four hours." The next morning he called and said, "I've got a producer: Marin Karmitz wants to do it, and can start right away! He doesn't need to wait for financing or an advance on box-office receipts or even a co-producer." "But" I replied, "I want to be done by Christmas and it's already July." "No problem," said Livi, "he's OK with that and likes the project." So I met Karmitz and we hit if off immediately. And suddenly I was trapped in this project that I'd proposed as a whim, and yet was very happy to be doing it!

I have to add that the other miracle that allowed the film to be made was that Henry Bernstein's daughter, Georges Gruber, lent us her support right from the beginning and, in a sense, joined our enterprise.

FT: So the challenge of *Mélo* was that you had to shoot the film very quickly?

AR: Well, the greater challenge was to realize that this type of project could only appeal to a small number of spectators—let's say, about one hundred twenty thousand in Paris—and, given that number, we could only allow a budget of about seven million yet not have that small a budget impair our work. Karmitz was able to focus his input on this problem and we decided that we could manage the film if we calculated a maximum of twenty days in the studio—since both Marin and I wanted to use a studio. If we'd been forced to use natural decors, I don't think I would have been interested. It would have taken forty days and cost twice as much. My average output per day (which has never varied) is one minute, forty-seven seconds of film, and we realized that at that rate we could never do a film lasting an hour and forty-five minutes in only twenty days of shooting. So we had to do longer takes, that often got up to four or five minutes, and there was even one that lasted nine minutes during Marcel Blanc's story at the beginning of the film. Well, I have to confess that we went past our limit and took twenty-three days. The two scenes that were taken outside the studio (the Seine and the café, which would have been too expensive to reconstitute) took us nearly two days just by themselves.

FT: You've said that you wouldn't want to adapt a novel or an opera into a film. Why doesn't this reticence apply as severely to a stage play?

AR: Well, I would be interested in creating an opera on film, but the idea of filming an opera that already exists doesn't excite me. But I don't make an absolute distinction between film and theater; I refuse to think of them as inimical. I've always rejected the opposition between theater and film, and even between music hall and film; for me, as I've often said, there's just the idea of entertainment. It seems very important to me that my screenwriters be passionate about the theater even if they've written novels. After all, I discovered Marguerite Duras through her play *The Square* when it was presented at the Mathurins Theater. The novelist follows very different rules from the screenwriter or the playwright, and exercises a very different discipline. Moreover, I think that it's much more difficult to write a screenplay or a play than a novel. In the theater as in film, the author knows that he can rely only on the words of the dialogue to keep his storyline going, and he's constantly forced to take into account this other character, who's right in front of him—the spectator—and manage to hypnotize him, to prevent him from leaving the theater.

FT: Had you seen the play, or at least the films that were adapted from it?

AR: In 1929, I was too young to see the play. You mustn't forget that I lived in Brittany, and that the only time I spent in Paris consisted of a week at Christmas and a week at Easter. And it wasn't a play for children. People today can't imagine how strict the education was back then. Young people were protected from "bad influences." Naturally I wanted to see Paul Czinner's film [in 1933], but my family thought it was much too immoral, and I was not allowed to go see it. So I could joke that I made this film for two reasons: first because, not having seen the play, one of the only ways to be able to see it would be for my actors to play it for me: and then because, just as they were before the war, the adaptations of Bernstein's plays that I was able to see struck me as so absolutely off-target that I left the theater in such a state of violent fury (I was very sectarian and very intolerant in my tastes in movies) that I wanted to offer myself the adaptation I would have wanted to see before the war.

FT: You often say that you undertake each new film as the contrary of the preceding one. In what ways might *Mélo* be the opposite of *L'Amour à mort*?

AR: Well, it's the exception to the pattern. There's more continuity than opposition. At one point, I even remember saying that I couldn't shoot *Mélo* since there were too many things that resembled *L'Amour à mort*, but my four actors argued that such a reaction was silly and anyway everyone would have forgotten the other film. Pierre Arditi would have a headache again and that would be it. Ultimately, maybe that was what was funny. They easily persuaded me and I have to insist on the fact that *Mélo* was created by their association with the film and according to their wishes.

FT: Certain of the lines in *Mélo* ("What I fear about death is separation from you") could have been directly taken from *L'Amour à mort*.

AR: We couldn't avoid it. It was pure coincidence, but it amused us a lot. Once we had started the shooting, we didn't think about it anymore. On the other hand, we stopped two or three times and said, "Oh no! We can't do that shot, we'd be starting *L'Amour à mort* all over again!" That said, *Mélo* is the opposite, from the point of view of the way the dialogues are done, since the work we did with Gruault in *L'Amour à mort* was precisely to take out all the adjectives and anything we felt was superfluous. In order to leave as much space for Henze's music, we wanted a dialogue with a minimum of words, a minimum of syntactical ornamentation. When we were editing the scenes, we kept saying, "We're going to Webernize this!" So it was very different from the dialogues in the Bernstein.

FT: At the beginning of *Mélo*, Pierre Belcroix alludes to Marcel Blanc's valet, whose name is Zambeaux. This name figures in several of your films, beginning with *Muriel*.

AR: The name Zambeaux figures in the play, and can be found in all of Bernstein's plays. Zambeaux is a fetish name that Bernstein used in all of his plays to bring him luck! There was always a character named Zambeaux or Zambo but who generally didn't appear on stage. I don't know why I used it—maybe to bring me luck—but anyway I used the name in certain of my films. It's a private gag that's not meant to trouble the viewer, and which got Pierre Arditi and me laughing, and I said, "Pierre, if they'd told us when you were playing Zambeaux in *Mon Oncle d'Amérique* that one day you'd find yourself acting in a play by Bernstein, and with me, we would have been pretty surprised!" I'd forgotten that Zambeaux was already in *Muriel, ou le temps d'un retour*, but I do remember that I'd used it in what I persist in calling *Biarritz-Bonheur* (I never accepted the title *Stavisky*...) because I wanted to see how Charles Boyer would react. In the sequence where you see the actors auditioning, I stood where I could get a good view of Boyer's face when he heard them call, "Mademoiselle Zambeaux, please!" I wanted to see if that would jog his memory, since he'd acted in so many plays by Bernstein and, indeed, he was greatly amused. It was a purely personal pleasure, which allowed me to have a long conversation with Boyer. Bernstein and he had been great friends. Bernstein wrote *Mélo* especially for actors that he knew (Gaby Morlay, Boyer, and Pierre Blanchar), and it's certain that he used in his plays moral characteristics, personal memories, or even favorite phrases that his actors used in real life. It seems to me that *Mélo* put in Marcel Blanc's mouth phrases that Boyer himself tended to use, since, when we were shooting *Stavisky*... I heard him repeat them.

FT: When you were working on *Mélo*, did you have your actors or technicians look at films from that era?

AR: Yes, we had about a dozen films shown for us at the Cinémathèque and at the Film Archives at Bois d'Arcy, which were both very cooperative. Each of the actors and technicians was able to see at least half of these films, some because of the acting, some because of the theme, and others because of the period. We saw Charles Boyer, Pierre-Richard Willm, André Lefaur, Victor Boucher . . . One day André Dussollier asked me a bit anxiously, "But Alain, you're not going to ask me to play like that!?" I reassured him. We absolutely did not want to imitate, or be inspired by them, but to be aware of what we didn't like in certain kinds of adaptations or screenplays. We also watched Sacha Guitry's *My Father Was Right*, to show that, at that time, there were lots of films that were not embarrassed to show their theatrical roots. Another key film we screened was *Les Parents terribles*, since Cocteau was one of the first directors who didn't try to make his viewers believe that the film wasn't a stage play. (Of course, Guitry and Pagnol are the two other masters in this domain.) During that era, a considerable number of films were based on plays and, in general, the directors tried to disguise this by "airing out" their films (by filming some scenes in the garden or in the street or on a boat); and especially by rewriting—I'm tempted to say by sweetening up—the dialogue, and adhering to good taste. I'm terrified of good taste.

FT: Did the technicians attend the rehearsals of *Mélo* before the shooting?

AR: I always try—when the actors are free, which is rarely the case—to have them rehearse the essential parts of the film and whenever possible on set. When the actors are doing other films and can't arrive until the last minute, I have to content myself with individual readings. For *L'Amour à mort*, we had three days of real rehearsals that allowed us to do a lot of things. But this time, it was much more systematic, given, on the one hand, the nature of the subject, and on the other, the challenge of trying to shoot a film in twenty days. Marin Karmitz provided us a studio in Boulogne, a large windowless room where we could install projectors and rehearse for several weeks, bringing in all the props we needed and then taking photos that we could discuss. And then we rehearsed using Jacques Saulnier's sets. And during the last week, we had the cameraman, Charlie Van Damme, and the framer, Gilbert Duhalde, who worked with the actors, mingling with them on the set. That must have been a bizarre ballet, since the three technicians were dancing around amongst the actors who, themselves, had their own blocking, while the script girl and her assistants, Sylvette Baudrot and Florence Malraux, were there as spectators.

Sometimes, during these rehearsals, I would say to Gilbert Duhalde that a certain camera movement would be too difficult to do: "Given the actors' movements, we can't get everything in a single shot, so I'm going to cut here and then do the splice this way." But he'd reply, "That's a shame. I sense that you don't like that." Ready to abandon the idea, I insisted that we rehearse it another way, but

Duhalde came back to his position: "I think I can manage this, let me give it a try!" This was the kind of challenge we'd throw back and forth, and it was extremely stimulating. We always had a choice: either we'd do things perfectly, taking no risks on the lighting, framing, or acting, or else we'd let the actors' emotions take over and accept the fact that for a second or two there might be some technical imperfections. We adopted the same policy for the sound with Henri Morelle: we preferred small imperfections to "the right way."

FT: Did you shoot in continuity?

AR: Thanks to Marin Karmitz, we were lucky enough to have all the sets ready at the same time. So the film was shot 80 percent in continuity, which is amazing, given that the actors weren't always available at the right moment.

FT: Did the actors play in different registers from one take to the next?

AR: At the outset, we were committed to doing only one take. The risk that all of the actors had agreed to take was to continue, even if they made a mistake in the text, so that we could do just one take. But then we realized we had enough time to do three or four takes and sometimes even five, not so many fewer than we'd do in an ordinary film. So we were able to try variations, especially in intensity. Once the take is done, it serves as a springboard for the actors' imaginations, and there's electricity in the air that allows them to suggest other approaches. Then we do a second take right on the spot.

FR: Was it André Delvaux's *Benvenuta* that drew your attention to the chief operator Charlie Van Damme?

AR: *Benvenuta* is a film whose photography really struck me. When I spoke to Fanny Ardant, she told me she considered him a passionate technician, who worked extremely well with the actors. I attach a lot of importance to the relations between the cameraman and the rest of the team. Charlie Van Damme and I had been promising to work together for several years and now we'd have the chance to do so.

FT: You use a lot of lighting changes during the shoot that obscure the décor and isolate the characters.

AR: The decision I arrived at with Charlie Van Damme was that the light sources never be justified by lamps or windows on the set, and that they exist purely as pieces of the dramatic composition. The great rule of cameramen (though it depends on whom you're talking about, obviously) is that the light source should always be justified by a visible origin. So I try to break this rule every chance I get and to change light sources in the middle of a sequence. In *L'Amour à mort*, the natural sources are systematically undone right from the beginning. Given that in *Mélo* there were very long takes, we were led to modify the lighting according to the placement of the characters in the space, I want to say in the scenery. There was a play of electronic organs and a large number of rheostats that the lighting people were operating during the take, and these variations gave the impression of descending a slalom: given the little time we had and the emotionality of the roles, we wondered if the actors were going to arrive in their places at the right time . . . the engineer's task was complicated not only because the different positions of the camera created different shadows, but also because the boom operator also had to juggle his work with all of these lighting changes within a single take.

FT: The poisoning attempt is handled very discreetly.

AR: I didn't want to emphasize it but I think the viewers understand what's happening. You mustn't forget that Romaine is extremely ambivalent; by that I mean that she's not doing this for pleasure. You could even say that if Romaine attempts to poison Pierre Belcroix, it's also to spare him from the suffering and torture caused by their separation, which might well be more intolerable than death. Her motivations are very ambiguous. But I think that the moment that she does it is clear for the viewer, as well as the moment when she decides not to do it.

FT: What's more, at that moment, you have recourse to an acoustic effect that's almost musical and that seems to prolong the sound of the piano cover as Pierre Belcroix drops it over the keys.

AR: For me that acoustic effect translates the feeling that one might experience on suddenly coming upon a dead person, a feeling that time has stopped. It's not by chance that popular novelists use this kind of expression: "frozen in terror" since one has the impression that one has become as immobile as a statue. When Romaine hears Pierre Belcroix fall, she believes he's dead, and that she's succeeded in her attempt; there's suddenly a moment when everything is thrown into question. I wanted to give this impression that time had stopped. All we did was to manipulate the sound of the keyboard cover closing as we caught it in the shoot, prolong it, and cut it short at the moment when Romaine begins to speak, since, after all, this acoustic effect belongs to her character's point of view.

FT: That's one of two arbitrary formal effects in the film, the other being this sort of black interval that arises when Pierre reads the letter from Maniche. The camera cuts from Pierre Arditi in a slow pan, changes direction as the light fades, then slips onto the rug and, after a fade to black, pans back up to André Dussollier's face.

AR: I'd say that these two formal effects are, if not arbitrary, at least intentional. It seemed to me that we needed to give the sensation of time stretching or stopping during the reading—the "recitation"—of Maniche's letter. On the other hand, this letter is a bridge, a connection between Marcel Blanc and Pierre Belcroix, these two characters who love the same woman with such intensity—or, rather, who love a woman whom one calls Romaine and the other Maniche. Any shot, no matter how it were done, that seemed to prioritize one or the other of these characters, would have felt awkward, not to say out of place. This is also a way of reintroducing the theme of water, of evoking the darkness of the water in the Seine that engulfs Romaine. I didn't realize at the time that this effect resembles the two "fades to black" in *L'Amour à mort*.

FT: Except that this time you're inviting the viewer to listen to a voice rather than to music.

AR: And yet, this voice is a kind of music for me. What interested me in Bernstein's play was his music, the music of his words.

FT: Indeed, Romaine's suicide brings together, once again, the two colors from *L'Amour à mort*: the screen fades to black and a red curtain appears.

AR: That's totally unexpected, and I hadn't ever noticed it. I could have used a blue curtain, since, though I'm not positive, the curtain at the Gymnase Theater where *Mélo* was created was blue-black or navy. Our curtain was painted by Jean-Michel Nicollet. I didn't want a real curtain, I wanted there to be a hint of the theater without having the impression of being in a real theater. And then, that allowed us to change the form of the curtain as the film advanced.

FT: Since *Je t'aime, je t'aime*, suicide has recurred in almost all of your films: Gérard Départdieu in *Mon Oncle d'Amérique*, Sabine Azéma in *L'Amour à mort* . . .

AR: The actors and the script girl told me about this. Here again, I hadn't noticed it. I don't have the impression that I'm obsessed with this. It's true that it recurs in a lot of films, except in *La Vie est un roman*. I can't help it. I try to do films without thinking too much, I mean by thinking a lot about the form but just letting the plot develop freely.

FT: Did shooting in a studio help you avoid using post-synchronization?

AR: As in *L'Amour à mort*, there are just a few sentences that needed post-synch, and that was entirely because of noise made by the crew: in a rapid shoot, even if you put styrofoam on your shoe soles, you can't always take enough precautions to avoid noise when the actors are moving or when the camera is following them (since there are five or six people behind the camera). Henri Morelle, the sound engineer, had his mixing board and could choose various sources (besides the boom, there were several hidden mikes) as a function of the movement of the actors, which was, in this case, particularly complex given the length of the takes. I never made a principle of using post-synchronization, but I've used it a lot in certain films because it saved a lot of time. It's not really an aesthetic choice but an economic one.

When I shot *Hiroshima mon amour* with Emmanuelle Riva, we began in Tokyo. It was obvious that we'd need post-synch with all of the shots done in the street, but when we went into the studio, there we had a choice. I told Emmanuelle, "We're probably going to keep the sound, so let's just keep that in mind. If we're not happy with something, we can always start over and take another shoot."

She agreed, and so we begin to shoot. And then, the next morning, I go into the studio and I hear a camera motor making a gigantic whirring sound. I go see the engineer and say, "What are we going to do? Do you hear the camera?" "Yes, I sure do!" "But it's really annoying!" "Okay, but there's nothing I can do about it. I put every possible cover over the motor but it's a Bell and Howell and that's normal. But maybe you could use a filter." "If I try to filter out a sound like that, what's going to be left of the voices? I don't know whether it's the medium or the higher register that will be silenced, but there'll be no more emotion." So I had to ask him, "But since you shoot with this camera a lot, what do you normally do?" And the engineer answered, "Well, Japanese actors speak much louder!" So when we started our third day of shooting in the studio, I told Emmanuelle Riva: "So here's our choice: either you project a lot more, which shouldn't be a problem since you've done so much theater, or, you can continue to act as you've done so far, and we'll be obliged to post-synchronize everything because of the camera noise." After a try or two, she told me, "I can't project any louder. There's nothing I can do." And, indeed, we ended up with something that felt artificial. We're getting a bit far away from our point of departure, but I find this anecdote interesting because it contradicts the famous theory according to which a theater actor is so accustomed to the stage that automatically he'll speak too loudly for film. And, indeed, without our having agreed on it, once Emmanuelle Riva felt the presence of the camera, she began to speak in a different way.

In *Marienbad*, we also did a lot of post-synchronization for economic reasons since, in that case, we could save on film stock. I have to add that, at that time, we didn't have magnetic but used only optical sound. It was another set of rules entirely. Since the financial limitations of shooting didn't allow for direct sound that was free of flaws, we used post-synch a lot. That said, it didn't bother me, given the incantatory quality of both of these films, their opera-libretto side, especially in *L'Année dernière à Marienbad* (which was almost recitative). I even thought that it might be better to do the recordings calmly in an auditorium. In *Providence*, I reworked a large part of the sound because we were working in a studio that wasn't sound-proofed, but even in *La Guerre est finie* there was a lot of direct sound. In the last three films, it has practically all the time been direct sound.

FT: *Mélo* is the first film you've done without music, at least without a musical score.

AR: It seemed to me impossible, unless we wanted a lot of redundancy, to add music to a film in which you were already hearing some notes of Bach and Brahms played by the musicians who are characters in the film. It seemed to me that the clash of extra-diegetic music with the music we created diegetically would have been disagreeable and, what's more, since I felt, rightly or wrongly, that there was music in Bernstein's text, that it would make the addition of any complementary music very difficult. I had the impression, without having done any deep analysis of the play, that Bernstein works in a way that wouldn't be considered foreign to the way musical composers work. It's that, by the way, that gives his theater such a powerfully spellbinding charm. I have the impression that you discover in theater the same notions of exposition, development, and diminution, and of the inversion and retrogradation of themes that you find in music. In the first tableau in *Mélo*, there is Marcel Blanc's long exposition of the theme of lying, and the play ends with a final tableau in which the same character will be obliged to use, in a different context to be sure, the very lie that he has earlier condemned. I believe that this is what you call a reversal in music. There is also an ornamentation theme—the red roses—that recurs throughout the play. Or again, the theme of separation—first of Pierre Belcroix-Maniche, then of Marcel Blanc-Romaine—will be reprised with variations. I know that, in working with the actors, we found such themes repeatedly. I haven't done a written analysis of *Mélo*, but I'm pretty sure one could be done.

FT: The Brahms sonata didn't figure in the Bernstein play . . .

AR: Bernstein used a sonata by the Belgian composer, Guillaume Lekeu, doubtless on the advice of the pianist, Jacques Février, his friend, but I couldn't use it. Lekeu is known to a few specialists, but not to the larger public, and I could imagine the reaction of some people who would assume that Lekeu was a name we'd made up.[1] It would have created an awkward moment of uncertainty in the movie theater. What's more, Bernstein could use this sonata during scene changes, but I really didn't want there to be long interruptions between the tableaux. I wanted them to flow immediately from one to the next. I could have used only the very end of the last movement, to open the second tableau. But if I used Lekeu's sonata, these last measures wouldn't correspond to anything, and therefore wouldn't produce any impression: you would hear a series of chords, which, by themselves, might have sounded like a French fire engine in the street and caused some hilarity among the viewers. As if I were doing vaudeville and making fun of this kind of music. But I also have to say that I wasn't very moved by Lekeu's sonata, though maybe that's my fault, since I didn't have very good recordings of his work and no commercial recordings of it existed as far as I knew.

On the other hand, the Brahms sonata is very sentimental and seems to me to work very well with these twenty to twenty-five minutes of connection between Marcel Blanc and Romaine. I could easily imagine that something could have happened between the pianist and the violinist that was extremely sensual. I have to add that there isn't a very large literature of piano-violin duets since it's a combination that's difficult to play. The two instruments don't go together, I would say; they're difficult to combine.

FT: Was the tango by Philippe-Gérard composed for the film?

AR: Yes. I find that there's something very disturbing, even morbid—in the French sense—in the waltz or the tango forms. Maybe Bernstein felt this as well. Philippe-Gérard knew full well at what moment of the Bach sonata for solo violin they would do a lap-dissolve, so he could play with the precise modulation to the foxtrot that begins this next sequence. He knew in advance that the slow tempo would be sacrificed, and remain in the background, but he did me the favor of taking care of this transition. I thought that the music would go by unnoticed here, but I am absolutely delighted that, thanks to Philippe-Gerard's talent, this venomous tango should communicate the anguish of the ending of this scene, that I find very cruel.

FT: When I asked you, at the release of *L'Amour à mort*, how the fades to black were shot, the "particles" as you called them, that accompanied Henze's music, you answered that it was too soon to talk about it.

AR: I didn't want your readers to know about it at the time. Now, two years later, it's not such a big deal. What I was trying to do was to create non-figurative images that wouldn't distract the viewers from listening to the music, and yet that wouldn't make them think that the projector was on the blink, and go complain to the usher about it. I began by thinking about the little particles that you drop in the water in a kind of aquarium, but that felt too much like window-dressing and there was something about it that bothered me. I also thought about electronic solutions, but that posed two problems: on the one hand, given the current state of technology, using electronic video would be quite expensive and bring too much granulation. And on the other, we wouldn't be able to control it very well. What's more, just as in music where I have some difficulty using a synthesizer, it seems to me that there's something too precise when you seek an electronic solution. I wanted to get away from what we see on TV, those terrific titles but that are too perfect. I wanted to maintain in these "particles" a kind of artisanal quality that seemed better suited to the simplicity of the story. I asked the producer, Philippe Dussart, if he'd authorize an addition to the budget. So we used a studio in Boulogne. I can't remember if we painted the walls black, or whether we hung black drapes, but it was one or the other. With our set designer, Jacques Saulnier, we must have tried using plaster and flour, but it was too heavy, so in the end we used a product that produces artificial snow for farces and tricks: you light a wisp of paper, and a kind of smoke starts to rise that gives off little particles. With Sacha Vierny, we lit this device and then walked the camera in among these particles, combining camera movements with zooms. These optical variations created variations of size in the particles. When we printed these takes we saw there were also different colors, and so, of course, we took advantage of that, so that I can't say it was an effect we'd studied. Since the music wasn't written yet, we tried to invent a solution that we could use in one day in the editing room. We didn't want to use the same sequence twice, first of all because it wasn't "pure" but also because that would have changed the texture of the film. We must have shot more than forty minutes of the particles, which Albert Jurgenson and I then paired with the music, once it was incorporated into the film. That said, I was acutely conscious from the outset of the worries that the viewers might have that the projector was on the fritz, but a fade to absolute black would have worked if such a thing really existed in film. True black exists at the opera, but on film stock there are always scratches and dust that mean you never get a true black. Besides, when there's a fade to black, the moviegoers suddenly become aware of the "Exit" signs around them and the colored lamps in the aisles. If I'd used pure fades to black all the time in *L'Amour à mort*, it would have coincided with fifty-two views of the word "Exit," which would certainly have been a catastrophe.

Note

1. The name would have sexual connations for a French audience.

Interview with Alain Resnais

Birgit Kämper and Thomas Tode / 1995

Below are excerpts from a longer interview with Alain Resnais about his short films and his collaborations with Chris Marker from September 18, 1995. We have retained the segments where Resnais talks about himself in the context of his interactions with Marker. A different selection from this interview was published in Germany as "Rendez-vous des amis: Alain Resnais," in *Chris Marker—Filmessayist*, eds. Birgit Kämper and Thomas Tode (Munich: Institut Français 1997), pp. 205–17. Translated by T. Jefferson Kline. Printed by permission.

Birgit Kämper and Thomas Tode: What was the idea behind *Les Statues meurent aussi*, the first film that you and Chris [Marker] worked so long on—from 1950 to 1953?

Alain Resnais: Well, it did take a long time. We completed the first version within a year, but the second took another entire year and then some.

BK and TT: Who took the initiative?

AR: It was an invitation to Chris by the review *Présence Africaine*, and he simply asked me to join him in the enterprise. There was also an ethnologist named Balandier, who must have met Chris at the Work and Culture Center, where Chris had an office.

BK and TT: But you'd already done some films on art.

AR: Well, our idea was also to attract future producers and this was a way of getting started.

BK and TT: And an article in *Les Temps modernes* . . .

AR: Well, after fifty years . . . I must have thought at the time the film was censored, that, had it been an article in a journal entitled *Les Statues meurent aussi*, no one would have paid attention. But we made a film, and right away there were problems, which, among other things demonstrated to what extend cinema lagged behind writing. When you see the film today, you have to wonder what could have provoked such distress. It took the intervention of André Malraux as minister of culture to lift the censorship.

BK and TT: So was it a collaborative project?

AR: Chris [as scriptwriter] and I got together and agreed on which works to show, so yes, we worked together on it. We also worked with an artistic advisor named Charles le Raton, and it was not always easy agreeing on things. As for Chris and me, neither of us was a specialist in African art, so we discovered a great deal about the subject while working on this film. One of the advantages of undertaking a documentary is that you get to learn things that you might have put off to much later, thinking that some day you'd look into African art. So it was a wonderful chance to take on such a project. We went to see collectors in London and Brussels and gradually became pretty expert on the subject. In the end Charles le Raton congratulated us profusely on our taste. What we did not foresee was the waves of anger that the film was to provoke, because if we had, we'd have written a contract that protected us better. Indeed, there was practically no contract at all. Instead, as we pursued this interest in African art, we ended up with a presentation of the works that seemed to upset a lot of people at the time.

BK and TT: But even at the outset there was some friction with the group *Présence Africaine*...

AR: Well, not while we were shooting. We worked closely with *Présence Africaine* who decided to look for a producer to make the film, but at the outset, it was Monsieur Diop who initiated the project, and we had a very good relationship with him throughout the production stage, up until we released the first copy of the film. The problems began after that, when the film was banned and *Présence Africaine* didn't want to get involved. Even after it was banned, Anatole Dauman of Argos Films made us an offer, and suggested I buy back the film from the producer, Tadié Films, and was upset because he lost money in the process, and so did *Présence Africaine*. So I ended up buying the film and the negatives in the state they were in, but no one wanted to distribute it, given the fact that it had been banned. Chris and I wanted to get the film approved, but we didn't entirely agree on the way to proceed. We had an initial showing with different directors and technicians and film people—about eighty people all together—in a private meeting room. We asked them if we should drop the whole thing, but they said, "Oh, no!" So Chris and Ghislain Cloquet and I worked on the voice-over soundtrack and changed some sentences in such a way as to—well, not satisfy everyone, but at least rework things to avoid offending anyone and hoping to regain support for the film. And in the end, we managed to clarify things without beating a complete retreat. Then we had another meeting, this time asking people whether, now that we'd reworked the commentary, they'd want to come see the film. This time, there were about a dozen of us who worked on the revisions, but in the end, no one showed up for the presentation. We had spent weeks and weeks on this, since we didn't have any financial backing, only to have one of the directors say, "What! This is the same thing!" Which proves you should only try such a thing when there's a certain amount of enthusiasm. If we'd produced this commentary within a week, we might have won the battle, but over six months. . . .

BK and TT: So that's what caused the long delay?

AR: Well, we had no money, so we had to produce it at our own expense and evidently that didn't help things. That's what I remember, but there may be other factors that I'm forgetting.

BK and TT: We understand that you met Chris Marker when he was working at Work and Culture. What was Work and Culture exactly?

AR: It was an association that was located in the Fifth Arrondissement on the rue des Beaux Arts, if I'm not mistaken, and which hosted meetings, conferences, and sometimes showings of films that they sometimes managed to distribute widely in France. They also furnished theater and concert tickets at half price and other things like that, in order to enhance cultural awareness. It was a public service. Chris had an office there, and that's how I met him. I just chanced to go there once, back in 1946 or '47, for reasons I can no longer recall, probably as a member of a student association. I was supposed to do some film editing and work as the assistant editor on a film. Chris wanted to make some 16mm films and was looking for an assistant editor. So I heard there was this guy there named Chris Marker, but he wasn't in his office. There were lots of strange objects in this office: posters, and all kinds of film paraphernalia, and I remember vividly that I told someone there that I'd really like to get to know this guy.

BK and TT: So was Chris Marker an employee of the organization?

AR: Among the members of the organization were the writer, Benigno Cacérès, and the director was a specialist in popular culture named Joffre Dumazedier, all good friends of Chris. They were the people to see.

BK and TT: So right from the start it was clear that they wanted to make films?

AR: That must have been what attracted me. I must have gone there because I had a 16mm camera and wanted to begin making film the same way that you made 35mm films. There were articles in the paper saying that thanks to 16mm cameras, anyone could make films now. I was the first one to make this claim, since what's expensive in making films isn't the cost of the film negative, which is a tiny percentage of the overall budget.

BK and TT: Chris had been shooting in 8mm.

AR: Yes. I remember that the first film he showed me at his house in Ville D'Avray, was called, if I remember correctly, *The End of the World as Seen by the Angel Gabriel*. It was a sequence of images that weren't always identifiable, he used a lot of out of focus shots and techniques like that, but the commentary was fabulous, and I was completely swept away by this film. I don't know whether he remembers this.

BK and TT: But at that time he was writing a novel . . .

AR: Yes, it won a prize in Brussels, and, thanks to that, he was able to buy a small tape recorder—one of the first on the market. It was magical! He did a series of very funny interviews with everyone he met.

BK and TT: He never wrote more than that one novel?

AR: You should ask him about it. I wouldn't say that he's disavowed the novel, but I do know that he doesn't like to talk about it. I remember it as being very moving and exciting. He really liked the English translation because it had nothing in common with his text!

BK and TT: But he made his debut in films.

AR: Well, he found that the commentaries in his films were more interesting than his novels.

BK and TT: Tell us about your first meeting. Did you discover that you had common interests?

AR: Well, I don't know if we had common interests but there were . . .

BK and TT: Cats, comic books. . . .

AR: In our first meeting, I discovered he knew Milton Caniff, that he read *Dick Tracy* and *L'il Abner* by Al Capp. It was pretty rare that you could get hold of those items in 1946 and '47.

BK and TT: In France, at least.

AR: You had to go to the US embassy at that time, where you could buy the *Stars and Stripes* that regularly published fourteen-to-twenty comic strips. I don't know who put it together, but it was an excellent selection, really the best strips, and I think Chris got his comics there as well. And there was also the American Documentation Center, where you could consult the daily papers, for example, the *Washington Post*, which was not available in the kiosks. That's how I discovered the comics, as early as 1935 and '36.

BK and TT: So what was so striking about the comics.

AR: It's hard to say. . . It was the quality of the stories, the drawing, and then the fact that these stories were entirely different from what you found in the illustrated stories in Europe. Of course, there was Belgium and to some extent Italy, where there were some similar things. I read *Tintin* from its beginnings, but it was really the only comic strip of its kind. In France there were things like *Ziggy Puce*, but they were for children, whereas the American comics could evidently be read by children, but their level appealed also to the father who bought the paper and so they had to interest him before he gave it to his kids to read. There were experiments in graphic design that one simply didn't find in France. The Italians adopted this style very quickly and caught up with the Americans within a few months, but not the French.

I don't think there was anything like it in Germany either.

BK and TT: What about Marvel Comics?

AR: That was later. It was Chris who introduced me to the *Captain Marvel* comics since I hadn't picked up on them, and that's how I became a "Marvelite" ... and even went and met the original writer in New York. He wrote a screenplay for me, but we never shot it.

BK and TT: Do you see a connection between the comics and the cinema.

AR: Of course! But it's not so much a question of the storyboard, but of the script. Just as I don't see theater and film as so different, I don't separate comics from film or film from historical painting. Of course, in terms of the rules that we apply, each one has its own categories, its grammar, but ultimately, there are dramatic laws that are common to both, especially in Italian Renaissance painting, for example, and that you also find in the theater and in film.

BK and TT: So this passion was the unifying factor for the three of you, the third musketeer being...

AR: I met Rémo Forlani in the courtyard of the Work and Culture Center. I was working on my bicycle, since there were no motor bikes yet.

BK and TT: Weren't you three inseparable?

AR: Not really, they were separate relationships, that is to say, Forlani and Marker would see each other and I could see Forlani or Marker, but almost never all three together. I remember that we had a feeler from the Péchinay Corporation to do some promotional shorts. Pierre Braunberger, the producer set up a lunch date with the head of the company, plus Forlani, Marker, and me. Forlani and Marker never opened their mouths once during the interview. They were polite but totally reserved, and so I was a bit the same way, and it ended up being a complete fiasco. We never got together as a threesome after that.

BK and TT: We want to ask you about genres. In particular, what do you think of the cinematic essay?

AR: I think Chris practically invented it ... although it's true that Sacha Guitry pioneered it, and I'm not sure that he'd be pleased by the term. Certainly we can say that Sacha Guitry is historically the first person to make films in the first person. Chris has used this differently, of course, though I find the same degree of freedom in the work of both men and especially their way of affirming and pacing the editing through both written and spoken words. We can imagine a film by Chris Marker in which there would be only non-figurative images yet it would still be a film. He really understood that the soundtrack was not just an add-on, since it would then be merely a monologue, and a record would suffice in its place, but he has a unique way of creating a connection between words and images, a sort of ping-pong effect that, in my view, influenced television reporting. Sacha Guitry was the only one to attempt this before Marker.

BK and TT: And you?

AR: Certainly I wanted to copy this; I wanted to equal it.

BK and TT: And did he learn anything from you?

AR: I really don't think so. I'm ready to say that I owe everything to him. He influenced me enormously.

BK and TT: Tell us about *Nuit et brouillard* and Jean Cayrol.

AR: At the time, Chris was working as director of collections for Les Editions du Seuil, and had an office there. It wasn't far from the Work and Culture offices. He'd left Work and Culture, and I got in the habit of meeting him after work every day. Jean Cayrol was working in the office below him. So I read his works and was very enthusiastic about his writing. We frequently met Cayrol in the stairway, or he would come up to Chris's office to chat. The atmosphere at Seuil was very convivial.

BK and TT: So what was his role in *Nuit et brouillard*?

AR: He agreed to serve only as an assistant. He didn't want to be listed at all, but, in my view, his contribution was very important. I'd accepted to do *Nuit et brouillard*, only on condition that Cayrol write the scenario. I only did the film because of Cayrol. I refused to do it at first, but he insisted, saying, "You've got to do this, but don't show me anything before I do the writing, and I don't want to work on the editing." Cayrol saw the first edit and gave me some suggestions and then provided the text. He wrote a very beautiful text inspired by the memories he had of watching the thirty-five minutes of the film. There was no synchronization between his text and the film. He couldn't bear to see the film a second time.

And that's where Chris Marker stepped in and saved the situation, rewriting the text based on Cayrol's work, and adapting it to the editing we'd done. Afterwards we showed it to Cayrol, and he was so re-energized by watching this version of it, that he rewrote his text over Chris Marker's! Things ended up getting a little complicated, because there were other people who'd wanted to write the text, but I insisted the Cayrol be listed as the sole author. I would have quit if I'd been forced to alter that position. There was what you might call a fusion between Marker and Cayrol, since you absolutely couldn't tell which of them had written a given phrase. And, since they were such good friends, there were never any problems with this approach.

BK and TT: Tell us about *Toute la mémoire du monde*.

AR: Forlani wrote everything except the last sentence, which is by Chris Marker. That's why the author should be listed as Magic Marker, but Forlani wouldn't agree to this. You'd have to ask them about it since they have completely different versions of how it went. I can't claim to be certain about any of it.

BK and TT: And Semprun?

AR: Florence Malraux introduced me to Semprun around 1962 or so. I would just like to say that when I started making full-length films I'd been so sensitized by Chris Marker's way of making connections between images and words or metaphors, that I tended not to ask novelists to provide screenplays, but instead turn to people who'd done some theater, like Marguérite Duras, or who'd written plays that hadn't been staged, like Jean Cayrol, or had worked in theater and had plays in their desk drawers, like Jorge Semprun. I've always been interested in sound and not literature. I've often been asked, "Why didn't you work with such and such an author? He's a great writer." I would answer that, since theater doesn't interest him, I wouldn't be at ease with him and it wouldn't work.

BK and TT: Tell us about *Ciné-tracts* and *Loin du Vietnam*.

AR: I think it was Marker who had the idea of making short 16mm films in black-and-white. We wanted to try to make films that were shot in one take without any editing. No reworking in the editing room. Obviously, it was a challenge, but at least it got me out of conferences, discussions, and speeches, and activities like that. At least it was concrete work. Because in May '68, we heard a lot of speeches. I did one of the *Ciné-tracts*, but it has been lost without a trace.

BK and TT: That's not true.

AR: It was an anonymous poem that I'd transposed into images with documents. It was a short film [30 meters] and was shot in black-and-white. I thought it was completely lost.

BK and TT: Did you go to any showings?

AR: No, never. It was Marker who took care of everything.

BK and TT: What about *Loin du Vietnam*?

AR: Same thing.

BK and TT: But there must have been some meetings or encounters.

AR: Well, yes. They were looking for 100 directors. Chris's original idea was that each one should bring some material. But there were no specifics: only that each one would bring some footage, and that we'd try to organize it. The only directives were: donate your time, bring some images, and we'll figure it out from there.

BK and TT: And Marker? Did he do the final editing?

AR: I believe so, yes. But what has he said about it? He must have worked with other people, for example . . .

BK and TT: Jacqueline Meppiel?

AR: I remember her, yes.

BK and TT: How did Marker, make his mark, if you will, on all that?

AR: He's the instigator of the whole thing, in my view. It seems to me that he did a lot of the editing, and a large part of the commentary.

BK and TT: Did he have collaborators?

AR: Jacques Sternberg worked on my part, I recall, but then so did Marker. It seemed everybody did a bit of everything.

BK and TT: But you completed the editing of your episode?

AR: No, not completely, because my episode was originally intended to be fragmented. The character of Fresson was supposed to return, a bit like in an American musical. The guy was constantly coming back to complain about something. And then, at the end, it was changed, thanks to Marker, who thought that it would be better another way because of the other episodes, since we couldn't predict what the others would be like.

BK and TT: Was the film about memory?

AR: No, I never thought about memory, but I don't know if Chris thought about it or not. Memory isn't a precise theme, except if you treat it on the level of nostalgia, and I don't think Chris or I have much feeling about that. And then there's the imaginary. It seems to me that the animal who imagines the most would be man, perhaps, cats, dogs, or chimpanzees, but for us everything leads us to be conscious of our power of imagination. Man is the only one who does this to this extent. Inevitably imagination plays a huge role in film and elsewhere. So there's always an attempt to put imagination onto the silver screen.

It was Giraudoux who said, "Theater isn't an imitation of life, it *is* life." Robbe-Grillet would say that to make a description of our meeting, we'd be shown sitting around the table with the camera situated over there, but would it be realistic? It would be less realistic than if, at the same time, you could see images of what was going on in our heads at that moment. And there again, it puts the very notion of chronology into question, because we don't imagine things chronologically. I mean, if you think about the people you met this afternoon, or during the shopping trip you are going to take, you would not see yourself going down and getting on the subway, changing at such and such a station, and getting off at the Galeries Lafayette, or the Louvre. Instead, you leap instantly from one scene to another. So, essentially, we're trying to capture as closely as possible the work of the imagination. But I want to say that I'm not the first film director to have done that. Last year, I saw Lubitsch's *The Student Prince in Old Heidelberg* [1928], one of his last silent films, and there are imaginary leaps forward in time that are stunning. I did my film thinking that there had never been anything like it before.

BK and TT: When and why did you stop working with Marker?

AR: There are two or three producers who allowed him to write a scenario for me. But we would only meet a couple of times, and then he'd get discouraged because he didn't have complete freedom to do what he wanted, and I would say, "You're avoiding us! You avoid the studio, you avoid any constraints, and you give us the scenario and then disappear." I think he never felt independent enough. He's like Kipling's cat, who just wanders off alone.

BK and TT: So that's why you didn't collaborate any more?

AR: Right. It wasn't because of any misunderstanding or fight. But you know he was involved in the early stages of *Hiroshima mon amour*, though that wasn't yet the title. The original proposal from Anatole Dauman and Philippe Lifchitz, who were at Argos films, was made to Chris Marker and me. But after a couple of weeks, Marker said, "Hey, I'm out of here, but there's someone who could more than replace me and who's been in Japan," but things didn't work out there. So that's how Marguérite Duras came on board, almost by chance. I mentioned her name in a meeting with the producers, explaining that she was a writer that I liked a lot, and Duras learned of it and let me know she wanted to meet with me. I explained to her that we couldn't make a film on the atomic bomb, because there were a dozen good ones out there already that I'd seen, and there was no reason to do another. And from that meeting we set out to do . . . the opposite.

BK and TT: Do you think Chris Marker could make a popular film?

AR: Well, he certainly asks a lot of his audience. I think we both felt a need to challenge the pure formalism of the '50s. We have certain tastes in common but certainly not the same artistic capacities. I always feel that Chris is self-sufficient. He's an auteur, and I'm an artisan. On the other hand I wouldn't be interested in doing a film all by myself with no one to help me. I typically need about forty-five people around me.

BK and TT: Your team.

AR: Well, I never have the feeling of a coherent team, though maybe it's true of films I've done, but not of films I'd like to do. I'm not a member of a school.

BK and TT: What about the designation "Rive Gauche"?

AR: It was Richard Roud who came up with that term in an article and had the idea of linking us together. But I think he was doing it mostly because he knew all of us. We never got together as a group, there was never a meeting at which we agreed to have a genre "Rive Gauche."

BK and TT: Are there other groups? The *Cahiers* group?

AR: Well, it's really a different generation. I think it's as simple as that. We belonged to a period when there was an idea that if you did shorts you would never do full-length features. I don't really know why, but I recall there was a union of cameramen for shorts and another for cameramen of feature films, which shows that we didn't think they were the same type of films. Luckily, Chabrol and others ended those distinctions.

BK and TT: How would you characterize the differences between you and the *Cahiers* group?

AR: Simply a difference in age. We've had good rapport with each other.

BK and TT: So it wasn't about different themes, for example the war.

AR: Well, it's possible we were more marked by the war.

Alain Resnais: On *The Same Old Song*

François Thomas / 1999

From *Projections 9: French Film-makers on Film-making* in association with *Positif* (1999) Reprinted by permission.

Alain Resnais's best know films include *Hiroshima mon amour* (1959), *L'Année dernière à Marienbad* (1961), and *Providence* (1977), with Dirk Bogarde. His most recent films include *Smoking* and *No Smoking*, adapted from Alan Ayckbourn's plays of the same name, and *On Connaît la chanson (Same Old Song)*, a musical comedy that was the surprise hit of 1998.

Like Chabrol, Alain Resnais seems, in old age, to be turning to a peculiar Anglophilia. His previous films, *Smoking* and *No Smoking*, were based on Alan Ayckbourn's plays and preserved the English settings of the originals. In this interview, he explains how Dennis Potter's *The Singing Detective* provides the inspiration for the use of music in *Same Old Song*. But the setting, this time, is firmly French and the songs belong to the canon of French popular music. Resnais uses extracts from these songs as sung dialogue at significant plot points where the lyrics suit the character's mood.

François Thomas: What was the starting point for *Same Old Song*?

Alain Resnais: After *Smoking* and *No Smoking*, Bruno Pésery suggested making an opera specially commissioned for the cinema. But it takes a composer at least five years to fulfill a commission for an opera and that's supposing you find the right composer and that he is available. We might have managed with a libretto in English, but I didn't think my English was up to such an undertaking. So while I was waiting to meet a feasible French composer, I looked for another route.

The English dramatist and screenwriter Dennis Potter, who died three years ago, was an inspiration. I never met Potter but I find his narrative experiments fascinating. He is such a meticulous writer that, regardless of who directs his work, it always seems as if it was him who supervised the cutting. In some of his writing, such as *Pennies from Heaven* [1978], *The Singing Detective* [1986], and *Lipstick on Your Collar* [1993], Potter has the actors sing pop songs in playback, pushing the boundaries of this technique a little further with every production. I was also motivated by the fact that popular music plays such an important part in our imagination. The songs we like accompany us all our lives and provide us with a measure of the passage of time. I recall Nicole Vedrès, whose assistant I was in 1947 on *Paris 1900*, saying that pop songs are probably the most precise rendering of human emotion. [. . .] There is another factor as well: my own experience. I sometimes quote from pop songs, in my everyday life, without realizing I'm doing it. Which is interesting.

In the aftermath of *Smoking* and *No Smoking*, which had been adapted from Alan Ayckbourn's plays by Agnès Jaoui and Jean-Pierre Bacri, I decided that I wanted to work with them again. No one else working in theater in France today produces such musical dialogue. And this was to be their first original screenplay. They accepted on condition that they could write in parts for themselves. They hadn't performed in our previous "twin film" project, but I liked the idea. I stipulated that I wanted a part for André Dussollier, as I had not worked with him in *Smoking* or *No Smoking*. We spent three or four afternoons discussing character, structure, what film could do and not do. We rummaged through my story pile. I have a feeling that I even let them have a mad half-hour improvisation that I'd recorded on tape. Some of these elements survive in *On Connaît la chanson*: guided tours; a character who writes plays; another named Von Choltitz, and—most importantly, I suppose—the idea of depicting someone with the mindset of a hermit crab. We also decided that one of the main themes of our story would be how all of us live our lives in disguise. We abandon certain projects because of the way others would interpret them. We all attach a great deal of importance to ensuring that our self-image—usually, but not always, a positive image—is interpreted by others as we would like it to be, forgetting that we cannot control how others see us. We cannot control our appearance. From the start, we realized that, as our story developed, the various characters' self-images must be destroyed.

I played them Arletty's and Aquistapace's song, "Et le reste," that I'd already listened to with Bruno Pésery. I wanted to make room for this song. I have a feeling that is what clinched it for them. I also showed Jaoui and Bacri extracts from Potter's TV movies, translating the dialogue. We borrowed Potter's use of playback, although our use is somewhat different to his. Out of respect, I could not just copy his ideas.

FT: In *The Singing Detective* the way in which different timeframes and different levels of reality intermingle, and indeed the way the film is shot, are very reminiscent of your film *Providence*, and, indeed, some of the films you made in the 1960s.

AR: It did not occur to me that Potter might have seen my films and, at the time, I had not seen his. The fact is that, in his work, I felt on familiar ground. I feel comfortable with intricate time games, with sound slippage between scenes, with complicating editing and the whole abstraction of his world. I have always wondered why David Mercer, who wrote *Providence*, never told me about Potter. They must have known each other. I can picture the five main characters in *Providence* playing in a drama by Potter. Anyway, there is a connection between my discovering Potter and my working on Ayckbourn. I had enjoyed the movie version of *Pennies from Heaven*, directed by Herbert Ross, which in France never received the attention it deserved. But *The Singing Detective* captured my attention when I caught a few minutes of it on American television while staying in NewYork nearly ten years ago—because the actor was Michael Gambon, whom I've often seen on stage, including in Ayckbourn's plays. But I did not get to see the series in its entirety until many years later. The funny thing is that the bit I'd seen in New York had no songs in it. But it was written, acted, and edited in such a way that I was instantly absorbed.

FT: How did you depart from Dennis Potter's example in *Same Old Song*?

AR: Almost always, with Potter, existing records are used to illustrate the characters' imagined worlds. Sometimes, they break into dance. We chose to incorporate songs in everyday life, as ordinary text. The film does comprise three or four "imagined" scenes, for example, like Dussollier dressed as an honor guard, but these were not allowed to dominate. We weren't making a musical. Sometimes, on set, I'd shout, "Careful, this isn't a musical!" That was my red flag, a signal that it was time to try out something different.

FT: Presumably, the reason André Dussollier has to sing with his mouth full is to get across the point about songs cropping up in everyday life?

AR: Yes, it's a question of realism. It's not like he breaks into song when the buffet is over. Potter—and this is another big difference—uses whole songs, or nearly whole, complete with orchestral accompaniment. In that respect, too, we wanted something more realistic. Usually, when you recall a song, you remember the chorus. Nowadays, unlike in our parents' and grandparents' day, people don't really remember whole songs. I wanted very short excerpts, sometimes cut off in mid-line, like in real life. But then, some of the extracts are longer. There is no hard and fast rule.

Since we were going to chop the songs up, one of the main problems was going to be maintaining the harmonies. There would have to be a cadence, a harmonic solution, to avoid sounding like we'd just chopped a song in half. I assumed we could find a composer who could extend the songs thematically, to avoid the excerpts sounding too abrupt. I wanted the songs to appear and disappear harmoniously. I warned the producers that I could not sign a contract to do the film until I found a musician who would undertake to do this harmonic work. Work on the script was continued, but the question of harmony remained unsolved till a couple of months before shooting began. Then one day Lambert Wilson introduced me to his accompanist, Bruno Fontaine, who is also Ute Lemper's and Hanna Schygulla's arranger. His work is unique. His arrangements, the transitions he writes from one song to another, are so daring that he should really be called a composer in his own right. When we met, I played him the truncated songs and I explained what the problem was. He told me that what I wanted was perfectly possible and that he would do it. So that meant we could green light the project. Subsequently, I also asked Bruno Fontaine to write an original soundtrack. I was delighted to give him his first film music commission.

FT: The soundtrack is at a very low level.

AR: Yes. To avoid confusion with the songs. Otherwise, whenever the audience heard music, they'd immediately think one of the characters was about to break into song. I told Bruno Fontaine I didn't mind some of the themes from songs recurring elsewhere in the soundtrack, if that could provide an overall sense of unity. Consequently, he elaborated variations on "Avoir un bon copain" and a couple of other tracks.

FT: You say that you are wary of comparisons between *Same Old Song* and musicals.

AR: Yes. If anything, I'd rather my film was called a vaudeville. I don't mean it's a French farce, in the tradition of Feydeau. At the end of the nineteenth century, vaudeville was a specific form, distinct from comic opera. It was a prose drama that included songs. The characters would break into song without necessarily interrupting the plot. In order for that to seem acceptable, the songs had to be hits. The playwright would rewrite the lyrics and use the tune. In a way, that's what we have done.

FT: Dennis Potter is supposed to have loathed many of the songs he employed. Do you like the songs you use?

AR: Potter had a love-hate relationship with his material. He can be scathing, true. There is something derisive about his choice of songs. I wouldn't say we went as far as that. A raised eyebrow, perhaps. Certainly, we never chose a song because we loved it, or because we loved the singer. We turned to a song because it seemed appropriate in terms of a particular character's emotional progress, in terms of a scene and in terms of narrative economy. In that respect, we are close to musicals. A song can communicate in a very short space of time feelings which words would take several minutes to render. Songs are faster and, I think, more profound.

FT: Were there any other rules that governed your choice of songs?

AR: Given the age difference between me and Jaoui/Bacri, it is possible that I promoted songs from the 1935–45 period, while they lobbied in favor of more recent songs. If we'd been told to use only recent hits, songs of 1996-97 that the audience would have known of by heart, I wouldn't have been able to do it. Most of the songs had to be hits, not least because it was important the audience didn't think they were written specially for the film, but you can tell a hit even if you've never heard it. I might never have heard of a particular song put forward by Jaoui and Bacri, but if, just by listening to it, I could tell it was a hit, I'd give it the OK. Because of this factor, mixing different periods was not a problem. Though we weren't out to produce a selection of greatest hits, nor a history of French pop music since the earliest days.

FT: How did you set about matching the actors' performance with the singers?

AR: The actor had to refrain from being taken over by the singer's persona. You couldn't suddenly have a pastiche of Maurice Chevalier, Claude François, or Charles Azanavour's gestures and expressions appearing on-screen, or it would look like impersonation. The actor would have to stick to the rhythms of the song without imitating the singer's style. We had to be very careful about that.

FT: The film opens with the sound of a cricket chirping over the distributor's logo, AMLF. You asked Richard Pezet, the managing director, to re-record the logo using the full name (Agence Méditerranéenne de Location de Films), then we see dolphins—which crop up in the dialogue—an octopus and so on. You've put your fondness for the animal kingdom into *Same Old Song*.

AR: I was once told that in an anthill, 30 percent of the ants just rush around pretending to be unbelievably busy, and ever since I've been convinced that human beings are full participants in the animal world. Dolphins are pure Jaoui/Bacri. Stick insects, too. They told me, "You're going to like this." It was a joke. I must admit that, as we were dealing with the business of appearance, I did raise with them one of the great wonders of creation—namely, that animals should take on the outward appearance of other animals in order to stave off predators. For instance, there is a caterpillar that clings on to branches with its front paws, showing a tail that has the appearance of a poisonous snake. So it's hardly surprising we included a stick insect. But it is no more a symbol than the jellyfish in *Love Unto Death*. When we were doing *Last Year at Marienbad*, Robbe-Grillet and I had a rule that we would allow ourselves no symbols, even though our films were undoubtedly symbol-friendly. If the audience chooses to see something as symbolic, then what could we . . . ? As a child, I remember a giant, dead jellyfish stranded on our beach, on the island in southern Brittany where I grew up. Me and my mates, we thought it was the last jellyfish on Earth. There was no television then, no documentary films. How were we to know there were such things as jellyfish?

FT: Characters often appear in front of or behind glass, glazing, brass doors, and so on. You play with focus, including even the reflections in character's spectacles.

AR: The characters in this story—in this, they are like jellyfish—float indecisively. They are inconsistent. It is a kind of rhyme. I wanted a correspondence with the aquatic world.

FT: You hold your shots for a long time. You shoot whole scenes in a single shot, only in such a way as this is not noticeable.

AR: It seemed the most appropriate way of preserving a unity of acting styles, and emphasizing rhythms of speech. It seemed to fit the style of writing. Reverse angles would have seemed odd. But some scenes are shot more conventionally, like the scene with the three doctors. I'm not against reverses, but if I do use one, I try to make sure I never use it twice or return to the same master shot—there are exceptions. I don't like to cut into a take in order to show the reverse, and then return to the same take. I do anything I can to make sure I don't come back from one angle to the same angle—except for the last three shots when we come closer and closer to the father, shown alone in the main room of the apartment. A homage to Pudovkin, perhaps.

FT: *Les Statues meurent aussi* [*Statues Also Die*], *The War Is Over*, *I Love You, I Love You*, *La Vie est un roman* [*Life Is a Bed of Roses*], *I Want to Go Home*, *Same Old Song*. You seem to like set-phrase titles.

AR: None of the titles originated with me. *Les Statues meurent* is Chris Marker's homage to Brecht. *I Want to Go Home* is Feiffer. It's a very popular phrase in America, which I've often come across in strips like *Little Nemo* or *Gasoline Alley*. I often brought Feiffer funnies to show him he was on to something. *La Vie n'est pas un roman* is something my father used to say at dinner and which I asked Jean Gruault to use. *Je t'aime, je t'aime* sounded to me like a signal, a beep-beep launched into outer space by astronauts in distress. As for *La Guerre est finie*, that's something a twenty-four-year-old Spanish girl said to me when I was discussing a screenplay Semprun was writing with her. She said, "But Monsieur Resnais, the war is over!" I jumped at it, particularly as the English translation, "War is Over," was good. But neither in England nor in America was the title translated. They kept the French. And I realized I played a nasty trick on Semprun, because later, on tour, we kept having to explain that the title meant its opposite: the war is not over.

Alain Resnais's *Not on the Lips*

Pascal Mérigeau / 2003

From *Le Nouvel Observateur*, November 27, 2003. Reprinted by permission. Translated by T. Jefferson Kline.

Ever since Alain Resnais (born June 3, 1922 in Vannes) began making films, his work has always been experimental. Even in bringing a 1925 operetta to the screen, he delights in trampling on all the accepted rules without his audience being aware of it. You need about ten minutes to get your bearings in *Pas sur la bouche* (*Not on the Lips*)—figure out how seriously to take the singing and what touches Resnais has decided to bring to this film—and "get into the groove," as the director would say. Once there you just have to let yourself be carried away by this discreet and modest inventor, as nervous as if it were the first day of his first shoot.

Pascal Mérigeau: How did you come to make a film of this operetta?

Alain Resnais: It was accidental. In June of 2002, we decided to delay a project based on a scenario by Michel Le Bris, because we couldn't manage to reconcile our shooting dates with the weather conditions necessary to the film. So we had four months free to do something else, and with my producer, Bruno Pésery, we looked for a project that we could complete with the same team of technicians and the same group of actors. So the whole thing started off as a sort of joke: we had to find something that would not require writing a screenplay, since there wouldn't be enough time for that. So it either had to be a remake or a play. Bruno and I thought about doing one of the operettas from the '20s whose texts had become extremely difficult to find. Two days later, Bruno brought me some that he'd unearthed in the Arsenal Library. We both immediately liked *Not on the Lips*, and then Bruno Fontaine, with whom I'd worked on *On connaît la chanson* (*Same Old Song*), played some of the songs for us on the piano and we all agreed we should try to do it. The decision was made on July 14th and shooting started on December 15th.

PM: What memories do you have of operettas of the '20s?

AR: It's a repertoire that I learned mostly from street musicians. Often, in the late afternoon in Brittany, an accordion player appeared accompanied by a singer. They'd perform a few songs and then would sell what they called small formats—the music and words to the songs—for 1F25. I would buy these scores and then try to play them on the piano. And then, twice a year, at Easter and Christmas, my parents would bring me to spend ten days in Paris with my grandfather, who lived in Buttes-Chaumont. Once there, we'd go to the theater and the cinema, since in Vannes, theatrical performances were limited to the Baret touring company. So by the time I was about ten years old, I'd seen several operettas: *Le Bonheur mesdames* (*It's All about Happiness, Ladies*) at the Bouffes Parisiens, with Arletty and Michel Simon, *Toi c'est moi* (*You are me*), with Pills and Tabet, Simone Simon, and Pauline Carton. From about 1930 on, I was a total fan of Koval, one of the kings of operetta. One of his favorite stage tricks was raising one eyebrow, and I tried to copy him in class . . . And then, it's thanks to musical comedy, to films like *Le Congrès s'amuse* (*Congress is amused*) or *Le Chemin du paradis* (*Three from the Filling Station*), that I began to get interested in the talkies. It happened that I'd been hostile to the talkies for the first two or three years after they began; I found the films very static. Two actors would sit opposite each other and talk in front of a campfire, and the Western would just stop. I came back to the cinema thanks to the songs.

PM: So why did you decide to do *Not on the Lips* of all things?

AR: I thought it was completely crazy and even absurd at times. And when Bruno Fontaine played us some of the melodies, we realized that Maurice Yvain's score was very harmonically complicated and virtually experimental. He has a taste for aesthetic research which is unique. But don't go thinking I'm a huge fan of operettas in general; I've always been horrified by *Les Cloches de Corneville* (*The Bells of Corneville*). So I had to think about this for four or five days since I was afraid of doing a film that would be too close to *Mélo*, and then I made up my mind. I found that *Not on the Lips* had a fantastical quality to it which derives from a pretty absurd idea, and that reminds me of Raymond Queneau or Boris Vian. At the same time, it was distressing, since we didn't know whether such a film could be shown today. I'm going to quote a formula that I've come to like: I shoot (*tourne*) a film to find out how it will *turn* out.

PM: It's definitely a crazy film, and at times you worry about the mental health of the characters. . . .

AR: Yes, they're all a little bit crazy. Especially Valandray, who's obsessed with cleanliness, had theories about everything and doubts about nothing. He's the kind of person who could turn out to be a dictator, and he scares me a bit. But you'll notice that he's the only one in the film who gets punished. I don't know what could happen two or three months after the end of the film's events—he might end up strangling his wife. Each of his obsessions is a question of purity for him and a question of cinematic sound for me. At fourteen or fifteen, I was fascinated by the voices of the Pitoëffs and of Dullin. When you see *La Guerre de Troie n'aura pas lieu* (*The Trojan War Will Not Take Place*) with Jouvet, you have the impression that you've just had dinner with Jouvet. Why is it so rare in film to hear such particular sounds? I understand that the theatrical side of my films can shock people, but that comes from my desire to have my films *sound* a certain way. That's why I like American and British voices; English offers a palette of intonations that's much richer than French, and the harmonic possibilities are legion. The French speak in a monotonal way, whereas Anglo-Saxon rises and falls constantly.

PM: The particular sound in this film is that of actors who are not singers, and so you don't know whether they're going to be able to sing or not . . .

AR: Yes, that was part of the experiment. The only one I felt secure with was Lambert Wilson, who's also a singer, and Daniel Prévost who's tried everything at one time or another. Pierre Arditi, for example, told me that he'd never be able to sing, but that he was willing to try. That's what I was looking for: actors who would sing, not singers who would play comic roles. As a result, the actors sing the songs in *Not on the Lips* exactly the way I want to hear them sung. This comes from my love of genres: just as I expect a detective story to provide the pleasure of a good mystery, I don't expect a musical comedy to provide much psychological depth or any kind of social message. Kiri Te Kanawa interests me when she sings Richard Strauss, and not when she sings *West Side Story* . . . which I always enjoy when it's sung by other voices. Only a very few singers were capable of singing everything and anything: Frank Sinatra, Dean Martin, and Bing Crosby.

PM: What about the choice of Darry Cowl for the role of the concierge?

AR: I had no idea who to select for this role and someone said, "Why not Darry Cowl?" Indeed. When he arrived, he told me he was very flattered to be invited, but when he learned that he was supposed to sing, he refused. So I told him it was really a pity, since I would have loved to see him in the role of Madame Foin. At this he did an about-face and asked, "*Madame* Foin? Did you say *Madame* Foin? If it's a woman's role, that's different! I'll do it!" I find that he rescues the song from vulgarity and gives it a light, slightly off-color quality. Because, "Through the Keyhole" is really something! They dared incredible things back in the day: when the construction work on the Paris Metro caused a cave-in near the Orsay train station, Dranem sang: "Le trou de mon quai" [literally translated as "the hole in my train station," the song is a play on the French term for "asshole"].

PM: One of the most astonishing aspects of the film is that the actors move from dialogue to song without any interruption . . .

AR: Yes, I wanted the film to be fluid, and so we had to avoid any break between words and songs. It was one of the greatest challenges we faced. It's also for this reason that there is no choreography in the film—at times, I had to keep the actors from dancing while singing. I remember that one of the greatest shocks I had at the movies was the discovery of *42nd Street* with Busby Berkeley's routines: it was a music-hall number, and you had the impression of a kind of filmed theater, but then suddenly the camera flew off and we were transported into another dimension. That's what I was looking for.

PM: The film clearly plays with genre expectations without ever fooling the spectator. Is that why you included so many asides?

AR: I demanded of my film viewers a kind of joyful complicity. I had been very influenced by Maurice Chevalier in Lubitsch's *One Hour With You* when he asks the audience what he ought to do. This complicity makes my film different from the films of the '20s or '30s but not really contemporary, either. We could have dressed our actors in tight-fitting black outfits and put them in a décor of cubes and tubes, project images of crowds and Nazi atrocities in the background, to say: "Look at this frivolous world dancing on a volcano." But it seemed to me that humility was a better approach: the spectators may think this, but we certainly shouldn't be saying it to them!

PM: What connections do you see between *Same Old Song* and *Not on the Lips*?

AR: In my view, *Same Old Song* is a film with a message: the street songs come naturally to mind, where words spring from certain situations. But in *Not on the Lips*, it's very different, if only because the actors are really singing. Some might say that just as *Same Old Song* allowed me to reach a broader audience for the first time (and it was about time!), and that I was trying for box-office success, it wasn't really true at all. You could also just say that it was kitsch or in bad taste. As for me, there's only one criterion in art: it's either alive or it's dead. There's not "greater" or "lesser" painting: Norman Rockwell is great in his particular way, just as Tintoretto is in his. Once again, I believe in genres. A silly little comedy can delight me simply because the actors are so alive. As long as I'm not bored, I'm happy.

A Conversation with Alain Resnais: A Persistent Shadow

François Thomas / 2006

From *Positif* (November 2006). Reprinted by permission. Translated by T. Jefferson Kline.

François Thomas: After *Smoking and No Smoking* in 1993, how did you get the idea of going back to adapting another work by Alan Ayckbourn?

Alain Resnais: As in the case of several of my other films, it was decided in a "state of emergency": in the spring of 2005, we'd begun rehearsals for an adaptation of Kurt Weill's *The Tsar Has His Photograph Taken*, since Bruno Pésery, my producer since *No Smoking* and *Smoking*, had asked me to do an opera. But we had to stop production for financial reasons and Pésery suggested that, instead, we think about doing a remake of another film or a play. An original screenplay would have caused a nine- or ten-month delay and we wanted to get started on *something*, arguing that we could change the project and keep as many as possible of the actors we'd lined up. After having exhausted other possibilities, I realized that, because of my tight schedule, it had been five years since I'd done my annual pilgrimage to Scarborough, the resort town where Alan Ayckbourn staged his most recent play every summer. I have been a huge fan of Ayckbourn's work ever since 1973. I love the way he constructs his plays, the way he manipulates time, and his conception of mise en scène that puts a huge emphasis on the imagination. So we got hold of the manuscripts of the five plays that I hadn't been able to see since 2001. They were all excellent, and I was particularly attracted to *Private Fears in Public Places* [2004]. When I spoke with Pésery that afternoon, we discovered we'd made the same choice. It had been the same thing with *Not on the Lips* when we'd read through a dozen operetta libretti a few years earlier.

Private Fears is a very particular play since it includes less slapstick and burlesque than Ayckbourn's fifty other plays. Before this one, *Haunting Julia*, a ghost story that he'd written ten years previously, was almost free of any gags and was, in fact, quite tragic. I was struck in *Private Fears* by the characters' constant desire to escape from their solitude, with all the obstacles that such a desire implies. If one were to pompously examine the question of the difficulty of communication, the problem for us humans is not that we don't communicate, but rather that we communicate so well that, when such communication is diminished or disappears, it becomes unbearable and we try by every means imaginable to recover our former state. The feeling of solitude is irreversible; you can't heal the desire not to be alone. It's this eternal quest for happiness, this particular happiness, which we feel we could have achieved if we'd tried hard enough, but which we can't accept as deriving from imagination alone. This is a play in which the subtext is particularly important, where what one senses between the words is as important as what the words say. We're very close here to Harold Pinter, who's a friend of Ayckbourn's. The characters try to dissimulate their private lives. Their panic is strictly interior and they're very sparing in their confidences to the point that, if they feel themselves beginning to share their feelings, they quickly bottle them up.

Ayckbourn's construction is also very unusual with its fifty-three tableaux, some quite long, others very short, followed by an epilogue. Our destiny is made by people whom we never meet, whose very existence we never imagine. Ayckbourn manages extremely well in making us feel the constant relations that exist among these seven characters, even though some of them never meet. Their connections make me think of those spiderwebs we may come across in the woods that are woven between two bramble bushes, and on which the night's dew has been deposited in little pearls. The characters are like those insects that have been caught in this trap and are struggling to disentangle themselves. Each time one of them moves, it causes a vibration in some other part of the web, at which, another character, who has no relation with the first, becomes agitated. I wanted to create in visual form this feeling of the spiderweb, with all the trembling that such a phenomenon supposes in the light.

I became aware that I could take the opposite tack from *Smoking* and *No Smoking*. In those films that were a love letter to England, I'd pushed my obsession for detail to the point of a mania by insisting that all the props and costumes be authentically English, and by recording the seagulls and church bells in the little village in Yorkshire where the action unfolded. *Private Fears* takes place in London, and since it seemed to me that it didn't include many typically English details, that it would be easy to transpose the action to Paris. And so I proposed to make a French film with French characters. I immediately thought that the equivalent of the London setting would be the newly developing neighborhood of Bercy, between the Avenue de France and the huge National Library with its very particular light. It's a neighborhood that has conserved, unless it has recently developed it, a somewhat fantastical dimension. It exudes a feeling of solitude that is perfect for a contemporary story in which the central characters are real estate agents and their clients. So we asked Ayckbourn for permission to adapt his play, which he immediately granted, and we began to shoot. I suggested we situate the action in February 2006.

For the French dialogues, I thought of Jean-Michel Ribes. I believed he had a connection with Ayckbourn and that he could understand the workings of Ayckbourn's mind. Like Ayckbourn, he's written many plays, and, even better, he's also a director for the theater and a workaholic who seems always to be involved in one project after another. In his play *Musée haut, musée bas*, for example, there is a sort of skidding off into madness that reminds one of Ayckbourn's work. And I love his Alphonse Allais side. Ribes immediately read *Private Fears* and answered that he was already at work preparing a film shoot but would postpone everything else for a month in order to write the dialogues. In fact, he delivered them in three weeks. I proposed that we remain absolutely faithful to Ayckbourn's construction. As opposed to *Smoking* and *No Smoking*, where we had to shorten the works considerably to get from eight plays to two films, in this case, I felt we shouldn't cut anything out. Nor could we eliminate anything from the dialogues. His is a very economical style. So, essentially the screenplay was the play, but transformed to make it as French as Ayckbourn's was English, especially in terms of everyday spoken usage. We had to find an equilibrium between making no changes in the character's feelings, yet avoiding giving them a British psychology or imitating the rhythms of the English language. Ribes had to appropriate the language and be extremely creative in the domain of rhythms. We ended up making a minimum of cuts in the shooting or editing: shortening the beginning of a scene here, or eliminating a sentence there.

Luckily we were able to find most of the actors who'd played in *The Tsar Has Himself Photographed*, with Lambert Wilson and his friends who are familiar with Ayckbourn's work, Pierre Arditi and André Dussollier, who'd played in the show at the Montparnasse Theater, as well as Sabine Azéma, who'd acted under his direction at Scarborough. The challenge we faced in *Private Fears* was very stimulating: it's a form of chamber music where the actors play almost always alone or with one other person (the scenes involving three actors you can count on one hand), but the memory of the preceding scenes leads us to make the actors telescope in our minds since they don't all meet each other. Claude Rich worked with Arditi and Azéma, who helped him record the role of Arthur on the eve of the beginning of the shoot. When I read the play, I could immediately "hear" the voice of Rich, who, during *Je t'aime, je t'aime* was improvising the voice of crabby old man between takes. But *Je t'aime, je t'aime* was the opposite of *Private Fears* since the camera almost never took its eyes off of him.

FT: Nicole, the character played by Laura Morante, is not Italian in Ayckbourn's play.

AR: That's my free will at play: I really like foreign accents in a film. Whether it's Giorgio Albertazzi in *Last Year at Marienbad*, Ingrid Thulin in *The War Is Over*, or in others of my films. Ayckbourn is very sparing of information about his characters, so we know very little about where they come from. We don't even know what Nicole does for a living, or rather Nicola, as she's named in the play. So, I felt that I was at liberty to make her Italian.

FT: The cast that Ayckbourn assembled was, on average, younger than your actors. And, by the way, are Gaëlle and Thierry, who are played by Isabelle Carré and André Dussollier, meant to be sister and brother or half-sister and half-brother?

AR: Sister and brother. No age is indicated in the play, and we justified the difference in ages by recalling a Hollywood actress whose brother is thirty years younger than she and whose parents had separated when she was a child. Isabelle Carré also knew of a similar case, so I had her approval on this. I had wanted to work with her ever since I'd seen her in Philippe Harel's *The Forbidden Woman*, and I really liked the tandem of Carré/Dussollier. I was immediately seduced by the harmony of their voices.

FT: The painting hanging in their living room seems to infantilize Thierry and justify his living with his much younger sister rather than living on his own.

AR: This portrait does indeed seem to be watching and judging Thierry. I proposed the hypothesis that Thierry had moved up to Paris from Roscoff and was working only part-time in a real estate office, spending the rest of his time painting, but without much success. Which explains the presence in his house of paintings by Takeo Adachi and of Wong Moo-chew. You know about my mania, inspired by Sacha Guitry, of never putting a reproduction in my sets but always using real paintings. We have, for example, a Cremonini in Nicole's apartment and it's a real Cremonini, borrowed for twenty-four hours from the assistant set designer, Solange Zeitoun, whom I'd asked on a Thursday if I could borrow it the next day. The painting you were referring to came from the "Gachet Collection" that belonged to my maternal grandfather, François Gachet, who owned a pharmacy in the Buttes-Chaumont. I've lived with this portrait ever since I was six or seven years old. At Christmas and at Easter, thanks to the Rhône Aspirin Company that offered pharmacists a subscription to *L'Illustration* and a discounted trip to Paris, my parents could travel from Vannes to visit my grandparents, so I was able to spend a week in the capital on each holiday. (My obsession was to stay longer than a week, but I had to wait until I was fifteen to realize this dream and move in with them.) I was surprised by the way the subject of this painting never took his eyes off you: whether I moved to his right or his left, I couldn't escape from his stare. My grandfather found this painting in the Paris flea market and never wanted to have it authenticated, because if it turned out to be valuable, his life would be complicated by insurance and all the rest. He preferred not to know who'd painted it. During the shoot, we noticed that Dussollier began to take on the physical appearance of this unknown person. André himself felt that it was happening, and that amused us all a lot.

In Lionel's family apartment as well, we had pieces from the Gachet Collection. The painting of the small boat, the cow, and the cat, the parishioners going to vespers in a winter landscape—these are all Breton paintings. The sideboard comes from the same source. In my grandfather's little dining room, there was this immense china cupboard.

FT: So the general principle of the sets here is the exact opposite of the one in *No Smoking* and *Smoking* that were also shot in a studio and that figured completely exterior settings.

AR: Here, with the exception of the first shot, everything is situated in interiors in order to give a claustrophobic impression. At one point, I considered doing all of the connecting shots outside in the streets, or in a little nineteenth-century staircase that leads down to the entrance to the François Mitterrand Library Station of the Paris Metro, but that would have destroyed the cohesion of the film. Shooting in a studio allowed us to give a plastic unity to the film, as well as a unity of lighting and a unity of style for the actors. Another advantage of using studios was that you could design a shooting schedule that is adapted to the availability of the very busy actors rather than having to depend on the seasons, which facilitated choosing the cast. In any case, from my very first film on, I always loved working in studios because I'm so impatient. If I have to sit in a café waiting for the wind to die down, I very quickly lose patience. When the atmospheric conditions are not good, I try to adapt the scene to rain or a sunny day, but that isn't always possible. On the first day we were shooting *Providence*, in Belgium, we were supposed to begin with a shot of a gray day when they were taking prisoners out of trucks and moving them into a stadium. There were some half-dozen trucks, a hundred extras of which about twenty were armed, uniformed soldiers. And we had a beautiful, sunny day! I explained that this scene, however short it might be, simply couldn't be filmed in that lighting. We had no fallback strategy for this scene and this setting. So we all went off to have a picnic on the grass. I was sure I'd be fired. Ultimately the producers, Klaus Hellwig and Yves Gasser, were very plucky. But it was a very strange first day!

But to come back to *Private Fears*, shooting in a studio didn't prevent me from wanting the film to be steeped in real settings. From the first days of this project, I studied various locations and filmed shots of the neighborhood on several occasions. These images created the right climate. I conferred a lot with the actors and the cinematographer, Eric Gautier. I don't know if they all followed my advice, but I did suggest that the actors take walks around the area.

FT: If you walk around that section of Paris, you hear exactly the background noises that you put in the film and that added a kind of diaphanous, phantasmatic color, like the noises of a train shunting.

AR: The sound engineer, Thomas Desjonquères, made a bunch of recordings of street sounds there. When you're walking along the Avenue de France, you can't see that there are railroad tracks some fifty to a hundred meters away. I tried to capture this eerie feeling. When you're walking along this deserted avenue and you suddenly hear the sounds of trains passing, and you wonder, "Where can they be?"

FT: The various settings of the film are as different from each other as they could possibly be.

AR: Given the structure of the play, we had to establish complete breaks in style from one setting to the next, so that the audience is never unsure of where each new scene is unfolding. In his theater in the round, where the stage is surrounded by the audience, Ayckbourn probably imagined one single set in which all nine scenes were meant to be played (he uses minimal scenery and props and plays with variations in lighting), but we had to take a different tack. I very much wanted all of the sets, with the exception of Lionel's kitchen and his father's bedroom, to be modern: the bar-restaurant of the Globe Hotel along with the café on the rue Oberkampf and the real estate office. I furnished Jacques Saulnier, our set designer, a dozen kilos or so of documentation on the topic of great bars and restaurants, and he brought me a bunch of other materials. We took our inspiration from existing decors without trying for good taste. We had to decide on each set without any consideration of good or bad taste. Thierry's and Gaëlle's apartment is not so ugly.

FT: For the second scene in an apartment, how did you get the idea of showing the décor in an overhead shot with the ceiling "removed"?

AR: It was, as usual, to carefully distinguish the various decors from each other, since we had three real estate visits, and also to give a sense of each apartment's layout, so that the audience could realize that it's too small without taking our word for it. For the first apartment, Ayckbourn's dialogues clearly described a sash window. That fit right in with the Bercy neighborhood since there are some apartment buildings there with that type of window.

FT: In his preface to the collection of plays that includes *Private Fears in Public Places*, Ayckbourn writes that he directed the play so that each tableau gradually "dissolved" into the next "by following the fragments of the lives of the characters colliding with each other like so many fragments of solar debris drifting in space." You chose an image that's both related to but distinct from Ayckbourn's by replacing the solar debris with the snow that we see falling outside the windows and that accompanies each of the dissolves from one tableau to the next.

AR: One day in February 2005, standing on the terrace of the National Library, I was caught in a sudden snowstorm without any overcoat, gloves, or boots. I wondered whether I'd make it back to the Metro alive, since there wasn't shelter of any kind to be found. This memory must have left its mark on the film. This idea of snow was present in my very first reading of the play. The snow blanketing Paris allowed me to discover the bitter core that I sense in all of Ayckbourn's plays, and to echo the melancholy, sometimes even the desperation of his characters. It's not a violent snowstorm. I wanted gentle continuous snowfall, always there in the background of the shot. We didn't do a single day of shooting without the team from the Snow Makers, directed by Géraldine Banet. Each time there was an opening in the shot (window, bay window, or doorway), the snow began falling. The snow team was very excited by this experience since it was probably the first time they'd ever made snow fall throughout an entire film. Géraldine was able to propose a variety of types of snow, and we'd agree on which kind of snow best fit each circumstance to match the kind of lenses that Gautier was using. The most difficult aspect of this work was overcoming the noise of the snow machines in order to record the dialogues. Even before we started shooting, we reserved some dates with the mixer, Gérard Lamps, since I knew what miracles he was capable of. Thanks also to the sound engineer, Jean-Marie Blondel, we managed to get away with almost no post-synchronization. Another reason for the snow was that I wanted to solder all of these fifty-three tableaux into a kind of mosaic. Simple fades to black wouldn't have worked. The snow allowed us to emphasize the connections between the characters. We used fade to black only at the ends of each of the four days in order to discreetly indicate the overall structure.

FT: How did you come to choose CinemaScope?

AR: For me, it was an obvious choice, just as it had been for *Love Unto Death*. Right from the start I wanted to play a lot with the faces of the characters. CinemaScope is also a good way to capture large landscapes, caterpillars, or running leopards, but for me its greatest advantage is that you can get close to the actors without appearing to do a portrait. You can do head shots or body shots all the while situating them in the larger realm where the action is taking place.

FT: Even if sometimes in *Private Fears* the backgrounds are out of focus, an effect that accentuates the evanescence of the characters . . . For the most part, the essential scenes, if not the entire film, are shot in deep focus.

AR: Gautier's assistants never refused to attempt acrobatics that might have permanently given them a heart condition! It was terrifying. With the longer lenses, depth of field is so fragile that the least movement on the part of the actor can compromise the visual equilibrium of the shot. We had to play with variations of the longer lens, actors' movements, a very mobile camera, and constant adjustments in focus, since what I wanted to achieve was, frankly, so crazy. I think it all came from the influence of a show I'd seen in which Grotowski wanted to get all of us audience members on stage. There were thirty or forty of us, each sitting on a chair, and the actors moved about among us. It was very strange seeing them move about in the midst of these thirty chairs, and to have to follow their often very unexpected movements. Given the fragility of the characters in *Private Lives*, I wanted to recreate this impression. I played a lot with changes in focus, moving the focal point nearer to and then farther away from us during the shot. During the rehearsals, we would decide at which word or which gesture the assistant would modify the focus. We also made several very "hard-hitting" zooms, quite against my usual principles, although I'd used this technique to show the bursts of thought or imagination in *The War Is Over*.

FT: Besides Grotowski, what other influences might you identify on *Private Fears*?

AR: Well, I'm a great fan of Wong Kar-wai, Hou Hsiao-hsien, Arnaud Desplechin, and David Lynch, but I would especially hope to have been influenced by Kim Manners. He made about fifty episodes of the *X Files*, and the virtuosity of his editing technique and of his mise en scène, as well as the way he directs his actors, made a huge impression on me. He's the ace of aces. I'm not an expert on TV series, but in *Millennium*, *The Shield*, *The Sopranos*, *24 Hours*, and some others, I find the cinematic syntax much richer and more inventive than in the lion's share of the films I've seen. The funny thing is that the full-length feature film of the *X Files* is just like a normal film, with a very ordinary story, and standard shots and photographic choices. With my actors, Gautier, and other members of our team, we talked a lot about certain American series.

FT: Your composer, Mark Snow, is also a veteran of this world.

AR: His striking music for *Millennium*, especially the credit sequence, with its tender and despairing demonic theme, enormously intrigues me, and that's what made me want to work with him. Subsequently, whether it was in *The X Files* or elsewhere, the more I listened to his music, the more it thrilled me. When I was looking at the video mock-ups for the film and I put on one of Mark Snow's records, it worked perfectly. This discovery was decisive for the film. There seemed to be a feeling of mystery shared by the play, the Bercy section of Paris, and the tonality of Snow's music. What first stimulated my attention in Ayckbourn's play was that beneath its great simplicity, something very enigmatic was emanating from his characters. So, we had to have the kind of music that would alert the viewers, whispering, "*Careful. We take the people we meet for what they say they are or for what they appear to be, but there's always a shadow that persists.*" Snow's music perfectly communicates the feeling that there is as much shadow as there is light in the images we're watching. The same week that we asked for the rights to adapt the play, Julie Salvador, our executive producer, contacted Snow, and he responded immediately that he would join our adventure. One day he sent us a waltz that captivated us and that we used for the opening credits. I always want to have at least one, if not three waltzes in my films, didn't even have to ask for one this time! He had immediately grasped the tone of all the characters.

Snow's music haunted our entire shoot. There aren't many recordings available of his music, but I patched together a recording of the series soundtrack where there were no voices, only music. Often we would rehearse while listening to these pieces, alternating "Diabolical Music" with "Angelic Music." Gautier and the actors were immersed in Snow's music. For the shots of the epilogue during which we take our leave of each of the characters in turn, for example, we had them all filmed with the same melancholic accompaniment, which guided both their acting and the tempo of the crane movements; and we realized that during editing, these shots would be connected by the music.

After we'd finished the editing, Snow came to Paris for ten days. I knew that he'd studied at Julliard and that he had a very solid training. During our first dinner together, when I was telling him a story about Anton Webern, he launched into an animated eulogy of Webern, who is his favorite composer. His favorite living musician is Pierre Boulez. He knows an incredible amount about medieval music, and spoke knowledgeably about Ockeghem and Guillaume de Machaut. Normally, I don't like to do this, but this time, we "pasted" some of Snow's compositions over our images to inspire us as we worked. We showed the film to Snow without the music, but he asked to see our "tinkering" and his interaction with the film continued. He sent us his music via internet from his home in New Jersey. Occasionally we would ask him to emphasize something here or there, and he'd send us the modified score. Then we'd send him back the images with the new synchronization, and he'd approve it or perfect it. And now, when I watch an episode of *Millennium*, I'm thrilled to be able to say, "I too have my Mark Snow!"

FT: Who are the actors with whom you regret the most never having worked?

AR: The first names that come to mind are James Mason, George Sanders, Gregory Peck, Lee Remick, and Denholm Elliott, but there are many others as well.

An Auteur in Spite of Himself: An Interview with Alain Resnais

Gary Crowdus and Richard Porton / 2010

From *Cineaste* 35, no. 3 (Summer 2010). Reprinted by permission.

Despite his well-deserved reputation as one of the most acclaimed and innovative filmmakers in the history of French cinema, Alain Resnais has always humbly described himself as merely an "artisan" or a "craftsman." He is not a true auteur, he says, because he does not write his own screenplays. He instead conceives of his creative role as that of a *metteur en scène* (often using the on-screen credit of "mise en scène"), a director less concerned with imposing his personal world view on each of his films than with being at the service of the distinctive authorial voices of the screenwriters, playwrights, or novelists whose works he adapts for the screen.

For such a highly esteemed filmmaker, in fact, Resnais is astonishingly disarming in his disavowal of any personal passions that have motivated choices in his career. Each of the films he has made, he points out, originated with a proposal or an assignment from a producer, and for him, directing films is simply "a way to make a living." Throughout his career, Resnais has continually refuted auteurist critics' notions of the director's superior visionary role, arguing for the essentially more democratic, collaborative nature of film production. "During the shooting of a film," he has said, "there is something stronger than any of us, something which takes possession of the whole crew and that is the film itself. That is why it is difficult afterwards to know how much any one individual was responsible."[1]

Whether on a studio set or on location, Resnais has commented that while he feels everyone else—the performers, the camera and sound crews, and other technicians—are working hard and playing important roles, he feels useless. Even John Ford, who famously described film directing as "a job of work," a statement he intended as a denial of any artistic pretensions, was never that self-effacing about his creative talents.

This extraordinary humility is of course readily belied by frequent testimony about Resnais's ability to elicit the very best work from the writers, actors, cinematographers, editors, and others who have collaborated with him throughout a more than fifty-year career directing feature films, beginning with *Hiroshima mon amour* [1959]. One such corrective came from Anatole Dauman, whose Argos Films Company produced several of Resnais's earlier films. "At the risk of offending his sense of modesty, I declare that Alain Resnais is well and truly the real author of his films and that, although working with different scripts and with different writers, he addresses us with a unique style which belongs to him and to nobody but him."[2]

Nevertheless, when considering the stylistic and thematic disparities in the nineteen feature films that Resnais has directed to date, it is difficult to deny that while each project surely had qualities that personally appealed to him, were his name not listed in the credits, it would be difficult for the average viewer to conceive that the same man directed both *Last Year at Marienbad* [1961] and *Not on the Lips* [2003] or both *Hiroshima mon amour* [1959] and *Private Fears in Public Places* [2006]. This chameleonlike quality, this ability to authentically capture and convey the respective voices of *nouveau roman* author Alain Robbe-Grillet, the 1920s operetta writers André Barde and Maurice Yvain, experimental novelist Marguérite Duras, and satirical British Playwright Alan Ayckbourn, surely reflects the desire of a filmmaker to respect the authors of the original screen plays or literary works being adapted as opposed to attempting to impose his own personal stamp.

This artistic approach is readily apparent in Resnais's newest film, *Wild Grass* (*Les herbes folles*), which succeeds brilliantly in conveying cinematically the distinctive stylistic qualities and narrative strategies of the original author, novelist Christian Gailly. Gailly has been a popular, award-winning novelist in France for over twenty years, although only in recent years have English translations of some of his fourteen novels to date (e.g., *Red Haze, An Evening at the Club, The Passion of Martin Fissel-Brandt*) been published. His novels are characterized by a minimalist style, light on plot, usually with absurdist narratives, and are especially distinguished by their naturalistic dialogue, third-person narrator voices, and representation of stream-of-consciousness thought processes.

Although we had meticulously prepared for what we hoped would be a comprehensive career interview with Resnais (between us, we had five single-spaced pages of questions!), the restricting circumstances of the interview (we were joined by journalists from two other publications, with whom we had to share the allotted one-hour session), we were able to pose only a few of our many questions. Although Resnais occasionally spoke in English, most of his replies were in French, with simultaneous translation provided by Lucius Barre.

Cineaste: We hope you had as much fun making the film as we had in seeing it.

Alain Resnais: I'm very happy to hear that. We enjoyed a delightful and very friendly relationship with all the actors and technicians. That really good human contact was facilitated by the two months of rehearsals we did before we took the first shot. We also enjoyed a fine working relationship with the film's producers who were very high on the novel from which the film was closely adapted. In a way, it was the easiest film I've ever made. I hope I don't sound like a Boy Scout in saying all of this, but everyone was truly very happy and content. We had a few problems with the weather when shooting outdoors—many days it was too cold—but there were no technical difficulties or emotional problems with the actors.

The French word for rehearsal, *répétition*, is not precisely accurate, because every day that you come back to review the script, to work on it with the actors page by page, you're always adding something new to the work, not just repeating it. I'm really against the idea of rehearsing during the shooting, of rehearsing a scene ten times, for example, before doing the first take. But if an actor does retain something from the discussions during rehearsals two months earlier, it really adds a warmth and liveliness. I might be a more difficult director because of this, since it takes longer to make my films. I'm jealous of my fellow filmmakers who don't give a second thought to delivering the script pages to the actors the same day that they're shooting. Those filmmakers work with a great sense of urgency and maybe the results are good, but it's not my style. I'm from Brittany [the Northwest province of France, the coastal region on the French side of the English Channel], and, even if I'm not a sailor, I have the reputation of being slow.

Cineaste: You've said that what attracted you to Gailly's novel was the musical quality of the dialogue and language. Were you excited by the challenge of finding cinematic means to express those literary qualities?

AR: I didn't have any predetermined ideas about it. The twenty or so films that I've made have always come about by pure chance or as a commission from a producer. I've occasionally met with a producer or an actor over dinner and maybe we talk about getting someone to write a script for us. Sometimes it clicks and sometimes it doesn't. But never in my life has there been a film I wanted to make at any cost. I've never rung the doorbell of a producer, for example, and said, "Here I am and here is the scenario that I want to make." I've never conceived of a film before the actual work of making it was begun.

On *Providence*, for example, the producer recommended the author, David Mercer, to me, and I told the producer, "If you're happy to pay David Mercer to work on this, I'm happy to work with him." I must say, by the way, that I have nothing but good things to say about every producer I've ever worked with because they've always been very helpful and understanding. I've never considered myself the "author" of films. I think working as a director is quite enough of a contribution.

Cineaste: How did you work with Laurent Herbiet and Alex Réval, the screenwriters of *Wild Grass*, and how was that different from your collaboration with writers on earlier films?

AR: In the case of Jean Cayrol, Alain Robbe-Grillet, or Marguerite Duras, they were writing original screenplays for me, day after day, week after week, so we could discuss the written pages. Sometimes we saw each other every day, but sometimes we did not see each other for a month or so. The big difference with Christian Gailly is that it was a published novel we were adapting. When we met, he told me that I could have the choice of any of his thirteen novels, but that what was most important for him was to be able to continue working on the novel he was then writing. He was afraid of getting involved in the film, and he preferred to stay away from the film business in general. So I promised Gailly that I would not ask him to write an adaptation or to discuss casting, that I would not phone to ask him to write new lines or a new scene, and he beamed happily. I told him that when the film was finished, I would show it to him first and he could decide if he wanted to keep his name in the credits or not.

The same thing happened with the British playwright Alan Ayckbourn, who preferred to direct his own plays and was always afraid that with a film he would be bothered. For *Wild Grass*, I talked with Laurent Herbier every day, and I started to prepare the shot breakdown (*découpage*) but we didn't prepare any kind of synopsis or treatment, and the shooting script was ready in about six weeks. It was the first time in a way that I had a complete script before shooting. My feeling was that the sound of the dialogue in Gailly's novel was so attractive that we had to follow it.

Cineaste: Did Gailly like the completed film?

AR: I met him for the second time when he came to see the film but I have not spoken to him since then. According to his publisher, he seems to have enjoyed the film very much. That's all I can say. Of course, after the film opens in Paris, and he sees the reviews, who knows?

Cineaste: In addition to always working very closely with your writers, you've also worked very closely with your cinematographers, such as Ghislain Cloquet and Sacha Vierny. In that regard, how was your collaboration with Eric Gautier on *Wild Grass*, especially in getting the color scheme to reflect the various moods of the characters, such as the scene in Marguerite's apartment?

AR: When preparing the breakdown of the script, we try to put as many technical considerations into the mix as possible, keeping in mind the budgetary restrictions of the film. In the first draft of the shooting script, I put in some really fantastic shots, but something that would be both practical and practicable. Gautier and I spent five days in a Brittany hotel, going through the script page by page, and every time I said, "This can't be done," Gautier said, "Yes, we can do it with this camera or this crane." Gautier also read several of Gailly's novels, and liked his writing style, so we both wanted to be faithful to it.

I really like it when a film looks like a film. If we're shooting in an apartment, I really don't want the lighting to be just like that of a real apartment. The direction and color of the light can play like a musical accompaniment to the personalities of the characters. The lighting in the scene that you mentioned, in Marguerite's apartment, during which we change the color palette along the way, is done to enhance and depict the emotions the characters are going through. For example, even though the light is coming from behind me here [*during the interview, Resnais was seated with his back to a window*], I would not hesitate for a minute, if it would enhance the performance, to change the light and have it come from the other side of the room. I'm not the only filmmaker who does this, but I do have a penchant for this approach to lighting.

Cineaste: Is this why you prefer to shoot in studios rather than on location?

AR: I'm really uncomfortable shooting exteriors, not only because they're real streets, real houses, or real forests, but also because you can't actually turn the sun around. It really bothers me to have to put the actor in a specific place vis-à-vis the sun, and not the other way around. For exteriors, you might also have to wait an hour or two just to pull off a shot. It's really boring, so we go into the café and smoke and drink coffee.

Cineaste: You've often said that you consider your approach to filmmaking as "experimental," and that it's most fun for you when you can experiment when making a film. But, just as in the world of science, it's clear that some cinematic experiments succeed and others fail. What criteria do you consider when deciding if one of your films has succeeded or failed?

AR: It's nearly impossible to determine. You know, it was once thought that, after a film's initial release, it would never be seen again, but that's no longer true. I haven't made a lot of films, but thanks especially to TV and DVD, my films are still being shown and released decades later, even if they didn't originally bring in huge audiences or profits. Critical judgments and reactions to the films have also evolved or changed along the way. *Muriel*, for example, at the time of its release, was a major failure. Today, it's a film that people talk about quite frequently, in particular its superimposition of dialogue from one scene to the next, and that's an experiment that I'm happy we tried. *Muriel* is a film still being studied in classrooms.

Everyone second-guesses himself and says that perhaps I should have done this or done that. But I do go for experiments. I much prefer taking a scene and doing it in a way different from what's normally done. It all depends on the script. In *Marienbad*, there were lots of camera movements, but when Jean Cayrol wrote *Muriel* for me, the sound of his scenario—which portrayed the perpetual malaise of his characters, people devoid of human feelings—dictated a different style. There's only one camera movement in *Muriel*—the last shot. There are over 900 cuts in the film, but every single shot was filmed with a fixed camera. There were a few pans, but otherwise the camera was locked down. I really like what my friend François Truffaut said about this: always make your next film in opposition to the preceding one.

Cineaste: You talked about a struggle for dominance between the characters in *Wild Grass*. To some extent, that seems like a continuation of the themes that the French psychologist, Henri Laborit talked about in *Mon Oncle d'Amérique*.

Resnais: Yes, it's true that we've all had occasions to work toward dominating people with whom we're living or working. It could be a fraternal domination, or it could be a situation of violence and warfare. People on the Earth are always attempting to dominate each other, and there's always that sense in social situations. But during the shooting I didn't wake up in the morning and say that this is the subject of the film. It just comes with the territory. It might be pretentious to say this, but I don't like to reason with my film when I'm working on it. We'll discover the film's meaning when it's finished. In fact, I often say that I shoot the film in order to see what happens, to see what the final outcome will be. This is a problem confronting every filmmaker—what can I do to make sure that audience members don't get up and leave?

Notes

1. "Memories of Resnais," an interview with Alain Resnais by Richard Roud, *Sight and Sound* (summer 1996).
2. *Anatole Dauman: Pictures of a Producer*, written with Jacques Gerber, in the chapter entitled "King Resnais" (London: BFI Publishing, 1992), 48.

A Conversation with Alain Resnais on *You Ain't Seen Nothin' Yet*

François Thomas / 2012

From the pressbook of the film.

François Thomas: How did you decide to launch into an adaptation of Jean Anouilh?

Alain Resnais: When my producer, Jean-Louis Livi, and his colleagues Julie Salvador and Christophe Jeauffroy proposed that we make a new film with them in the aftermath of *Wild Grass*, we began looking for a play that would allow us to produce a screenplay very quickly. What I'm always looking for in my films is the language of theater, a musical dialogue that invites the actors to get away from daily realism and into a different sort of acting. I read and reread various playwrights before deciding on Jean Anouilh. I've been at the opening of at least twenty of his plays since the '30s. When I left the premiere of *Eurydice* seventy years ago, I was so moved that I rode my bike all around Paris and then went back to see the play again a week later. Just as I'd done for *Wild Grass*, I asked my friend Laurent Herbiet to work on an adaptation between his work directing two other films. Two or three days later, Laurent suggested that we mix *Eurydice* with *Cher Antoine*, another of Anouilh's plays that I'd asked him to reread. *Eurydice* would then be a play by the playwright, Antoine d'Anthac, an eternally dissatisfied man who doubts himself and doesn't feel loved. Antoine's actor friends, who had performed in the premiere of his play or performed it ten, twenty, or thirty years afterwards, would be watching the filmed rehearsals of a young troupe desirous of obtaining the rights to the play. During the projection of this film, they are so overwhelmed by their memories of the play, that they begin to play their former roles even though they are no longer the age of their characters. I always have particularly strong feelings when I see an actor redoing one of his former roles. The challenge of the film was to create drama from the back and forth between Antoine's friends and the actors in the filmed rehearsals. This seemed to me a way of heightening the emotion in the reunion of Orpheus and Eurydice, these two mythological characters rendered immortal by the force of the imagination and the popular unconscious.

FT: You came back to a number of actors who had already had roles in your films, recently or as long ago as the '60s, but you also chose four newcomers: Denis Podalydès, Andrzej Seweryn, Girardot, and Michel Robin.

AR: As much as I dream of working again with actors I've already used, I also dream of working for the first time with many others. I was fascinated by Denis Podalydès's delivery in films by Bruno Podalydès and Arnaud Desplechin, and by his chameleon-like qualities when he gives readings of books on the radio. I had admired Hippolyte Girardot in *Kings and Queen* and *A Christmas Tale* by Desplechin, and in Pascale Ferran's *Lady Chatterley*. Andrzej Seweryn was extraordinary as Molière's Don Juan, and I've seen Michel Robin countless times on and off stage ever since he signed on with Roger Planchon in the late '50s. But I was also delighted to reunite with the eleven others, both actors I'd worked with recently and others I hadn't seen for ages but whose careers I had continued to follow.

FT: Why did you ask Bruno Podalydès to make the film of the Compagnie de la Colombe that was rehearsing the play?

AR: It was an experiment, a game. If I'd had to invent a mise en scène for a theatrical performance by a young troupe in 2012, I would have felt I was cheating, that it wouldn't be sincere. It was much more exciting to ask a colleague and close friend who belongs to that younger generation. The script indicated the passage from *Eurydice* that should be filmed, but otherwise I gave Bruno carte blanche for the staging as well as for the casting, the crew, and the style. He asked me for some instructions but I insisted: "No, I don't want to be involved at all in the acting in the film that you're going to direct. The more different it is from what I would have done the more it will reflect the spirit of our enterprise." The wager that most amused me was to wait until we began editing the film to discover the juxtaposition of his images and mine.

FT: After *Private Fears* and *Wild Grass*, this is your third collaboration with the American composer Mark Snow. You've never before worked so consistently with one musician.

AR: I wanted the music to be the kind of hypnosis that plunged Antoine's guests into the memories that overcame them. Mark Snow was therefore ideal. I had been struck by the tender and desperate, ultimately demonic theme that he'd written for the TV series by Chris Carter, *Millennium* (no connection with Stieg Larsson's novels), and that's what made me want to work with him. He knows marvelously well how to combine light and shadow, simplicity and enigma. I was delighted that he'd accept to come over from Connecticut to see the film and discuss what he was going to do. As with my two previous films, I shot certain scenes while playing recordings of some of his previous compositions on the set in order to help the actors and the team find the right tone. The editor, Hervé de Luze, and I also played some of his pieces with the provisional edit to best set the rhythm of the film. When we showed *You Ain't Seen Nothin' Yet* to Snow, we left those original pieces in. His reaction was, "If I understand you correctly, I have to do better than myself!" And in my view, that's exactly what he succeeded in doing!

A Conversation with Alain Resnais on *The Life of Riley*

François Thomas / 2014

From *Positif* (April 2014). Reprinted with permission. Translated by T. Jefferson Kline.

François Thomas: After *No Smoking* and *Smoking* in 1993 and *Coeurs* [*Private Fears in Public Places*], *Aimer, Boire et Chanter* [*The Life of Riley*] is your third adaptation of a play by Alan Ayckbourn.

Alain Resnais: Ayckbourn is very prolific and writes a play a year. His official catalogue now includes seventy-seven plays. I must have seen twenty-five of them on stage whether in London or Scarborough, the little town in Yorkshire where he produces them himself, but it's been years since I've been able to escape to England during the summer. In 2010, after we shot *Vous n'avez encore rien vu* [*You Ain't Seen Nothin' Yet*], my producer, Jean-Louis Livi was able to acquire the five last plays of Ayckbourn that had never been published, and, when we read them, we fell in love with the very last one, *The Life of Riley*. A year and a half later, Livi suggested that we make it our next film. As in Ayckbourn's other plays, the unpredictable behavior of a character (here, George Riley) unleashes in couples, who were routinely chugging along, the discovery of their deep dissatisfactions and of the errors they'd committed. In the same way that Colin's clocks chime at the wrong time, these six characters are mistaken about others and about themselves. The play poses the question: Are we what our friends and enemies believe us to be? Do we have a personality that's different from the description they give of us? This theme is very close to the one Philip Roth has his characters say: that every biography is a string of errors and the very idea of a biographical novel is fallacious. I was also very aware of a certain melancholy that Ayckbourn expresses repeatedly: over time, all lives are evidently failures. And the worst of life's dirty tricks is the knowledge that there will be separations: we invented attraction, love, the couple, but we all know in advance that sickness and death will eventually separate every couple.

Ayckbourn loves to do what is normally forbidden in the theater. In *Life of Riley*, the real action is always happening off stage and the characters are always talking about what the audience doesn't see and never will see. In principle this way of writing should be avoided! So it was a stimulating challenge to adapt the play, and I had the impression of being in unknown territory.

When you adapt a play, since you have to depend firmly on the theatrical text and respect the way the dialogue is constructed, you're obliged to play with the form in a way that differs from an original filmscript. I worked with Laurent Herbiet as we did for *Les Herbes folles* [*Wild Grass*] and *Vous n'avez encore rien vu* [*You Ain't Seen Nothin' Yet*]. We developed a technical storyboard, using the English dialogues in the first draft. Then we cut down the play so as to have a film of less than two hours, but we managed to do this with only one modification of the dialogue: we switched an allusion to hang-gliding to scuba-diving. We also changed the first name of one of the characters, but gave him a name that had been mentioned at some point during the play. Then we had to find someone to write the French dialogues. I really like the vivacity of Jean-Marie Besset's dialogues in his own plays as well as his French adaptations of Alan Bennett and David Hare: they're fluid, supple, and written to be played by good actors. Besset always has the sense of the actor's breathing, which is why his actors delight in his work. When I met him, we talked about all of the English playwrights of the '50s and '60s—and of today—who so fascinate us, and I discovered that he was really in his element with Ayckbourn. This was the man we needed! The phrasing and cadences of his dialogues would encourage the actors to invent an edgy style of delivery.

We had to look for a French title since the pun on *The Life of Riley* (which means both "the life of Riley" and "the life of a knockabout") was untranslatable. Ultimately, we thought of the Johann Strauss waltz, *Aimer, Boire et chanter* [*Wine, Women and Song*]. That captured the sense of the play.

FT: How did you select your actors, grouping actors you've already used with a newcomer, Sandrine Kiberlain?

AR: I was very moved by Sandrine Kiberlain's performance as a schoolteacher in love with a mason in *Mademoiselle Chambon* [directed by Stéphane Brizé in 2009]. It seemed to me that Sabine Azéma, André Dussollier, Hippolyte Girardot, and Michel Vuillermoz would surprise me in roles that were very different from anything we'd done before. I hadn't worked with Caroline Silhol since *I Want to Go Home*, but I remembered her performance in Philippe Claudel's *Parlez-moi d'amour* [*Tell Me about Love*] at the Comédie des Champs-Elysées, a play about a couple who decides to get even with each other. She managed to communicate a great variety of feelings that bourgeois couples experience. Several of these actors already knew Ayckbourn's work so our preparation was quite easy: Dussollier had premiered one of his plays at the Théâtre Montparnasse in the '70s; Ayckbourn had directed Azéma in a play in Scarborough twenty years later; Vuillermoz had wanted to stage one of his plays; and Silhol loved *The Life of Riley* and would have produced it as a play if we hadn't made a film of it.

FT: The couple formed by Sabine Azéma and Hippolyte Girardot [Kathryn and Colin] seem to be competing for an award for physical activity! Their hands are constantly in motion and they manage to bring the space around them alive through their gestures and movements.

AR: This was something they invented by themselves. What I worked on, as usual, was the combination of voices and the harmony of these two particular voices that worked well together. Anything beyond that was brought by the actors themselves. Azéma and Girardot never appear together in the same scene in *You Ain't Seen Nothin' Yet*. But I easily imagined them playing this couple that is so threatened.

FT: In Ayckbourn's play, the action never unfolds indoors. With the exception of the final scene, everything takes place in four different gardens, or, if you prefer, three gardens and a barnyard.

AR: I think that the best way to do justice to Ayckbourn's dialogue was to enclose them in a transposed studio décor. This basic approach was inspired by the memory of Georges Pitoëff's staging of Chekhov's *Sea Gull* at the Théâtre des Mathurins in 1939, when I was seventeen. That was the performance that inspired my lasting and devouring passion for the theater. Georges Pitoëff played Trigorine, Ludmilla Pitoëff, Nina, and Louis Salou, Sorine. Héléna Manson was also in that cast and agreed forty years later to play a role in my film *Mon oncle d'Amérique* [*My American Uncle*]. Ayckbourn is not without similarities to Chekhov, and I wasn't surprised that he staged *Uncle Vanya* at Scarborough recently. When Pitoëff didn't have enough money for the sets, he collected bits of fabric, of felt, of old curtains, and, with these materials, created a suggestion of the suggested sets for the play. I suggested to our chief set designer, Jacques Saulnier, that he use this idea of strips of fabrics schematically representing the gardens, façades, forests, and horizon. In the theater, they use strips of black felt to hide the offstage areas and block the light, so why not give them back their prominence? With his assistant Matthieu Beutter and his team of painters, Saulnier succeeded in effecting this. From time to time, you feel as if you're looking at paintings by such "naïve" painters as Le Douanier Rousseau, as in the shot in the farmyard where Jack comes to ask Monica to return to her life with George. I said, "We're going shoot this the way D. W. Griffith would have done it."

In the second act, I dragged our characters indoors for a few scenes in order to give a certain whip-like rhythm to the film. This is the reverse of the habitual rhythm, where you give a film breathing room by transposing the action to exterior shots when everything takes place indoors. In this case, in the first instance, we enter Jack and Tamara's house for Tamara's hysterical outbreak. I expected that Ayckbourn would condemn the liberties I'd taken with his play, but when he saw the film, he gave me his blessing. In like manner, I also wanted that increasingly high gradation of the three staircases (at Jack and Tamara's house, at Simeon's place, and then at the home of Colin and Kathryn) as the film progressed.

FT: So even though, judging by their façades, these three houses get progressively smaller, the diminutive exterior of Colin's and Kathryn's townhouse opens into an interior worthy of a manor.

AR: I'll give you my usual answer: dramatic progression is more important than realistic credibility. Indeed, it's perhaps this contradiction that creates surprise.

I also had fun making certain elements of the décor disappear at will: a rose garden, a glass door in an absurd location behind which Jack and Monica can retreat to have a thorny conversation while watching the birthday party outside. I may have been influenced by certain plays that I saw in New York that treated the décor in a very free and inventive way, such as Arthur Miller's *After the Fall* as staged by Elia Kazan in the '60s.

FT: Ayckbourn's play is composed of about forty scenes that alternate among the four gardens. At Scarborough, where the set was divided into four spaces of equal dimensions, repositioning the lights moved us from one garden to the next. When you adapted the play you created these transitions by using drawings by Blutch or shots of natural decors that situated these gardens in larger spaces.

AR: I'm very impressed with Blutch's graphic innovations and by the expressivity of his characters. I especially enjoyed his last album, *Pour en finir avec le cinema* [So Long, Silver Screen], where I reread several times the discussion between the antihero and the young woman on the differences between theater and film. The idea of asking him for drawings that would clearly differentiate the four gardens came to me very quickly. His drawings also allowed us to mark the passing of the seasons. Blutch worked a lot with Saulnier. He was inspired by his sets but took them in a very different direction. The shots of streets and roads in Yorkshire were shot at the very end. With my editor, Hervé de Luze, for both the illustrations and the shots of Yorkshire, we had to find the right equilibrium, the right dosage, without getting systematic about it.

FT: *Mélo*, with its seventy shots, had the fewest edits of all your films. This time the number was one hundred fifty shots.

AR: It happens that I also admire George Stevens, who broke up his fights into numerous different shots: what I loved about his films was that you could never be sure what the next shot would be. But in this case I wanted to do the opposite. We made a film that didn't have a single shot-countershot or very nearly so, with shots that sometimes lasted more than three minutes. Each time I told the director of photography, Dominique Bouilleret, that this or that complicated shot, where both camera and actors were moving constantly, seemed impossible to do and that we'd better cut it into two or three shots he'd say, "No, we're going to manage fine!" He's an ace.

FT: How did you choose him?

AR: I love the made-for-TV films that Laurent Herbiet directed, and Bouilleret had done the lighting for three of them. I was particularly struck by the lighting of *Manipulations*, which was particularly vivid and dramatic. It was all the more sensational in that the film was shot in very few weeks. When I met Bouilleret, we immediately hit it off. What I like in his lighting of *The Life of Riley* is that he manages to flatten the shots to make them look like they're laminated, making them feel like graphic literature. And yet, we never said a word about comic strips with Bouilleret. Our first discussions focused on the question of how to make a film that would be both hyper-theatrical and hyper-cinematic. As far as the editing was concerned, I tried to be at times excessively traditional and at other times introduce unorthodox subtleties, hoping that this antagonism between timidity and audacity would create an emotive shock for the viewers and that the shock of this contradictory style of editing would reflect the contradictions in the characters. After the prologue in Yorkshire, we began with a shot where Kathryn and Colin are in their garden rehearsing the play that their friend Peggy Parker is directing, so we're practically filming amateur theater. And progressively we begin to use effects that are impossible in the theater.

FT: So your actors had to simulate the acting of amateur players.

AR: For Kathryn and Colin, yes, but Tamara seems to have been an actress in her youth. As for Jack, he's never done any theater, so he simply reads lines to Tamara to help her learn her role. I loved the way Vuillermoz imitated the diction and false gaiety of people who are not in the theater and don't know how to act.

The play they're rehearsing is *Relatively Speaking*, Ayckbourn's first great success that launched his career in London in 1967. Our actors have the original brochure in hand. The amusing thing is that the characters in *The Life of Riley* are not nearly as young as those in *Relatively Speaking*. Tamara and George are playing lovers who are in their twenties. We're not far from *You Ain't Seen Nothin' Yet*.

FT: In *The Life of Riley*, Tamara's dialogue during her daughter Tillly's birthday party does not in the least anticipate the explosion of rage that Caroline Silbol displays.

AR: I told Silbol about two or three other Ayckbourn plays containing such terrifying explosions of lunacy where a woman has a nervous breakdown and becomes completely irrational, generally at the beginning of the second act. In

Absent Friends, when she realizes the failure of all her aspirations, a woman who is welcoming a few guests to her house for tea suddenly recounts how, as a child, she had wanted to enter the Royal Canadian Mounties and wear a red coat. When it was explained to her that this wasn't a career for girls, she marries her husband instead. Why isn't she the queen of the Mounties? This woman suddenly regresses to childhood, cries, screams, and they end up dragging her off stage. Tamara's despair in *The Life of Riley* is directly inspired by this moment. Silhol had lots of latitude. Azéma went much further in *Smoking*, when she loses her mind in the tent. I was also tempted to adapt the play that Ayckbourn wrote after *Life of Riley*, *Neighborhood Watch*, in which there's also a dramatic nervous breakdown at the beginning of the second act that is very striking.

With my actors, I talked a lot about Ayckbourn's other plays and it turned out to be a useful guide for them. In his theater, the actors must play with great intensity. The characters are never trying to make people laugh, they're unaware that they're crazy. In *Absurd Person Singular*, there's a scene in the kitchen, when the hostess, dressed in a formal gown for Christmas Eve, without saying a word, makes a whole series of suicide attempts by various means, but her guests never notice a thing. The audience dies laughing at something that's actually quite tragic.

FT: According to Blutch, the mole that doesn't appear in *Life of Riley*, and that you have come up out of the ground at the end of the first act, represents the director.

AR: Why not? I don't like to be in the sun and prefer to live in semi-darkness. When I read the play, I thought that, since everything took place in the gardens, we needed the point of view of the mole. You could say that everything is told by this burrower, who finds humans so bizarre that she returns to her hole.

I wanted to put a mole at the beginning of *No Smoking* and *Smoking*, thinking of a film by Clarence Brown with Mickey Rooney, *And Life Goes On* [1943], co-authored by William Saroyan, whose work I like a lot. After the invasion of Normandy, the American army planes brought a dozen or so films to France, and I saw this one privately with a couple of journalists. At the beginning, you hear the voice of a dead man through images of clouds floating across the sky, and then you see an airplane flying over the California countryside. You fly over a town (that is clearly a miniature model) and then beneath you, you see a farmyard and you descend toward a child who is watching a mole emerge from its hole, and the camera keeps moving downwards until it frames just the mole. What I loved and wanted to imitate was the disproportion of scale, the conclusion of this great voyage ending with the image of a mole scraping in the dirt. Ultimately, we found another way of beginning: for *Smoking* and *No Smoking*, it was films with seagulls.

FT: If my memory serves me well, the animal in *And Life Goes On* is not a mole but a gopher.

AR: I haven't seen that film since 1944! I don't know if I would have derived the same pleasure working with a gopher. The mole was great. We filmed her on the last day.

FT: One of the most astonishing choices in the film, mostly in the long monologues, is the use of close-ups with abstract backgrounds of black-and-white from which the character emerges without entering the light of the shots around him.

AR: We called that "rips" or "ripping." I wanted to make a film with abrupt changes of speed. When the characters were in their most intimate and private moments, the décor would disappear and the characters could act differently. I wanted a neutral and discreet background that might simulate a cartoon.

FT: The concept of a two-dimensional image, without depth, leads you to play with the soundtrack. Colin and Kathryn's little village, and the countryside surrounding the other characters are alive with distant and muffled tones that characterize each place.

AR: Gérard Hardy, the sound editor for most of my films since *Not on the Lips*, brought a selection of soundtrack possibilities. I'd made my usual request: "Don't tell me where the sound is coming from, whether you fabricated it artificially or whether you recorded it in a real street or on a real farm." Hardy is obsessively meticulous. He is a master of sonic ambiguity and chiaroscuro.

FT: Strauss's waltz, "Aimer, Boire et Chanter" ["The Life of Riley"], provided not only the title of the film, but you hear excepts from it at various times in the film.

AR: For the scenes in which George, isolated in his cottage, is listening to a record or to the radio without answering the phone when his friends call him, I hesitated a lot: what music should I use? In Ayckbourn's play, it was Pink Floyd that you also heard at the cemetery. On set, we put on AC/DC to avoid having silent rushes. I wondered what music I would listen to in this situation. Stephen Sondheim's bitter song "The Road You Didn't Take"? The opening music to *The Mary Tyler Moore Show*? I finally noticed that I had the solution right in front of me with Strauss's waltz that propels the changes of scene. Luze and the composer Mark Snow both liked the effect, and so we kept it.

So we had "Aimer [Love] and Boire [Drink]" all right (of the French title), but we didn't have "Chanter" ["Sing"] to complete the program. We could have put in a song during the final credits, I suppose. But without knowing anything about scales, a tune came to me in a dream that wouldn't go away for weeks. One day I sat down at my desk in front of my notebook and wrote the lyrics to a sad song and sang it for Snow when he came to Paris. It began "George Riley is not the title of a sweet little songlet / George Riley's the name of the tale of a comet," and it ended "George Riley has committed hara-kiri / Eleison!" Snow played my tune on the electric piano, noted it down and intended to use it in the film's score. I might have been listed as co-composer! But ultimately, we chose a recording of the Strauss Waltz by the tenor, Georges Thill, in 1935, with French lyrics by Lucien Boyer to open the credits before giving way to Snow's score. Bye-bye, career change! I'll have to make another film to earn my bread.

I was blown away by the evocation of a clock ticking in the music Snow composed for the beginning of the film, inspired by Colin's mania for clocks. The credits are displayed over a fixed shot of a road in Yorkshire, with trees reaching out to embrace over the roadway. And then, once the credits have rolled, the film begins to run as the musical carillon starts. I asked Snow to write music only for the scenes transitioning between the gardens. Afterwards, I relaxed a bit about this, but, except for the last scene, the music can be heard during the dialogues only two or three times.

FT: For the final burial in *You Ain't Seen Nothin' Yet*, Mark Snow wrote a very solemn piece for the violin, as tragic as the opening theme in the TV series *Millennium*, which was what attracted you to this composer. For the final burial scene in *The Life of Riley*, he composed a very lively air, a lot like Nino Rota.

AR: When de Luze and I chose the provisional music to help us with the editing, we tried some melancholic and some dramatic music by Snow, including his music for *Millennium* and also some crepuscular music by Miklós Rózsa, but none of that worked. As soon as we tried something lighter and a bit more fantastic, almost slapstick, I could breathe more easily. The contrast between the music and the sinister story worked much better. Snow was delighted to go in this direction.

FT: When your earlier films are edited for DVD, you often request that the soundtrack not be remastered. Why is that?

AR: Many editors have a tendency to clean up the sound beyond what is necessary. But how can you dissociate the style of acting from the techniques of recording and mixing? They didn't perform in 1930 or in 1960 the same way we do today. In the DVDs of films that are remastered according to the tastes of the present, the actors tend to appear to be performing in an affected way, giving the impression of watching a dubbed film, or someone reciting or reading his lines. If you take the breath out of the epoch, you remove all the harmonics from the actors' voices. Charles Boyer, Louis Jouvet, Sacha Guitry all lose their bass tonalities. Whether it's the bass, the middle register, or the high notes, the voices become neutral, flattened, all mixed together. The sound of laserdiscs was much more lively than the sound of DVDs. I tested this by playing the same Woody Allen film simultaneously on DVD and laser: the laser was better. I almost think that remastered sound is worse than VHS. The videocassettes of Guitry's films were better than the French DVDs that I listened to. I made the same comparison with a film by Pierre Chenal, where the conversations at a bar in the background were intelligible on the VHS but not on the DVD. By correcting what are thought to be defects, you can upset the equilibrium among the voices, the sounds, and the music in the film and destroy its style. If you correct a distortion the music risks being deadened. Once someone said while we were looking at a computer screen, "You see! There's a distortion on the curve; I'll correct it." But once it was retouched, all the life was drained from it, and the music was killed. I prefer to respect the sonorous characteristics of the period, especially since the viewer stops noticing these "defects" after a few minutes. When I hear the unrestored soundtrack of my films, I like it a lot. As a viewer, I always prefer the original version. As a director, I'm not opposed to a thoughtful remastering of my films as long as it's not mechanical. But I think we ought to leave the spectator the freedom to choose between the remastered and the original soundtrack.

Additional Resources

Armes, Roy. *The Cinema of Alain Resnais*. New York: A. S. Barnes, 1968.

Benayoun, Robert. *Alain Resnais: Arpenteur de l'imaginaire*. Paris: Stock, 1980.

Douin, Jean-Luc. *Alain Resnais*. Paris: Éditions de la Martinière, 2013.

Kreidl, John Francis. *Alain Resnais*. Boston: Twayne, 1977.

Liandrat-Guigues, Suzanne, and Jean-Louis Leutrat, *Alain Resnais: liaisons secrètes, accords vagabonds*. Paris: Cahiers du Cinéma, 2006.

Lindeperg, Sylvie. *Night and Fog: a Film in History*. Translated by Tom Mes, foreword by Jean-Michel Frodon. *Visible Evidence* 28. Minneapolis: University of Minnesota Press, 2014.

Lindeperg, Sylvie. *Nuit et brouillard, un film dans l'histoire*. Paris: Éditions Odile Jacob, 2007.

Monaco, James. *Alain Resnais*. New York: Oxford University Press, 1979.

Raskin, Richard. *Alain Resnais's "Nuit et Brouillard": On the Making, Reception and Functions of a Major Documentary Film, Including a New Interview with Alain Resnais and the Original Shooting Script*. Aarhus, Denmark: Aarhus University Press, 1987.

Regazzi, Jean. *Le roman dans le cinéma: retour à Providence*. Paris: L'Harmattan, 2010.

Sweet, Freddy. *The Film Narratives of Alain Resnais* Ann Arbor: UMI Research Press, 1981.

Thomas, François. *Alain Resnais, les coulisses de la création : Entretiens avec ses proches collaborateurs*. Paris : Armand Colin, 2016.

Thomas, François. *L'Atelier d'Alain Resnais*. Paris: Flammarion, 1989.

Ungar, Steven. *Critical Mass: Social Documentary in France from the Silent Era to the New Wave*. University of Minnesota Press, 2018.

Van der Knaap, Ewout. *Uncovering the Holocaust: The International Reception of Night and Fog*. Wallflower Press, 2006.

Ward, John. *Alain Resnais or the Theme of Time*. New York: Doubleday, 1968.

Wilson, Emma. *Alain Resnais*. Manchester and New York: Manchester University Press, 2006.

Index

Anouilh, Jean, xviii, xix, 173–74
Ardant, Fanny, xvi, 97, 127, 132
Arditi, Pierre, xv, xvi, xviii–xix, 89, 97, 129, 130, 133, 156, 160
Ayckbourn, Alan, xvi–xix, 148–50, 158–61, 163–65, 168, 170, 176–82
Azéma, Sabine, xv–xvi, xviii–xix, 89, 129, 134, 160, 177–78, 181

Bacri, Jean-Pierre, xix, 149, 152
Bazin, André, ix, xx, 45, 53
Belmondo, Jean-Paul, xii, xv, 5, 59, 71–72
Bergman, Ingmar, 10, 25, 44, 59
Bernstein, Henri, xvi, 4, 112, 118, 127–30, 134, 136–37
Bogarde, Dirk, xiv–xv, 62, 122
Boyer, Charles, 72, 79, 130–31, 183
Bresson, Robert, viii, 24–26, 31, 52–54
Breton, André, xiv, xx, 17, 19, 42, 51

Cahiers du cinéma, ix, 65, 147
Cayrol, Jean, x, xii, xvi, 5, 8, 37, 40, 43, 48, 65, 117, 144–45, 170, 172
Clair, René, 18, 111–12
Cocteau, Jean, 9, 17, 52–54, 112, 131

Dauman, Anatole, viii, 121, 140, 147, 168, 172n2
Deleuze, Gilles, xv, xxi
Demy, Jacques, 40, 52, 66, 126

Dickson, Harry, viii, xvii, xxin2, 21, 48, 59, 114, 121–22
Duras, Marguerite, xi, xvi, 4, 8, 10, 21, 28, 34, 37, 43, 57–59, 65, 124, 129, 145, 147, 168, 170
Dussollier, André, xv–xvi, xix, 97, 131, 133, 149, 150, 160–62, 177–78

Eisenstein, Sergei, xx, 9, 19, 45, 66
Epstein, Jean, 45, 51–52, 66
Expressionism, 49, 51

Fantômas, viii, xiv, xvii, 8, 49–51, 109, 111
Feiffer, Jules, xviii, 153
Feuillade, Louis, viii, 48–50
Fontaine, Bruno, 151, 154–55

Gailly, Christian, xix, 168–71
Giraudoux, Jean, xiii, 53–54, 80, 112, 146, 156
Godard, Jean-Luc, 5, 39–40, 43–44, 49, 56–57, 66, 72, 115, 125
Griffith, D. W., 66, 85, 178
Gruault, Jean, 78–80, 84–85, 88, 98, 130, 153
Guitry, Sacha, xiii, 52, 54, 70, 104, 112, 123, 131, 143, 161, 183–84

Henze, Hans Warner, 90–93, 130, 137

Jaoui, Agnès, xix, 149, 152
Jurgenson, Albert, xvi, 90, 93, 138

Kundera, Milan, 105, 111, 126–28

Laborit, Henri, xiv, xvi, 67, 77–79, 82–86, 125, 172
Lee, Stan, 62–63, 105, 125, 126n1
L'Herbier, Marcel, 40, 50–51, 56

Malraux, Florence, xvi, 85, 114, 131, 144
Marker, Chris, ix, xiii, 3, 26, 40, 43, 54, 66, 139–47, 153
Montand, Yves, xii, xv, 24, 26, 27, 63

Pésery, Bruno, 148–49, 154, 158
Proust, Marcel, xii, 10, 80
Pudovkin, Vsevolod, 19, 45, 66, 153

Queneau, Raymond, x, xvi, 6, 155

Renoir, Jean, viii, 25, 41, 54–56, 111
Resnais, Alain: on actors, 24–27, 39, 45, 61, 71–72, 79–80, 89, 93–94, 96–97, 119, 125, 130–32, 135, 156, 160, 162, 165–66, 169, 174, 177–78, 183; on automatic writing (*écriture automatique*), 7, 14, 39, 88, 100; on censorship, 11, 12, 24, 40, 139; on CinemaScope, 6, 94, 164; on colors (use of), 6, 40, 64, 75, 115, 119, 134, 137–38, 171; on comic strips, 81, 105–6, 142–43, 153, 179–80, 182; on imagination, 4–5, 31–32, 78, 117, 123, 132, 146, 149, 158–59, 165, 174; on improvisation, 3, 61, 82, 96–97, 149, 160; on memory, 9–10, 20–21, 35, 42, 63, 78, 84, 91, 103, 122–23, 146, 160, 164; on mise en scène, 7, 25, 40, 45, 58–59, 86, 93, 119, 158, 165, 167, 174; on music in film, 34–35, 37–38, 72, 75, 87–93, 105, 118, 130, 135–38, 148–51, 165–66, 174, 182–84; on musical comedy, operetta, 4, 44, 146, 148, 150–51, 154–56, 168; on musical structuring of film, 4, 13, 35, 38, 52, 87, 92, 96, 98, 100, 105, 133, 160, 171, 173; on musicality, 25, 28, 53, 95–97, 118, 124, 134, 136; on opera, 28, 124–26, 129, 135, 138, 148, 151, 158; on painting and painters, 7, 18, 21, 25, 37, 42, 44, 59, 80, 93, 101, 115–16, 123, 143, 157, 161–62, 178; on politics, 12, 17, 20–24, 30, 33, 35, 38–39, 41, 65, 73; on post-synchronization, 49, 94, 134–35, 164; on rehearsing, 18, 94, 96, 125, 131, 165–66, 169, 173, 180; on sound, 15, 44, 49, 53, 89, 94, 132–35, 140, 143, 145, 150–51, 156, 163, 182–84; on sound films, 6, 110, 112, 116, 155; on television, 44, 94, 114–16, 122, 137, 143, 149–50, 152, 165, 171, 174, 180, 183; on theater (early love of, inspiration from), 30, 80, 112–13, 129, 155, 178; on theater (film modeled on, adapted from), 5, 34, 36–37, 119–20, 124, 131, 134–36, 145, 148–49, 156–58, 163, 173–74, 177, 179–81

Films: *Aimer, boire et chanter* (*The Life of Riley*) (2014), xix, 176–78, 180–83; *L'Amour à mort* (*Love Unto Death*) (1984), xvi–xvii, xix, 87, 97–100, 109, 127, 129–32, 134, 137–38; *L'Année dernière à Marienbad* (*Last Year at Marienbad*) (1961), vii, xi–xii, xiv, 13–19, 20, 27–28, 33–34, 37–38, 48, 57–58, 60, 63, 68, 77, 98, 101, 103, 108, 116–17, 124, 135, 148, 152, 161, 168, 172; *Le Chant du styrène* (1958), vii, x, 6, 21, 98; *Ciné-Tracts* (1968), xiii, 145; *Cœurs* (*Private Fears in Public*

Places) (2006), xvii–xviii, 158–60, 162–65, 168, 174, 176; *Gershwin* (1993), x; *Guernica* (1950), ix, 124; *La Guerre est finie* (*The War is Over*) (1966), xii–xiii, 20–35, 41, 43, 48, 60, 63–64, 70, 104, 116, 124, 135, 153, 161, 165; *Les Herbes folles* (*Wild Grass*) (2009), xix, 168, 170–74, 177; *Hiroshima mon amour* (1958), vii, xi–xii, xix, 4–6, 9–11, 20–21, 27–29, 34, 43, 59–60, 65, 68, 103–4, 116, 124, 134, 146, 148, 168; *I Want to Go Home* (1989), xviii, 153, 177; *Je t'aime, je t'aime* (1968), xiii, xix, 44, 60, 63–64, 93, 104, 122, 134, 153, 160; *Loin du Vietnam* (*Far from Vietnam*) (1967), xiii, 145; *Mélo* (1986), xvi–xvii, 115–20, 127–32, 134–36, 155, 179; *Mon Oncle d'Amérique* (*My American Uncle*) (1980), xiii–xvi, 67, 77, 82–83, 86, 100, 102, 125, 130, 134, 172, 178; *Muriel, ou le temps d'un retour* (1963), xi–xii, 20–22, 27–28, 37–38, 40, 43, 48–49, 60, 63–65, 78, 92, 108, 116–17, 130, 171–72; *Nuit et brouillard* (*Night and Fog*) (1956), vii, x–xi, xvi, xxin5, 5–6, 8, 124, 144, 185; *On Connaît la chanson* (*Same Old Song*) (1997), xv, xix, 148–54, 157; *Paris 1900* (1947), 149; *Pas sur la bouche* (*Not on the Lips*) (2003), xviii–xix, 154–58, 168, 182; *Paul Gauguin* (1950), ix, 8, 104; *La Pointe courte* (1955), viii; *Providence* (1976), xiii–xv, xxin9, 78, 108, 122–23, 135, 148–50, 162, 170, 185; *Smoking/No Smoking* (1983), xvii–xix, 148–49, 158–60, 162, 176, 181; *Les Statues meurent aussi* (1950–53), ix–x, xxin5, 139–41, 153; *Stavisky . . .* (*Biarritz-Bonheur*) (1974), xii–xiii,

xvii, 60–64, 68–76, 79, 86, 104–5, 130; *Toute la mémoire du monde* (1956), x, 4, 108, 144; *Van Gogh* (1948), ix, xiv, 18, 95, 101, 104; *La Vie est un roman* (*Life is a Bed of Roses*) (1983), xvi–xvii, 87, 97, 134, 153; *Vous n'avez encore rien vu* (*You Ain't Seen Nothin' Yet*) (2012), xviii–xix, 173, 175–78, 180, 183

Réval, Alex (Resnais pen name), xix–xx, 73, 170
Rich, Claude, xiii, xv, 160
Riva, Emmanuelle, 27, 134–35
Robbe-Grillet, Alain, xi, xvi, 5, 8, 13–17, 19, 27, 34, 37, 43, 57–58, 78, 101, 103, 124, 146, 152, 168, 170

Saulnier, Jacques, xvi, 131, 137, 163, 178–79
Semprun, Jorge, viii, xvi, xxi, 22, 24, 26, 28, 34, 37, 61–63, 69–73, 144–45, 153
Seyrig, Delphine, xi–xii, xv, 27–28, 58
Snow, Mark, 165–66, 174–75, 182–83
Sondheim, Stephen, xiii, 72, 74–75, 182
Surrealism, vii, viii, xii, xiv–xv, xvii, xx–xxi, 19, 39, 51, 101–2

Towarnicki, Frédéric de, viii, xxin2, 121
Truffaut, François, viii, 15, 40, 43, 62, 65–66, 85, 113, 172

Vannes (Brittany), vii, 28, 52, 111–12, 154–55, 161
Varda, Agnès, viii–ix, 3, 40, 66
Vedrès, Nicole, 77, 80, 149
Vierny, Sacha, x, xi, xvi, 17, 64, 75, 137, 170

Webern, Anton, 101, 130, 166
Welles, Orson, 9, 55–56
Wilson, Lambert, xviii, 151, 156, 160

About the Editor

Lynn A. Higgins is Edward Tuck Professor of French and professor emerita of comparative literature and film studies at Dartmouth College. She is author of books on the New Wave and the New Novel and on Bertrand Tavernier. She is coeditor of *Bertrand Tavernier: Interviews*, published by University Press of Mississippi.

About the Translator

T. Jefferson Kline is professor emeritus of French at Boston University. He has written five books on French cinema, film, and intertextuality in screenplay. He is editor of *Agnès Varda: Interviews* and coeditor of *Bertrand Tavernier: Interviews* and *Bernardo Bertolucci: Interviews*, all published by University Press of Mississippi.

www.ingramcontent.com/pod-product-compliance
Lightning Source LLC
Chambersburg PA
CBHW021840220426
43663CB00005B/333